Changing Contexts in Spatial

This book considers the major forces that have emerged to reshape planning following 2010, including national infrastructure project delivery, the Localism Act (2011) and neighbourhood planning. This period also saw the introduction of the replacement of regional plans by new strategic sub-regional approaches in combined local authorities for functional economic areas. All of this is set within the UN's New Urban Agenda, Brexit, the changing programme for the EU post 2021 and the likely effects that these will have on UK planning practice. There is also a discussion on the evolving planning policies in Scotland, Wales and Northern Ireland and the ways in which the UK nations are beginning to work together more closely and with Ireland, Jersey, Guernsey and the Isle of Man through the spatial planning group in the British–Irish Council. Although primarily focused on the UK, the text sets some of the policy discussions in a wider international context including agreements on the environment and the emerging alignment of governance and economies in newly recognised sub-regional spaces. It follows *Effective Practice in Spatial Planning* (2011), which addressed the developments in planning in the UK between 2004 and 2010, and discusses the major changes in all aspects of planning policy in the following period.

Janice Morphet has been engaged in planning practice and research for nearly 50 years. She has worked in local, regional and central government organisations and been employed as a consultant. She has been a trustee of the RTPI and TCPA and was a member of the ODA's Planning Decisions Committee for the London 2012 Olympic Games. Janice has been involved in planning education and research throughout her career. She was the head of a large school of planning and landscape and has been a visiting professor in the Bartlett School of Planning at University College London, UK, since 2005. Janice holds degrees in sociology, politics, management and literature and is a fellow of the RTPI and of the Academy of Social Sciences.

Changing Contexts in Spatial Planning
New Directions in Policies and Practices

Janice Morphet

Routledge
Taylor & Francis Group

NEW YORK AND LONDON

First published 2019
by Routledge
711 Third Avenue, New York, NY 10017

and by Routledge
2 Park Square, Milton Park, Abingdon, Oxon OX14 4RN

Routledge is an imprint of the Taylor & Francis Group, an informa business

Library of Congress Cataloging-in-Publication Data
Names: Morphet, Janice, author.
Title: Changing contexts in spatial planning : new directions in policies and practices / Janice Morphet.
Description: New York, NY : Routledge, 2018.
Identifiers: LCCN 2018007115 |
ISBN 9780815365044 (hardback) |
ISBN 9780815365068 (pbk.)
Subjects: LCSH: City planning--Great Britain. |
Housing policy--Great Britain. | Urban policy--Great Britain.
Classification: LCC HT169.G7 M67 2018 | DDC 307.1/2160941--dc23
LC record available at https://lccn.loc.gov/2018007115

ISBN: 978-0-8153-6504-4 (hbk)
ISBN: 978-0-8153-6506-8 (pbk)
ISBN: 978-1-351-20311-1 (ebk)

Typeset in Sabon
by Taylor & Francis Books

MIX
Paper from
responsible sources
FSC   FSC® C013056
www.fsc.org

Printed and bound in Great Britain by
TJ International Ltd, Padstow, Cornwall

To Dylan, Phoebe, Charlotte, Sophie and Robin

Contents

Illustrations

Tables

Boxes

Preface

When spatial planning was introduced into England in 2004, through the Planning and Compulsory Purchase Act, there was far more interest in the structural reforms to local development plans than the implications of this new type of planning. The focus of many practicing planners in local government was on the form of the Local Development Framework (LDF), with its Core Strategy that could be prepared in parts to form the local development plan. Much of this initial focus was the requirement to set out a programme for the delivery of this LDF rather than the more fundamental changes that were to be used in the examination of the plan. These introduced both the tests of soundness against which all submitted plans were to be assessed by a Planning Inspector and shifted this examination process from adversarial to inquisitorial in its conduct. The Inspector, having assessed the submitted plan and accompanying evidence and statements of community consultation, could now decide which, if any, parts of the plan needed to be tested and how this would take place in an examination framework. Inspectors in this role could stop the process and eventually make proposals for changes. No government explanation was given for these changes in the examination process and from the outset, initial local authority expectations that these were changes in name only were quickly challenged.

Nearly fifteen years later, it is these processes of examination that have remained the same within the operation of the 2004 Act while other elements of document structure and government guidance on form and content have changed. The legislation has been robust enough to withstand the abolition of parts of the policy framework included in the Act – that is, of Regional Spatial Strategies. It has survived two Labour, one Coalition and two Conservative governments. It has been able to absorb a much greater weighting towards housing than other planning matters and integrate within itself the introduction of a Community Infrastructure Levy in the 2008 Planning Act and the subsequent tests of viability that followed the economic downturn. It has also survived the introduction of the National Planning Policy Framework in 2012 and its review in 2018. It has also been able to operate a new system for nationally significant infrastructure projects introduced in 2008 and the creation of combined authorities with directly elected mayors in 2017.

Yet even after this time and with the planning system's ability to absorb change, some of the basic tenets of spatial planning are only just being understood and reinforced. Spatial planning has been criticised as being a post political neo-liberal tool that has supported private sector development over the role of the public sector. However, while successive governments have listened to the criticisms of the planning system made by the development industry, it has now become clear that planning is not the deterrent to development that has been suggested. Indeed, it maintains value by ensuring quality and scale of development. Private sector developers have a role to play but they cannot provide all the housing and other development that the country requires either for future growth or to retrofit places to address longstanding needs. The public sector has become directly involved in the delivery role that is at the heart of spatial planning. In adopting plans, local authorities are now being expected to support their delivery through all the means available to them. This may be through their own land and funding, using their convening capacity to work with other providers for infrastructure, utilities and public services and using their legal powers to acquire land for development, if this is needed.

The legal framework of planning changes nearly every 15 years and is frequently linked with changes in local government structures – 1974, 1990–1991 and 2004. The next turn is likely to introduce new forms of strategic planning in functional economic areas – both cities and polycentric ruralities – with a focus on programmes and projects as well as policies. This book examines the ways in which planning processes are being practiced now, their changing context and how planning is dealing with longstanding issues using new forms of data and a return to mixed economy values. It sets this discussion within some of the key issues facing society, including public health and an ageing population. It also recognises the changing governance context that has been provided by austerity since 2010 and the role of the UN's New Urban Agenda from 2016. As this book demonstrates, planning continues to respond to change and to the economic, social and environmental challenges that it faces on a daily basis.

Part I
Planning's Changing Context

1 Planning and Austerity

Introduction

Austerity has been an overriding narrative in the UK since the economic crisis of 2008. It has created the context within which planning practice is conducted within England. In particular, the private sector has an expectation of a continuing low economic performance. The recovery from the 2008 international economic crisis has not reflected what occurred following earlier crises and has been slower in the UK. It has not seen a return to the growth in income trajectories that were the norm before 2008.

This has put pressure on governments to reduce public sector expectations for developer contributions for social and affordable housing, while providing financial incentives for housing supply despite increases in company financial performance (Walsh 2017). While commentary on the effects of austerity has primarily focussed on the consequences of reduced budgets in the public sector (Lowndes and McCaughie 2013; Peters 2012; Grimshaw 2013), it has also had a considerable influence on the context for development and places in the operation of planning and delivery. Austerity has influenced investment confidence and levels of construction activity, which in turn have encouraged successive UK governments to increase their efforts to deregulate planning (Laffin 2016). Austerity has also made institutions, including pension funds, more risk averse in making capital investment.

The private sector has also changed during this period, particularly through its expansion in staff and consultancy firms (Geoghegan 2016). Since 2010, the government has adopted a more *laissez-faire* approach to regulation on developers for financial contributions. The government has promoted deregulation through the increased categories of development that have deemed planning consent including changes from offices to residential use (Clifford et al. 2018).

In this chapter, there will be an initial review of austerity practices in the public sector within England, particularly since 2010, when a Coalition government was formed and operated for five years, until 2015. It will consider the effects of this culture and narrative on planning. It will also consider what may be emerging as public-sector bodies, including local authorities, seek to regain some control over their own activities and policies, particularly using planning tools that are available to them.

The Coalition government (2010–2015) pressured local authorities to increase the number of planning consents approved for housing (Wilcox and Perry 2014). At the same time, there was a reduction in staff in the local authority planning departments to deal with these promoted upsurges in planning applications (Arup 2015; NAO 2014a). However, planners and local politicians have been frustrated to see that planning permissions have not been converted into development and stay on the desk (McAllister et al. 2016; Burroughs 2015). At the same time, pressures on welfare services, the loss of EU workers following the Brexit referendum (Mohamed et al. 2017) and the rise of the gig economy have all contributed to lower levels of unemployment than those experienced in the UK since 1977 (Taylor 2017). Notwithstanding this, there have been major consequences on the revenue budgets of public services, where failure to maintain levels of income from government has had major effects on service delivery and, in some cases, the availability of facilities such as libraries and children's centres. While all services have suffered from financial pressures and cuts, planning staff have been reduced more than other services (NAO 2016).

Why Austerity?

Austerity is a political choice (Bailey et al. 2015) focused on reshaping the state. Its role in determining the priorities, programmes and expenditure of local authorities has been concerned both with the specific choices (Overmans and Noordegraff 2014) but also the wider blame-shifting culture that this has posited (Hood 2010; Cochrane 2016). In England, it has primarily been associated with attempts to change the underlying philosophy of the welfare state away from meeting need to more minimal and market-based services, frequently provided by contractors. The effects of the 'age of austerity' on local government since 2010 have focussed on the efficiencies and cuts that have been made in specific services (Lowndes and Pratchett 2012; Lowndes and McCaughie 2013) and draw upon the legacy of similar practices that have been in operation since the International Monetary Fund (IMF) crisis in 1976 (Pierson 1994; Morphet 2008). It has also focussed on the transfer of services and social responsibility to voluntary and community organisations that have taken on the operation of libraries, food banks and other social support (Clayton et al. 2016), including neighbourhood planning (Brownill 2017). Lowndes and Gardner (2016) have also argued that local authorities have been nudged into innovating through new institutional structures. These have been both within the organisation and externally with neighbouring local authorities in larger functional economic areas (FEAs) to improve their efficiency but also to increase their voice with government. Other commentators suggest that this scalecraft (Fraser 2010) has been a means of shifting blame for decision making (Haughton et al. 2016) in a form of 'scalar dumping' (Shaw and Tewdwr-Jones 2017).

Osborne's Austerity 2010–2016

In the 2010 general election campaign, the Conservative Party used the economic crisis narrative as a means of promoting change and then used the Coalition government as a means of underpinning its credibility (Hayton 2014). The austerity programme introduced by the Coalition Chancellor of the Exchequer, George Osborne, was a political rather than an economic programme. Gamble (2014) argues that the narrative of austerity was an important exercise of statecraft to assist Conservative politicians in gaining popular confidence in their responses to the 2007–2008 economic crisis. They did this by creating distance between the incoming Coalition and outgoing Labour governments. There were also wider implications of this approach. The Chancellor used the mantra of austerity to promote a reduction in the size of the state, based on a long-held view that the public sector 'stole' resources from the private sector and did not allow it access to the labour market (Skidelsky 2015). Osborne also argued that greater budget cuts would lead to a speedier reduction in the national debt (Gamble 2014).

The 2008 global budgetary crisis was amplified by the lack of preparation for the crash by the leading Western economies represented in the G20. The US, Germany, the UK and France together with Japan had to take immediate action to prevent financial catastrophes. Once this period had stabilised, each country then took its own action to deal with the issues that had contributed to the crisis – banking practices, unsecured loans and housing bubbles. Within the European Union (EU), the European Commission (EC) has responsibility for macroeconomic policy with the European Central Bank. The EC undertook a review of member state macroprudential policies and adopted a pan-EU policy framework that has been reviewed annually (CEC 2017). It also commissioned an assessment of the effectiveness of the operation of the single market (Monti 2010) that was followed by *Europe 2020* (CEC 2010), a programme of action across all member states that included specific objectives to remedy the weaknesses in each of them. This was also accompanied by the Territorial Agenda for the European Union, which set out some of the spatial approaches to achieving this wider economic agenda (CEC 2011). The EC adopted national reform programmes accompanied by six monthly reviews of progress (CEC 2017).

As part of this process, the EC diagnosed the UK's macroeconomic weaknesses as the operation of the housing market, the delivery of infrastructure and the operation of the planning system together with weaknesses in youth skills. The weaknesses in the housing market were identified as a lack of flexibility in the housing stock, which did not support labour mobility, a practice that has always been associated with the success of the US economy and higher productivity. The role of planning and the slow preparation of local plans by local authorities and incipient Nimbyism were also identified as restrictive on the provision of new housing to support the UK's growing population. These findings on the working of the UK housing market were also supported by the work of the Organization for Economic Cooperation and Development (OECD) (André 2011; Havrylchyk and Kierzenkowski 2015). Infrastructure and delivery were addressed through the 2008 Planning Act but as Morphet and Clifford (2017a) show, reforming the planning system does not necessarily provide more infrastructure delivery.

This EC diagnosis was significant, as three of four UK economic weaknesses identified had a strong relationship with local government core responsibilities. During Osborne's tenure as Chancellor, until July 2016, the EC maintained their assessment of the weaknesses in the UK economy despite many initiatives and speeches on the part of the Chancellor, particularly in his hard hat, Hi-Viz jacket mode, to talk up confidence about his actions and the effects they were having in addressing them.

In addition to these concerns, austerity policies were focussed on reducing expenditure on government programmes. The triple lock guarantees on income for pensioners made by the Prime Minister in 2010 meant that the austerity focus was placed on other major areas of public expenditure, including welfare benefits and local authorities. Although some funding was protected for major infrastructure projects, the pressure to deal with the housing market was largely focussed on two elements: expanding the volume of housing in the private rented sector and building new housing to maintain political commitments to home ownership (Hodkinson and Robbins 2013; Taylor-Gooby 2012). The government also intervened through a range of policies to remove security of tenure for existing local authority housing tenants, to stimulate local authority rights to buy sales and to make housing association properties subject to right to buy, thus removing even more dwellings from the social and affordable housing stock. The government also provided regulatory support for those purchasing housing for rent – 'buy to let' – that increased the relative proportion of renters in the UK (ONS 2017).

The pressures on local government services were increased through the course of the 2010–2015 Parliament, both directly through cuts to local authority budgets and also through the pressures placed on other areas of public expenditure, including benefits and other measures of financial support for the unemployed and disabled. These central government welfare reductions also placed pressure on local authorities not least for accommodation for the homeless. As Morris (2016) demonstrates, the re-construction of government policy has been a product of statecraft where specific groups have been promoted or vilified using austerity narratives as a means of achieving underlying structural shifts in institutional relationships between the central state and local governments.

The effects of austerity on individual local authorities have varied. One study (Zurich Municipal with Solace 2016) demonstrated that the differences in approach and culture within local authorities have had major implications between those pursuing more innovative approaches to finance and others regarding these as risky, preferring to take more cautious and traditional approaches. However, all local authorities responding to this survey identified risks inherent in the government's imposed austerity approach.

Austerity in the Public Sector: The Response from Planning?

While much of planning in the public sector is undertaken by local authorities, there are several other public bodies that have planning functions. These include government agencies and bodies that have legal functions in relation to the environment. All have been affected by government austerity policies. The path to austerity in local government was set by Secretary of State (2010–2015) Eric Pickles, who was deaf to concerns about budget reductions on local authorities and firmly held the view that local authorities should be generating more funding through their own activities (Morphet 2016). These focussed on two key areas. The first was using financial balances and assets and to create more finance through income generating activities. The second was through joint work between local authorities to save costs, including creating single or joint management teams or creating new combined authorities. Groups of local authorities were expected to operate more efficiently by securing the benefits of scale but they also could be more effective in raising funds through bonds secured on their assets.

The financial freedoms that allowed local authorities to use their assets in this way were included in s1–7 of the 2011 Localism Act, although it has taken a while for local authorities to adapt to generating income. These new legal freedoms for local authorities (Hope 2010) included the creation of companies, banks and other legal entities singly or with other local authorities or partners. Many local authorities have established housing companies as a means of generating income (Hackett 2017; TCPA/Nationwide Foundation 2017; Morphet and Clifford 2017a). When the Act was discussed in Parliament, these new powers were overlooked, with a much greater focus on the proposed planning, housing and neighbourhood reforms. They were also coupled with the introduction of new accounting practices for International Financial Reporting Standards (IFRS), introduced across the public and private sectors in all OECD countries. The IFRS combines public and private accounting standards in the UK for the first time and means that, in addition to the creation of whole government accounts, local authorities can operate in the same way as the private sector.

Since 2010, the public sector has had several responses to austerity, when they have been able to use some of these financial reforms. Since 2010, the budgets of local authorities in the UK have been cut in all four nations (Innes and Tetlow 2015; NAO 2014b). These cuts have primarily been to revenue budgets – that is, the funding that supports specific services such as planning, social care and libraries. It may have been a simple approach to consider raising income or fees for these services to maintain them, but in the cases of both planning and social care, fees that can be levied for services are set in part by the government. In local government, expenditure on planning services was reduced by 56 per cent on outturn figures between 2009–2010 and 2013–2014 (Fitzgerald and Lupton 2015). While local authorities have been able to increase prices for services, such as for pre-application planning advice, charging for the administration of developers' contributions through planning performance agreements and Community Infrastructure Levy (CIL), their core income on planning is through planning application fees that are controlled by the government.

The public sector has had several responses to austerity, which have been able to use some of these financial reforms. Public sector bodies responsible for planning have responded to austerity in several ways. Hastings et al. (2015) identified three headline strategies that local authorities have used to cope with austerity: efficiency, which has been concerned with reducing the costs of services, retrenchment, which has sought to reduce the local authority's role in service delivery and investment, which has been used as a means of reducing the need for a service in the future. Of these three approaches, it can be argued that retrenchment involved greater responsibilisation – that is, personal accountability for managing problems – and was one of the government's preferred outcomes of austerity and its political objective. However, the backlash against austerity in all its forms, including personal liability transfer to individuals in greatest need, was one of the driving forces behind the Brexit vote in 2016 (Ashcroft and Bevir 2016).

In planning, strategies of efficiency and investment in back office systems are the most frequently applied, as the planning services are statutory responsibilities. Local authorities have implemented a range of approaches to dealing with austerity in the planning services:

(i)   Downsizing Permanent Staff

Most public-sector bodies have responded to reduced budget availability by reducing their staff or by changing its composition. In the period immediately after the recession of 2008–2010, the number of planning applications declined (HBF 2016), which meant that public bodies often did not fill vacancies or made staff redundant. This was an issue where there had been a shift towards funding all or part of the planning development management team through planning application fee income. Planning application fees are set by central government and while local authorities can increase the fees for other services, the core income remains relative to the levels of development activity. A study undertaken for the Royal Town Planning Institute (RTPI) by Arup in 2015 found that in North West England, there was an average of four fewer staff in development management, or -29 per cent, between 2006 and 2015 (Arup 2015). At the same time, numbers of planners in the private sector increased (Geoghan 2016). Consultants are primarily working on development for the private sector but many consultancies will also provide specialist advice for local authorities and, in some cases, provide short term staff to meet gaps.

One of the consequences of the downsizing of planning staff has been the loss of specialist staff, including those who had expertise in urban design, conservation or aspects of research. These include reduced numbers of planners to cope with heritage protection reforms (IHRC 2009). Historic England (Reilly 2016) assess that 32 per cent of heritage staff have been lost since 2006. Some public-sector bodies have decided to manage without these specialist skills, while others have become more reliant on consultants to provide these services when needed. Consultants may be specialists who work on household projections, assess housing needs or provide design or archaeological advice. In some local authorities, specific types of planning applications such as the smaller household applications were given to consultants. However, there are always doubts and uncertainties about the extent to which consultants know the area and are committed to it. There is also a fear amongst practitioners that knowledge gained by consultants within a local authority will later be used against it.

In many local authorities, reduced staffing budgets led to changes to the schemes of delegation. These delegate powers for decision making from elected councillors to planning officers and can be made without the need for formal meetings in pubic. The government also made changes to permitted development rights, removing several types of development temporarily outside the planning application system. Reducing permanent staff numbers has some impact on both salary costs and also the other costs associated with employing staff (Morphet 2015). While these costs are reduced as the planning system returns with the market, these returning pressures are met by staff employed through agencies. These staff are more expensive, as they are available for a brief time and include costs of accommodation, but they do not have associated costs for pensions, etc. This also means that they are not included in the overall departmental headcount, allowing managers to demonstrate that they are not increasing staff overall.

The reduction in the number of permanent planning staff has a range of potential consequences. Firstly, there are concerns about the pressures on remaining staff and their ability to deal with increased workloads. These staff reductions have raised concerns for quality vs quantity in any planning process. This is particularly the case in development management. At the same time, the number of planners in plan preparation and policy has also had an associated effect, as their lack of policy advice and plan making progress has been a major issue for the government. In research undertaken by Planning Futures (2017), it is stated that 'Cuts to planning department staff over the last decade have restricted the abilities of local authorities to offer an efficient and robust planning service' (p3).

Another consequence of this reduction of the employment of planners is that planning graduates entering the profession have found it difficult to obtain a job, with applications for roles frequently in the hundreds. Also, as more qualified planners may have been made redundant, those vacancies available were filled by those with greater amounts of experience. Those graduates who entered the profession during this period were those who had gained more experience though vacation or intern jobs during their training and may have established relationships with potential employers.

(ii)   Reducing Management Teams

The overall effects of austerity budget reduction on public bodies has led to a streamlining and reduction of the management levels, usually by incorporating services and functions into larger groupings within the organisation. This has frequently been through combining planning with other services and then placing the head of this combined service on the management team of the organisation rather than the head of planning. While the head of the new combined department or directorate might be a planner, the role of planning is essentially diluted. This has led to its being more frequently considered as a regulatory function, which has skewed the perception of the role of planning. However, elsewhere local authorities are considering their own roles in developing land for housing and other uses. The presence of a planner on the management team of any public organisation considering this approach may be a significant factor in achieving these ends (Hall 2017; Morphet and Clifford 2017b; RTPI 2018).

(iii)   Back Office Efficiencies

Local authorities have been attempting to be more efficient using technology in the back office over many years (Slay and Penny 2013) and this has been accelerated by austerity. A focus on efficiency frequently includes reviews by management consultants assessing the whole organisation or the use of specific techniques including business process reengineering and lean methods, both of which have been popular in planning (Morphet 2015). Other back office technology improvements have included moving services online and using work flow and other business process solutions to integrate data and files on sites and performance-manage the processing of planning applications to ensure that government deadlines are met.

(iv)   Reducing Services

Reducing costs in planning has been achieved by withdrawing services available to the public, the community and developers. In some cases, this might mean a more minimal approach to providing advice to developers or the community about specific applications. This may also lead to reducing availability of planning staff in the office and public access times to meet planners. In some authorities, there have been reductions of specific services, including enforcement, which has always been a poorly resourced area of planning activity. Other areas that have been reduced include environmental and community engagement although as local authorities now have neighbourhood planning responsibilities since 2011, this might mean that what resources are available are diverted to these specific areas (Brownill 2017).

(v)   Reducing Service Outlets

Some public bodies are reducing the number of locations where they offer services. This might have an effect in areas that are more geographically dispersed although there may be improvements in digital delivery as a result. However, this may also mean a reduction in consultation locations or spaces for exhibitions or other planning service events.

(vi)   Combining Services

In addition to combining services within the local authority, under larger management groupings, some local authorities have been combining their services with those of other local authorities (Sandford 2016). This approach has been supported by the government although this has not necessarily been a driver except for the combined approach of three London boroughs (LBs): Westminster, Kensington and Chelsea and Hammersmith and Fulham. However, after political changes, this partnership for sharing staff has now been dissolved. Another approach has been taken by LBs Wandsworth and Richmond-upon-Thames where there is a single management team and staff but the two councils are operating separately with different policies. These two LBs are sometimes the same and sometimes different political majorities.

In Suffolk, two local authorities that have been working together have now applied to become a new single authority, whereas in Dorset, the whole county has applied to become two unitary local authorities. Elsewhere, councils have been sharing specific staff, for example, for enforcement or legal advice, or there may be shared procurement contracts for advice services from third parties. In the East Midlands, the Welland Partnership has now been operational for 20 years between five authorities maintaining arrangements in which one council may supply any of the others with services. This has the benefit of longstanding arrangement and trust and confidence and knowledge of the area. The introduction of more strategic government levels, such as directly elected mayors of combined authorities, may lead to integrating planners in joint teams in the longer term. However, this has not occurred in London, where the Mayor of London has specific planning functions and a directly appointed team to lead them (Morphet 2017), while the LBs retain their own planning powers and staff.

(vii)   Generating Income

One of the major pressures on public sector planning services has been generating income for wider council services and infrastructure. Planning provides several opportunities to create income. This may be through charging for specific consultations on planning applications of all sizes but has been primarily focussed on larger developments. This approach has also been taken by many public statutory consultees on environment and transport issues Morphet and Clifford 2017b). The government has supported this approach through the introduction of planning performance agreement (PPA) frameworks that allow the local authority to offer specific service delivery tables in return for a developer fee (DCLG 2015; LGA nd). In some cases, these agreements have supported the appointment of staff within the local authority planning team who are dedicated to these specific projects. However, these agreements can be sporadic in their use and not used at all by some local authorities where there are major planning applications (Morphet and Clifford 2017b).

The second way in which the planning system is being expected to generate income for the local authority is through the increased number of planning permissions for housing, which, once completed, will provide local authorities with a New Homes Bonus. This is a temporary government incentive that is followed in the longer term by increasing income through council tax. The third way that planning is being expected to generate income for local authorities is through the negotiation of developer contributions and CIL (Squires and Lord 2017). Lastly, local authorities are generating income by providing their staff to other organisations in return for a fee.

(viii)   Transferring Responsibilities to the Voluntary Sector

While transferring service responsibilities to the voluntary sector has been used by several local authorities to reduce operational costs (Fitzgerald and Lupton 2015), this has been stimulated in planning through the use of legislation to introduce neighbourhood planning. While neighbourhood planning places some responsibility for determining planning priorities within defined and agreed neighbourhood areas, there is a still a responsibility for local planning services to support neighbourhood planning activity. At a time of high resource constraint, this may move attention and staff time to serve those areas with neighbourhood plans, frequently the most wealthy or engaged, leaving areas with greater needs with fewer resources (Brownill 2017).

(ix)   Innovation and Experimentation

Innovation in local government may require cultural change that drives the achievement of other agendas. When used by central government to promote change in local government, innovation, like austerity, can be viewed as a form of statecraft focusing on prompting and promoting change without having any explicit narrative that has been discussed within a wider policy framework of the state. Rather, the notion of innovation is wrapped in a fuzzy promotion of doing public good (Harris and Albury 2009).

Innovation in organisations may be stimulated by internal or external factors (Baldock and Evers 1991). Local authorities may respond to external responses to innovate because these are rewarded in some way by central government. Innovation is driven by improvements in efficiency and performance and the austerity narrative has also been pervasive in the 'innovation imperative' (Bartlett (2016 p2). While much of the literature on public sector innovation has been conceptual (de Vries et al. 2016; Bartlett and Dibben 2002), there is some evidence that the innovation that has emerged within local authorities and is directed towards the direct provision of housing has been internal within the organisation (Hill et al. 2016) and has been introduced by those who understand the organisation and its needs. The role of internal innovator may come from a variety of places within the organisation and the extent to which their proposals for innovation are adopted may depend on the relative weighting that this individual or their department has in the culture of the local authority as a whole. As de Vries et al. (2016) show, service innovation only accounts for 22 per cent of the range of innovation types in the public sector and is more likely to be reliant on foregoing organisational antecedents than other factors.

Has austerity led innovation in planning? Since 2010, local authorities have been faced with a series of housing challenges. Firstly, housing need and the number of homeless have grown while local authorities have primarily had to find accommodation to meet these needs on the private rental market. Here they have found that the rental property available largely comprises former local authority housing that has been bought through right to buy provisions and is now let out. Some landlords have targeted the acquisition of former local authority dwellings for this sole purpose. Given other pressures on the housing market, including those of citizens from elsewhere in the EU coming to Britain to find work, the housing rental market had been subject to continuing rises in rent costs.

Secondly, local authorities have found that there is increased pressure on their normal housing stock as it dwindles through right to buy programmes and, despite government rhetoric to the contrary, housing units lost to the social housing stock are not being replaced through other means. Thirdly, political pressures are raised by parents whose children are no longer able to rent or buy property because of lower pay rates, unstable and flexible employment contracts and rising prices and are living at home longer. Many local authorities have started to consider ways, in addition to the specific schemes supported by government to assist young people buying new homes, that assistance can be given to young people. Finally, the government measures have dealt with only part of the housing market. The mobility in the housing market has been static since there have been new taxation measures at point of house sale and no specific incentives for older people to downsize.

Some local authorities have gone beyond these measures to establish their own wholly owned housing development companies. In a survey of all local authority leaders in England in 2015, nearly 50 per cent stated that it was their intention to establish a housing company and local authorities of diverse types all over England are taking this approach (Sharman 2015). In some cases, local authorities are establishing housing companies to provide affordable housing. Elsewhere, local authorities are establishing companies so that they can retain control over their housing stock and not lose dwellings through right to buy initiatives (Hackett 2017).

As local authorities take a more pro-active approach to housing provision, this will have some important implications and outcomes for planning (Morphet and Clifford 2017a). The first is that this approach does not remove requirements on local authorities for effective plan making and efficient development management. However, where local authorities are directly involved in the provision of housing, it can enable a more secure estimate of housing delivery rates, which can provide evidence for appeals and inquiries. If local authorities start to provide more housing in locations where there are many unimplemented planning permissions, then it may encourage those holding these permissions to bring forward their own development programmes or sell them to local authority housing companies or housing associations.

Direct provision of housing also enables local authorities, including planning professionals, to consider how they can change areas to bring forward more investment. In acting as patient developers, local authorities might start to assemble sites for development. Local authorities could also look at the role of existing land uses. Many larger inner-city sites were put into lower value uses when the property market collapsed in the 1980s. Although they provided relatively low employment rates, large retail sheds and car showrooms were an effective way of filling land and removing blight. However, with the current land pressures for housing in cities, it is time to consider whether these uses are still optimal at a time when housing on brownfield land is more important. Concentrations of lower density uses can be overlooked and neglected but can be brought back into more productive and efficient uses. However, local authorities must demonstrate that they would welcome such changes of use. Despite severe shortages and price rises, in some locations, the housing market remains dominated by fashion that influences investors, tenants and purchasers. In areas that have been neglected, there needs to be some indication that new housing is supported by wider planning for the area. This may not be regeneration so much as re-planning.

Conclusions

The fundamental issues facing planning relate to the longevity of austerity practices and whether there will still be a primary focus on private sector delivery of housing and infrastructure. Through the establishment of a new government agency, Homes England, there still appears to be a focus on using public funds to support low density, private housing development accessed by car. It is uncertain whether these approaches will be supported in the longer run. The fire and loss of life at Grenfell Tower in 2017 placed the government under pressure to increase funding for social housing, currently at 20 per cent of the total housing expenditure budget. For all the government's actions, planning permissions do not automatically increase delivery but rather site value (Whitehead 2017a). Recently, over 90 per cent of new houses sold received some form of public subsidy (Whitehead 2017b) and there are increasingly calls for the government to change its priorities. While this might result in developers' building fewer dwellings, it could reassert the role of the public sector, which would have a greater influence on what type of houses are built, for whom and where, allowing a more diverse offer for those who have children or are approaching retirement. So, while austerity has started to reshape public sector services in local authorities, there has been some evidence of consequent adaptation and innovation in response in planning. This greater engagement is not restoring all the housing powers and funding that have been lost but it suggests a more reinvigorated public sector with a key role for planning.

References

Arup (2015). Investing in delivery: How we can respond to the pressures on local authority planning. RTPI Research Report no.10, October.London: RTPI.

Ashcroft, R., & Bevir, M. (2016). Pluralism, national identity and citizenship: Britain after Brexit. *The Political Quarterly*, 87(3), 355–359.

Bailey, N., Bramley, G., & Hastings, A. (2015). Symposium introduction: Local responses to 'austerity'. *Local Government Studies*, 41(4), 571–581.

Baldock, J., &Evers, A. (1991). Innovations and care of the elderly: The front line of change for social welfare services. *Ageing International*, 18(1), 8–21.

Bartlett, D. (2016). Champions of local authority innovation revisited. *Local Government Studies*, 43(2), 142–149. doi:10.1080/03003930.2016.1245184.

Bartlett, D., & Dibben, P. (2002). Public sector innovation and entrepreneurship: Case studies from local government. *Local Government Studies*, 28(4), 107–121.

Brownill, S. (2017). *Localism and Neighbourhood Planning: Power to the People?*Bristol: Policy Press.

Burroughs, L. (2015). *Getting Houses Built*. London: CPRE.

CEC (2010). *Europe 2020*. Brussels: CEC.

CEC (2011). *Territorial Agenda of the European Union 2020*. Brussels: CEC.

CEC (2017) *European Semester: Country Specific Recommendations*. Council Recommendations. Brussels: CEC. https://ec.europa.eu/info/publications/2017-european-semester-country-specific-recommendations-council-recommendations_en (accessed 4 July 2018).

Clayton, J., Donovan, C., & Merchant, J., (2016. Distancing and limited resourcefulness: Third sector service provision under austerity localism in the north east of England. *Urban Studies*, 53(4),723–740.

Clifford, B., Ferm, J., Livingstone, N., & Canelas, P. (2018). Assessing the impacts of extending permitted development rights to office-to-residential change of use in England. RICS. www.rics.org/uk/knowledge/research/research-reports/assessing-the-impacts-of-extending-permitted-development-rights-to-office-to-residential-change-of-use-in-england/ (accessed 4 July 2018).

Cochrane, A. (2016). Thinking about the 'local' of local government: A brief history of invention and reinvention. *Local Government Studies*, 42(6), 907–915.

DCLG (2015). Planning performance agreements. www.gov.uk/guidance/before-submitting-an-application#planning-performance-agreements (accessed 4 July 2018).

de Vries, H., Bekkers, V., & L. Tummers. (2016. Innovation in the Public Sector: A Systematic Review and Future Research Agenda. *Public Administration*, 94(1), 146–166.

Fitzgerald, A., & Lupton, R. (2015). The limits to resilience? The impact of local government spending cuts in London. *Local Government Studies*, 41(4), 582–600.

Fraser, A. (2010). The craft of scalar practices. *Environment and Planning A*, 42(2), 332–346.

Gamble, A. (2014). Austerity as statecraft. *Parliamentary Affairs: A Journal of Representative Politics*, 68(1), 42–57.

Geoghegan, J. (2016. The Planning Consultancy Survey 2016. *Planning Resource*, 18 November. www.planningresource.co.uk/article/1415798/planning-consultancy-survey-2016-leading-employers (accessed 4 July 2018).

Grimshaw, D. (2013). Austerity, privatization and levelling down: Public sector reforms in the United Kingdom. In Vaughan-Whitehead, D. (Ed.), *Public Sector Shock: The Impact of Policy Retrenchment in Europe* (pp. 576–626). Cheltenham: Edward Elgar.

Hackett, P. (2017). *Delivering the Renaissance in Council-Built Homes: The Rise of Local Housing Companies*. London: Smith Institute.

Hall, K. (2017). *Local Authority Planning in Context*. Oxford: JPLC.

Harris, M., & Albury, D. (2009). The innovation imperative: Why radical innovation is needed to reinvent public services for the recession and beyond. London: Nesta. http s://media.nesta.org.uk/documents/the_innovation_imperative.pdf (accessed 4 July 2018).

Hastings, A., Bailey, N., Gannon, M., Besemer, K., & Bramley, G. (2015). Coping with the cuts? The management of the worst financial settlement in living memory. *Local Government Studies*, 41(4), 600–621.

Haughton, G., Deas, I., Hincks, S., & Ward, K. (2016). Mythic Manchester: Devo Manc, the Northern Powerhouse and rebalancing the English economy. *Cambridge Journal of Regions, Economy and Society*, 9(2), 355–370.

Hayton, R. (2014). Conservative Party statecraft and the politics of coalition. *Parliamentary Affairs*, 67(1), 6–24.

HBF (2016). *New Housing Pipeline Q3 2015 Report*. London: HBF.

Hill, A., Mellon, L., Laker, B., & Goddard, J. (2016). The one type of leader who can turn around a failing school. *Harvard Business Review*, 20 October 2016.

Hodkinson, S., & Robbins, G. (2013). The return of class war conservatism? Housing under the UK Coalition Government. *Critical Social Policy*, 33(1), 57–77.

Hood, C. (2010). *The Blame Game: Spin, Bureaucracy, and Self-Preservation in Government*. Princeton: Princeton University Press.

Hope, C. (2010) Local authorities can set up their own banks. *Daily Telegraph*, 13 December. www.telegraph.co.uk/news/politics/8199173/Localism-Bill-councils-can-set-up-their-own-banks.html (accessed 4 July 2018).

Innes, D., & Tetlow, G. (2015). Central Cuts, Local Decision-Making: Changes in Local Government Spending and Revenues in England, 2009–2010 to 2014–2015. IFS Briefing Note BN166. London: Institute of Fiscal Studies.

Laffin, M. (2016). Planning in England: New public management, network governance or post-democracy? *International Review of Administrative Sciences*, 82(2), 354–372.

LGA (nd). Planning performance agreements. www.local.gov.uk/sites/default/files/docum ents/good-practice-advice-and–fcb.pdf (accessed 4 July 2018).

Lowndes, V., & Gardner, A. (2016). Local governance under the Conservatives: super-austerity, devolution and the 'smarter state'. *Local Government Studies*, 42(3), 357–375.

Lowndes, V., & McCaughie, K. (2013. Weathering the perfect storm? Austerity and institutional resilience in local government. *Policy & Politics*, 41(4), 533–549.

Lowndes, V., & Pratchett, L. (2012). Local governance under the coalition government. *Local Government Studies*, 38(1), 21–40.

McAllister, P., Street, E., & Wyatt, P. (2016). An empirical investigation of stalled residential sites in England. *Planning Practice & Research*, 31(2), 132–153.

Mohamed, M., Pärn, E. A., & Edwards, D. J. (2017). Brexit: measuring the impact upon skilled labour in the UK construction industry. *International Journal of Building Pathology and Adaptation*, 35(3), 264–279.

Monti, M. (2010). *A New Strategy for the Single Market: At the Service of Europe's Economy and Society*. Report to the President of the European Commission. Brussels: CEC. http://ec.europa.eu/internal_market/strategy/docs/monti_report_final_10_05_2010_en.pdf (accessed 4 July 2018).

Morphet, J. (2008. *Modern Local Government*. London: SAGE.

Morphet, J. (2015). *Applying Leadership and Management in Planning: Theory and Practice*. Bristol: Policy Press.

Morphet, J. (2017). Sub-regional strategic spatial planning: The use of statecraft and scalecraft in delivering the English model. *Town Planning Review*, 88(6), 665–682.

Morphet, J. R. (2016). Local authorities build housing again... *Town and Country Planning*, 85(5), 170–177.

Morphet, J., & Clifford, B. (2017a). *Local Authority Direct Provision of Housing*. London: NPF and RTPI.

Morphet, J., & Clifford, B. (2017b). *Infrastructure Delivery: The DCO Process in Context Main Report*. London: NIPA.

Morris, Z. (2016). Constructing the need for retrenchment: disability benefits in the United States and Great Britain. *Policy & Politics*, 44(4), 609–626.

NAO (2014a). *The Impact of Funding Reductions on Local Authorities*. London: National Audit Office.

NAO (2014b). *Financial Sustainability of Local Authorities*. London: National Audit Office.

NAO (2016). *Financial Sustainability of Local Authorities: Capital Expenditure and Resourcing*. London: NAO.

ONS (2017). Number of buy to let investment properties 2000 to 2015. www.ons.gov.uk/aboutus/transparencyandgovernance/freedomofinformationfoi/number ofbuytoletinvestmentproperties2000to2015 (accessed 4 July 2018).

Overmans, J. F. A., & Noordegraaf, M. (2014). Managing austerity: Rhetorical and real responses to fiscal stress in local government. *Public Money & Management*, 34(2), 99–106.

Peters, J. (2012). Neoliberal convergence in North America and Western Europe: Fiscal austerity, privatization, and public sector reform. *Review of International Political Economy*, 19(2), 208–235.

Pierson, P. (1994). *Dismantling the Welfare State? Reagan, Thatcher and the Politics of Retrenchment*. Cambridge: Cambridge University Press.

Planning Futures (2017). *Delivering the Planning Service We Need: Building Planning Department Capacity*. London: Planning Futures.

Reilly, S. (2016). *An Eighth Report on Local Authority Staff Resources*. London: Historic England.

RTPI (2018). Research paper. London: RTPI. http://www.rtpi.org.uk/knowledge/research/projects/chief-planning-officers/ (accessed 19 August 2018).

Sandford, M. (2016. Local government: Alternative models of service delivery. House of Commons Library Briefing Paper No.05950, May 20. London: House of Commons Library. https://researchbriefings.parliament.uk/ResearchBriefing/Summary/SN05950 (accessed 4 July 2018).

Sharman, L. (2015). Half of councils setting up companies to tackle housing. https://www.localgov.co.uk/Half-of-councils-setting-up-companies-to-tackle-housing-shortage/39171 (accessed 19 August 2018).

Shaw, K., & Tewdwr-Jones, M. (2016). Disorganized devolution': Reshaping metropolitan governance in England in a period of austerity, [„Desorganisierte Devolution": die Umgestaltung metropolitaner Governance in England in einer Phase der Austerität. Raumforschung und Raumordnung] *Spatial Research and Planning*, 75(3), 211–224.

Skidelsky, R. (2015). Austerity: The wrong story, *The Economic and Labour Relations Review*, 26(3), 377–383.

Slay, J., & Penny, J. (2013. *Surviving Austerity: Local Voices and Local Action in England's Poorest Neighbourhoods*. London: NEF.

Squires, G., & Lord, A. (2017). *The Uneven Geography of Financing Cities through a Betterment Tax: Using the Community Infrastructure Levy (CIL) in England*. Reading: European Real Estate Society (ERES).

Taylor, M. (2017). *Employment Practices in the Modern Economy*. London: HMG.

Taylor-Gooby, P. (2012). Root and branch restructuring to achieve major cuts: The social policy programme of the 2010 UK coalition government. *Social Policy & Administration*, 46(1), 61–82.

TCPA/Nationwide Foundation (2017). *How Can Councils Secure the Delivery of More Affordable Homes? New Models, Partnerships and Innovations*. London: TCPA.

Walsh, D. (2017). Taxpayers help to buy £100m bonus for Persimmon boss Jeff Fairburn. *The Times*, 27 November 2017. www.google.co.uk/search?ei=kkZGWtKXJYnZgAa Kr7zoAQ&q=persimmon+bonus&oq=persimmon+bonus&gs_l=psy-ab.3.. 0l3j0i22i30k1l3.8598.12160.0.13517.17.17.0.0.0.0.85.1177.17.17.0....0...1c.1.64.psy-ab..0. 17.1144...0i131i67k1j0i67k1j0i10k1.0.cWkH_NLCiA0 (accessed 29 March 2017).

Whitehead, C. (2017a). Breaking down the barriers to housing delivery? *Journal of Planning and Environment Law*, 13, OP26–OP39.

Whitehead, C. (2017b). Breaking down the barriers to housing delivery. Paper presented at Joint Planning Law Conference, Oxford Union, 16 September 2017.

Wilcox, S., & Perry, J. (2014). *UK Housing Review*. Coventry: Chartered Institute of Housing.

Zurich Municipal with Solace (2016). *Worlds Apart the 2016 Senior Managers' Risk Report*. Fareham: Zurich Municipal.

2   Planning and the New Urban Agenda

Introduction

While much of the planning context for England is set by the UK government, this includes the incorporation of agreements that the UK has made internationally, which are then integrated within planning legislation and practice. The implications of these agreements are seldom transparent and infrequently mentioned at the point of delivery. However, this does not remove their power and influence over government policy or the modes set out for its delivery. Central government has a range of powers, although since the 2007 EU Lisbon Treaty these are less binding on local government (Morphet 2013) and it has to achieve its outcomes though nudged compliance, frequently included within deals and competitions for resources. The underlying shifts for the application and implementation of the New Urban Agenda (NUA) set out in this chapter are in process but not yet fully applied. This is, in part, because the United Nations (UN) and other bodies involved in their delivery have yet to finalise how compliance with the agreement will be assessed although the UK, along with other countries, will be seeking to influence these processes to their own benefit.

The Role of the United Nations in Framing Planning Policy

The UN, since its foundation in 1945, has always had the improvement of society's wellbeing and protection as its charter responsibilities (Thakur 2016). These have included the provision of humanitarian aid in response to disasters and the work of the World Health Organization (WHO) in combatting disease and attempting to reduce poverty across the globe. The UN has pursued these objectives in a variety of ways but since the Brundtland Commission in 1987, the UN has increasingly become engaged in promoting environmental, economic and social sustainability as a principle means of dealing with economic differences and poverty. At the first Earth Summit in Rio in 1992, the UN brought together a range of actors under the banner of thinking globally and acting locally and encouraging all local authorities to adopt a Local Agenda 21 (LA21) action plan.

Sustainability was also taken up by the European Union (EU), which has been engaged in supporting the implementation of the UN's agenda in a positive way since the Scandinavian countries joined the EU in 1972 (Morphet 2013; CEC 2013a; CEC 2016a and b). The Earth Summit objectives were also taken up by other international bodies. The EU, for example adopted its Fifth Environmental Action Programme (CEC 1992; Jordan et al. 2003), which was significantly more ambitious than the preceding ones. The EU took the opportunities provided by the Single European Market, also adopted in 1992, to consider how sustainable approaches could be adopted through trade as well as through environmental and redistribution programmes to promote economic and social cohesion.

LA21 was very actively taken up by local governments within the UK. In the early 1990s, local authorities had been through a period of Thatcherism since 1979, with reductions in their budgets and powers. The opportunity to work across the public, private and third sectors to adopt LA21 targets and programmes was different. LA21 offered more local activity that could be embraced and managed within whatever resources were available. Further, it did not need any new powers. By 1996, nearly 40 per cent of UK local authorities were actively supporting LA21 and nearly 50 per cent provided more tentative support (Tuxworth 1996). This support focused primarily on preparing a strategy to put LA21 principles into action in the local authority through changing approaches to waste management and energy conservation, with a number adopting a more systematic approach to environmental auditing (Morphet and Hams 1994), including a few that applied an international standard, including a few that applied an international standard for environmental auditing (BS EN ISO 14001 2015). BS7750 for Environmental Auditing. LA21 was implemented through a range of local authority services, including planning, anti-poverty programmes and regeneration, but also included tendering and procurement. Local authorities also took the opportunity to establish LA21 fora and engage directly with business and community groups in a joint approach to adopting more sustainable places that would be recognised as such by their citizens.

While there were criticisms about the extent of the penetration of LA21 throughout local authority organisations (Selman 1998), its adoption marked a considerable revitalisation in local government. The integrating approaches generated at the Earth Summit for local government influenced subsequent government policy, which required all local authorities to prepare a community strategy, from 2000 onwards, that was specifically to include the LA21 Action Plan. Although there was some resistance to this initially (Williams 2002; Morphet 2008), this was later reduced when the community strategy was changed to a Sustainable Community Strategy (SCS) in 2007. Local authority SCSs were for all internal services. They also set the framework for work with partners, including setting strategic objectives. The SCS was the strategy of strategies. This also included the direction and priorities of the local plan (Morphet 2010). The requirement to use this local authority SCS to identify the priorities for the local plan was further adopted in the Planning and Compulsory Purchase Act in England and Wales (Lambert 2006); it was also incorporated for community planning approaches in Scotland.

The government added the requirement for local authorities to commit to a specific number of targets set out through national indicators, so local plans not only had to meet the objectives of the SCS but also had to specifically demonstrate how they would achieve progress on the targets for the local authority. These targets were based on issues where the local authority had specific problems such as health, poor housing or educational attainment. In a study commissioned by the Department of Health in 2010, it was found that local authorities had started to take innovative approaches in addressing their health priorities in their local plans. However, much of this innovation was subsequently lost as government priorities for local plans switched towards housing after 2010. Planning also had to operate within the priorities set out by the government's Sustainable Development Strategy (ODPM 2006), which included commitments to environmental standards, transport and housing. Gradually, the role of LA21 was absorbed into the Local Plan and it was lost as a freestanding local authority policy statement.

UN Millennium Development Goals 1992–2000

In 2000, the UN followed the Earth Summit in Rio with the adoption the Millennium Development Goals (MDGs). These comprised of eight goals to be achieved by 2015, as shown in Table 2.1. The MDGs focused primarily on poorer countries and from the outset, differential rates of take up and delivery were noted (Sachs and McArthur 2005). The focus of the approach was for each country to adopt its own national programme of action and mobilise its own resources as well as an aid to achieve these ends. However, as it was difficult for poorer countries to meet these goals, there were concerns expressed that these countries would be identified as failing in their inability to do so (Easterly 2009), even if they had made substantial progress (Sachs 2012), particularly in relation to reducing poverty and gender parity (Bourguignon et al. 2010).

The MDGs have been regarded as an important framework to set out targets for change with investment from donor countries and internal policy changes. At the same time, more investment was required from the private sector, specifically for infrastructure that would allow poorer countries to grow their economies.

Table 2.1 UN Millennium Development Goals

Beyond 2015

1. To eradicate extreme poverty and hunger
2. To achieve universal primary education
3. To promote gender equality and empower women
4. To reduce child mortality
5. To improve maternal health
6. To combat HIV/AIDS, malaria and other diseases
7. To ensure environmental sustainability
8. To develop a global partnership for development

Towards the end of the target period, attention started to switch to the adoption of a new set of Sustainable Development Goals (SDGs) from 2015 onwards, which would apply to all countries.

The UN's Sustainable Development Goals

The UN developed its SDGs in a more open and inclusive way than that adopted for the MDGs. Sachs (2012) identified the need for a key shift in focus between the MDGS and SDGs. Whereas the MDGs were primarily focussed on less developed countries, he argued that the SDGs should apply to all countries, regardless of their economic position, and that they could act together. While important environmental issues were identified, Sachs also placed an emphasis on the role of governance from national to local scales as being an essential feature in delivering change. The role of cities was also particularly identified and has its own agreement within this programme – the NUA – which is discussed further on.

The SDGs were developed through consultative processes and, as a result, there were eight goals that, between them, included 18 targets and 48 indicators (UN 2009) and were addressed to all nations in a normative way (Watson 2016). While poverty was a primary focus in the MDGs, the SDGs are generally targeted at achieving more sustainability. Griggs et al. (2013) have argued that the SDGs can no longer be an extension of what was there before but need to convey a significant shift into a more integrated approach that appreciates the move into a new geological era of the Anthropocene, which includes the influence of man-made changes.

Since the SDGs were adopted in 2015, national delivery assessments have commenced. One of the key challenges in the SDGs, compared with the MDGs, is the integration and overlapping nature of the goals and how they can be delivered. In a working paper for the UN, Le Blanc (2015) indicates that these goals are best seen as a network rather than as silos. However, as Nilsson et al. (2016) discuss, it is difficult for policy makers to work in an integrated way when delivery programmes frequently operate within specific, silo-based goals. It would be more integrating if the mutual benefits created across different localities and policy areas could be measured. There has been considerable discussion about the ways in which these SDGs can work together (see, for example, Waage et al. 2015) and a concern that these goals will be managed in a top-down way by governments (Hajer et al. 2015). Lu et al. (2015) also identify that the SDGs place much more responsibility for their achievement on the role of scientists' developing ways of achieving and monitoring those goals. However, as Parnell (2016) indicates, academics are not always comfortable with having a direct role in delivery. Further, Le Blanc (2015) argues that the SDGs should be enablers for integration and has identified how this could be examined in practice, as shown in Table 2.2. The interrelationships between these goals are shown on Table 2.3.

Table 2.2 Links between the SDGs through Targets: An Aggregated Picture

Rank	Sustainable Development Goal	Number of Other Goals to which the Goal Is Connected
1	12 – Ensure sustainable consumption and production patterns	14
2	10 – Reduce inequality within and among countries	12
3	1 – End poverty in all its forms everywhere	10
4	8 – Promote sustained, inclusive and sustainable economic growth, full and productive employment and decent work for all	10
5	2 – End hunger, achieve food security and improved nutrition and promote sustainable agriculture	8
6	3 – Ensure healthy lives and promote wellbeing for all at all ages	8
7	5 – Achieve gender equality and empower all women and girls	8
8	4 – Ensure inclusive and equitable quality education and promote lifelong learning opportunities for all	7
9	6 – Ensure availability and sustainable management of water and sanitation for all	7
10	11 – Make cities and human settlements inclusive, safe, resilient and sustainable	6
11	13 – Take urgent action to combat climate change and its impacts	6
12	15 – Protect, restore and promote sustainable use of terrestrial ecosystems, sustainably manage forests, combat desertification, and halt and reverse land degradation and halt biodiversity loss	6

Rank	Sustainable Development Goal	Number of Other Goals to which the Goal Is Connected
13	16 – Promote peaceful and inclusive societies for sustainable development, provide access to justice for all and build effective, accountable and inclusive institutions at all levels	6
14	7 – Ensure access to affordable, reliable, sustainable and modern energy for all	3
15	9 – Build resilient infrastructure, promote inclusive and sustainable industrialization and foster innovation	3
16	14 – Conserve and sustainably use the oceans, seas and marine resources for sustainable development	2

Source: Le Blanc 2015.

The New Urban Agenda

As part of the adoption of the SDGs, Goal 11 has focussed particularly on the role of cities. In this, through the delivery of their targets, city governments are asked to make cities 'safe, resilient, sustainable and inclusive'. Much of the world's population now lives in cities and, as with LA21, there is a strong focus on the influence and effectiveness of local action to make change. These approaches for change can be adopted across all cities. Action can be taken from the city's current position or base line and localised, rather than suggesting a common approach for all. However, the UN will be adopting methods of assessing progress towards achieving the principle targets within the NUA for each city and ranking their comparative progress through bench-marking.

The declaration of the NUA, which was made in Quito (UN 2016), states that its delivery will require a paradigm shift from what has been before. This shift is represented through planning, developing, governing and managing cities in ways that are different. While relying on the roles of local government and communities, the NUA also recognises the need for leadership from central governments for the development of urban policies and support for their implementation. To achieve this, the NUA includes 'transformative commitments' to achieve the reduction of poverty through a range of measures, including supporting policies for older people and for housing. These

Table 2.3 The Influence of One Sustainable Development Goal or Target on Another Can Be Summarised with this Simple Scale.

Interaction	Name	Explanation	Example
+3	Indivisible	Inextricably linked to the achievement of another goal.	Ending all forms of discrimination against women and girls is indivisible from ensuring women's full and effective participation and equal opportunities for leadership.
+2	Reinforcing	Aids the achievement of another goal.	Providing access to electricity reinforces water-pumping and irrigation systems. Strengthening the capacity to adapt to climate-related hazards reduces losses caused by disasters.
+1	Enabling	Creates conditions that further another goal.	Providing electricity access in rural homes enables education, because it makes it possible to do homework at night with electric lighting.
0	Consistent	No significant positive or negative interactions.	Ensuring education for all does not interact significantly with infrastructure development or conservation of ocean ecosystems.
−4	Constraining	Limits options on another goal.	Improved water efficiency can constrain agricultural irrigation. Reducing climate change can constrain the options for energy access.
−2	Counter-acting	Clashes with another goal.	Boosting consumption for growth can counteract waste reduction and climate mitigation.
−3	Cancelling	Makes it impossible to reach another goal.	Fully ensuring public transparency and democratic accountability cannot be combined with national-security goals. Full protection of natural reserves excludes public access for recreation.

Source: Nilsson et al. 2016 p321.

transformative approaches are also linked to economic growth that is related to spatial and territorial integration across borders. The role of planning in setting out policies and regulatory frameworks for density and polycentric urban and rural relationships has been identified as a core institutional component. The NUA includes the issues of ethical business operation as part of the growth agenda and the local provision of goods and services to improve sustainable delivery. There is also the recognition of the need for urban resilience against a range of potential environmental and economic disasters. There is also a commitment to a smart city approach to improve service delivery and this is discussed further in Chapter 14.

The implementation plan for the NUA was also adopted in Habitat III in Quito in 2016. In the period before the meeting in October, there were preparatory sessions between selected member states charged with putting together the agenda. In addition, the EU made its own contribution to the debate through its adoption of an Urban Agenda in the Amsterdam Pact (CEC 2016c). The EU also identified the role of cities and urban governance as being critical dimensions of achieving the changes that are being sought. Like the adoption of LA21 at Rio in 1992, there is a much bigger push towards identifying the role of sub-state governments, which generally have lower levels of recognition in international organisations and agreements. This also coincides with the policy approach being undertaken by the OECD, which is emphasising the role of strong city leadership and the alignment of economic and administrative boundaries as mechanisms to improve national GDP (OECD 2015). Cities are also being encouraged to work in vertical contracts between national, local and community governments (Charbit and Romano 2017).

Delivering the New Urban Agenda in the EU

The EU has expressed its commitment to delivering the NUA though its own priorities and programmes since 2013 (CEC 2013a). The EU's Urban Agenda (UA), also known as the Amsterdam Pact (CEC 2016c), recognises of the role of cities in the EU and their role in achieving this agenda and incorporates the component policy areas, as shown in Table 2.4.

The European Commission (EC) is holding a wide range of conferences and discussions on the UA and these will feed into the formulation of programmes and legislation. In line with the NUA, the EU is promoting an integrated approach as part of its key objectives. The EC is not proposing to provide additional funding for the UA, but to better focus the funding and policy programmes on achieving these objectives. These will have an increasingly spatial turn from 2021 and will be allied to the more integrated approaches for other, more strategic investment programmes and, like other EU activities, it will set out how these goals can be achieved through an Action Plan.

In developing the UA, the EU has located its provenance in an extensive line of territorial and planning activities. These include:

the Leipzig Charter (2007)
the Toledo Declaration (2010)
Europe 2020 (2010) and *Europe 2020*, the territorial agenda (2011) (CEC 2007, 2010a and b, 2011).

The Toledo Declaration was important but initially overlooked in the UK, as it was made at a meeting a few days after the 2010 general election and while the Coalition government was being formed. From this, initiatives such as City Deals in the UK (O'Brien and Pike 2015) perform as territorial pacts or contracts between localities and the state (Camagni and Capello 2010).

Table 2.4 EU Urban Agenda Policy Areas

- Urban mobility
- Digital transition
- Circular economy
- Jobs and skills in the local economy
- Urban poverty
- Inclusion of migrants and refugees
- Housing
- Air quality

Source: CEC 2017a.

In the current EU programme period, 2014–2020, the focus is on the partnerships established to take forward key issues identified in the Amsterdam Pact, but also those in the NUA. It is interesting to note that while planning is not identified as a specific issue in this list, housing enters as a priority for the first time. This will be developed though member state-led partnership to propose ideas for wider consideration. The housing partnership that is led by Slovakia is particularly focused on the provision of affordable housing and has already prepared a toolkit that can be used (CEC 2017b). This toolkit comprises examples and is also linked to the Geneva UN Charter on Sustainable Housing (UN 2016). Finally, it has linked to the EU's policy on corporate social responsibility to housing provision (CEC 2017c). Other partnerships that relate to the practice of planning including those for urban mobility and local transport provision principles and practices, the digital and circular economies and a partnership to tackle urban poverty.

There have also been calls for the EC to consider territorial impact assessment (TIA) for EU policies as they are developed and delivered in practice (CEMR 2015). This would also be an integrative approach (Charbit and Romano 2017) serving to reduce the effects of silo working within EC directorates and starting to meet the integrative priorities of the NUA. The role of TIA (Camagni 2006; CEC 2013b) and the methods that could be used to consider policy impacts on localities have been developed by the EC in conjunction with the OECD Urban Policy programme. A review of potential TIA methodologies has been funded by the EC and developed though ESPON (Medeiros 2015). This has now moved to the next stage in consideration of draft legislation (Fischer et al. 2015).

NUA and Planning

The mechanisms for delivering the NUA, as set out, focus primarily on the role of planning at all spatial scales. This includes a requirement for a national spatial plan – something that has not yet been prepared in England although available in Scotland, Northern Ireland and Wales. The UK is the only EU member state without a state spatial plan (Barca 2009). While not specifically mentioning the need for vertical and horizontal integration between plans at different scales, these are also an essential feature of the approach. There is a specific commitment to city regions and functional economic areas and their governance. This suggests a much greater focus on strategic planning approaches that can include the integrated policy frameworks for decision making and investment. Within the EU, this broader context has been provided through mega regions such as the Baltic, Adriatic, Alpine and Danube regions (Stead 2014), while the OECD has praised the approaches being adopted in Manchester and London in the UK (OECD 2015). The four key drivers of change that are included within the NUA are set out in Table 2.5.

One of the key dimensions of the NUA, for planning, is a focus on strategic planning and its links with governance both within and between countries. This is seen to be both within functional urban areas and in relating cities with their peripheries (ESPON 2017; Morphet 2017). Another key dimension for planning is the relationship between spatial planning, governance and participation in decision-making (Evans et al. 2016). As Watson (2016) points out, achieving the NUA requires a strong approach to spatial planning at all territorial scales through what she describes as the adoption and delivery of a state agenda. This includes a strong set of national level plans but is later to be replaced by policies that will provide strong structures to support increasing levels of decentralisation. The approach to spatial planning coincides with OECD and EU approaches.

> We will implement urban and territorial plans including city-region and metropolitan plans, to encourage synergies and interactions between and among separate urban areas, and their surroundings, including the cross-border ones and develop regional infrastructure projects that stimulate sustainable economic productivity, promoting equitable growth of regions. In this regard we will promote urban-rural partnerships.
>
> (UN Habitat 2015 para 81)

This approach to planning also includes transport and mobility, affordable housing, access to green space and culture and heritage.

Table 2.5 The Four Drivers of Change in the New Urban Agenda

i.	Developing and implementing national urban policies within a renewed local–national partnership building integrated national systems of cities and human settlements, toward the achievement of national development targets;
ii.	Strengthening urban legislation, providing predictability and order in the urban development plans to enable social and economic performance and wealth creation;
iii.	Reinvigorate urban and territorial planning in order to optimise the spatial dimension of the urban form and deliver the urban advantage;
iv.	Supporting effective financing frameworks, enabling strengthened municipal finance and local fiscal systems in order to create, sustain and share the value generated by sustainable urban development.

Source: UN Habitat 2016 p11 para 11b.

There are also issues that arise from deriving delivery programmes to meet targets based within international agreements. While there is an intense pressure to deliver the outcomes through subsidiarity, that is at the lowest level of government that is appropriate and through partnerships, the pressures for compliance on states that have signed the international agreements tend to push them towards a more statist and top-down approach (Schreiber et al. 2016). It also means that there is a need to establish methods through which compliance can be measured and direct action taken if the goals are not being reached by the times anticipated. It can also mean that there will be greater reliance on intermediary bodies such as the EU for indicating methods of delivery. There is some commonality of approach and methodologies can be compared. There are also similar government frameworks for issues such as subsidiarity that will support delivery.

One of the key issues for the implementation of the NUA through planning is the challenge of measurement and what is regarded as being successful. In considering the application of the NUA in specific cities and their degree of success in achieving the targets through criteria-based measurement, a main consideration will be the extent to which there are existing statistical monitoring systems available that will be able to meet the criteria-based approach. As Simon et al. (2016) point out, what is measured is usually what is easiest to capture through data, although these factors may not be the most important ones to consider. Yet there are no standardised metrics across cities for the measurement of responses to the NUA criteria.

A second issue for the NUA is that it has gone beyond sustainability. In the NUA's original 1992 approach, 'sustainability' included social, economic and environmental dimensions, but it has increasingly been associated only with the environment. The term 'environmental sustainability' is used to characterise this diminished form and positively excludes the social and economic aspects. This makes it difficult to undertake assessments of choices and the consideration of effects through techniques such as cost–benefit analysis or the balanced score card technique of comparative analysis. Other concepts such as life cycle analysis or natural capital are also considerations in evaluation (Neuman and Churchill 2015) but again, these may be too generic to provide any useful approaches to systematic consideration of issues for policy and decision making.

In developing the NUA, Satterthwaite (2016) asks how much of the agenda is new and differentiated from the agendas that were put forward in Habitat I and Habitat II. He mentions the range of initiatives such as LA21, as well as the healthy cities movements, support for participatory budgeting and the need for resilience. He also mentions the way in which cities have supported approaches to carbon reduction in principle. But in these approaches, how many have been successful and what difference have they made in improving sustainability and reducing the negative effects that they have been targeted to deal with, including poverty?

While there have been commitments to earlier NUA approaches in Habitats I and II, Buckley and Simet (2016) also argue that there is now evidence that urban growth has a positive relationship with economic growth, thus making the NUA more acceptable to global governments. These approaches have also had the effect of making the cities and their economic roles more important to state governments. Since Habitat II, the world has had a major economy recession and growth has been more difficult to find, with levels creeping back to pre-2007 levels only ten years later. In some cases, growth in wages has yet to be restored, as in the UK (ONS 2017). Therefore, the potential of city growth to support the additional economic growth of national economies ensures that there is a considerable focus on cities' roles. This also means that, unlike the preceding agreements, there is a new priority to consider the methods of delivery, as well as goals and targets. However, this may lead to a more standardised approach to city policy across the world (Caprotti and Cowley 2017; Caprotti et al. 2017).

This may be further captured through the creation of an International Standards Organization (ISO) standard for smart cities in 2014 (Lazarte 2015), which has been followed by other international standards. In this way, smart cities are now seen as a practical manifestation of the NUA and this international standard is a technical means of comparing programmes. However, it is unlikely that all aspects of the NUA can be represented in smart city analytics and even this nomenclature might discourage some city governments and citizens from engagement with measurement. The use of the standard approach also depoliticises the agenda and any redistributive effects. By following a standard, this reduces the political responsibility for the outcome and yet can demonstrate 'progress' towards technically defined ends. A standard also provides an objectified reason for action, which may not relate to the needs of specific localities and reduces the effectiveness of devolution and local prioritisation.

Not all cities want to adopt the same approaches and see the use of indicators and policy initiatives such as smart cities adopted though the NUA as being a formulaic approach to achieving change. Kaika (2017) has called this approach 'greening by numbers', where adherence to achieving the technical standards specified may be undertaken but at the same time, the city may become more inequitable or less resilient to environmental disasters. In focusing only on some indicators, there is a danger that the wider scale impacts are overlooked or appear as an unintended consequence of applying such approaches. As part of the work on developing the NUA, the paper of the Focus Group on Smart Sustainable Cities stated that it is 'a truth universally acknowledged that a (smart) city in possession of a good information and communications technology (ICT) infrastructure must also be sustainable' (Araña and Myhili 2015 p9).

Conclusion

Does the NUA suggest a different approach for planning within the coming period to 2030? There are some shifts that are likely to be important for the UK. The first is the need to produce a spatial plan for the whole territory that encompasses spatial priorities for investment, growth and attention, particularly where there is an economic and social difference from national averages. The production of a national infrastructure plan or national infrastructure strategy does not provide enough detail of priorities, nor the integration between objectives and programmes that is required.

Secondly, there is a focus on strategic planning within functional economic areas that are supported by governance structures and institutions. If cities are the major contribution to achieving inclusive growth, then they need to be able to work with their peripheries to incorporate a common approach. These arrangements also need to be set out in contractual form that allows governments at each scale to pursue their own priorities but also to determine where joint working will provide significant benefits for all geographies. Both outcomes will have significant implications for planning practice. The development of strategic plans that incorporate vertical and horizontal policies and programmes for functional economic areas will require a major shift in culture, particularly for those who are still arguing for the return of regional or structural plans (Colomb and Tomaney 2016).

References

Araña, S., & Menon, M. (2015). Smart Sustainable Cities: A Guide for City Leaders. ITU-T Focus Group on Smart Sustainable Cities technical report.

Barca, F. (2009). *An Agenda for a Reformed Cohesion Policy*. Brussels: CEC.

BS EN ISO 14001 (2015). Environmental management systems: Requirements with guidance for use. https://shop.bsigroup.com/ProductDetail/?pid=000000000030281203 (accessed 23 July 2018).

Bourguignon, F., Bénassy-Quéré, A., Dercon, S., Estache, A., Gunning, J. W., Kanbur, R., & Spadaro, A. (2010). The millennium development goals: An assessment. *Equity and Growth in a Globalizing World*, 17.

Brundtland Commission (1987). Our common future: Report of the World Commission on Environment and Development. UN Documents Gathering a Body of Global Agreements. New York: United Nations.

Buckley, R. M., & Simet, L. (2016). An agenda for Habitat III: Urban perestroika. *Environment and Urbanization*, 28(1), 64–76.

Camagni, R. (2006). Territorial Impact Assessment-TIA: A methodological proposal. *Scienze Regionali*, 5(2), 135–147.

Camagni, R., & Capello, R. (2010). Macroeconomic and territorial policies for regional competitiveness: An EU perspective. *Regional Science Policy & Practice*, 2(1), 1–19.

Caprotti, F., & Cowley, R. (2017). Interrogating urban experiments. *Urban Geography*, 38(9), 1441–1450.

Caprotti, F., Cowley, R., Datta, A., Broto, V.C., Gao, E., Georgeson, L., Herrick, C., Odendaal, N., & Joss, S. (2017). The New Urban Agenda: Key opportunities and challenges for policy and practice. *Urban Research & Practice*, 10(3), 367–378.

CEC (1992). *Fifth Environmental Action Programme*. Brussels: CEC.

CEC (2007). Leipzig Charter on sustainable European cities. http://ec.europa.eu/regiona l_policy/archive/themes/urban/leipzig_charter.pdf (accessed 23 July 2018).

CEC (2010a). Toledo informal ministerial meeting on urban development declaration. www.mdrap.ro/userfiles/declaratie_Toledo_en.pdf (accessed 23 July 2018).

CEC (2010b). Europe 2020 strategy. https://ec.europa.eu/info/business-economy-euro/economic-and-fiscal-policy-coordination/eu-economic-governance-monitoring-prevention-correction/european-semester/framework/europe-2020-strategy_en (accessed 23 July 2018).

CEC (2011). Territorial agenda of the European Union 2020. http://ec.europa.eu/regional_policy/en/information/publications/communications/2011/territorial-agenda-of-the-european-union-2020 (accessed 23 July 2018).

CEC (2013a). *EU Contribution to the Millennium Development Goals Key Results from European Commission programmes*. Brussels: CEC.

CEC (2013b). Assessing territorial impacts: Operational guidance on how to assess regional and local impacts within the Commission Impact Assessment System Brussels. Brussels: CEC. http://ec.europa.eu/smart-regulation/impact/key_docs/docs/cswd_ati_en.pdf (accessed 4 July 2018).

CEC (2016a). The 2030 Agenda for Sustainable Development. https://ec.europa.eu/europeaid/policies/european-development-policy/2030-agenda-sustainable-development_en (accessed 4 July 2018).

CEC (2016b). Key European action supporting the 2030 Agenda and the Sustainable Development Goals. Strasbourg: CEC. https://ec.europa.eu/europeaid/sites/devco/files/swd-key-european-actions-2030-agenda-sdgs-390-20161122_en.pdf (accessed 4 July 2018).

CEC (2016c). *The Urban Agenda for the EU: The Amsterdam Pact*. Brussels: CEC.

CEC (2017a). Urban Agenda for the EU. https://ec.europa.eu/futurium/en/urban-agenda (accessed 4 July 2018).

CEC (2017b). Affordable housing toolkit. https://ec.europa.eu/futurium/en/housing/toolkit-affordable-housing-policy-0 (accessed 22 October 2017).

CEC (2017c). Responsible housing. www.responsiblehousing.eu/en/. (accessed 22 October 2017).

CEMR (2015). Territorial Development An EU Urban Agenda Should Facilitate Local Authorities' Action on the Ground: Position Paper. Brussels: CEMR.

Charbit, C., & Romano, O. (2017). Governing together: An international review of contracts across levels of government for regional development. Regional Development Working Paper 2017/04. Paris: OECD.

Colomb, C., & Tomaney, J. (2016). Territorial politics, devolution and spatial planning in the UK: Results, prospects, lessons. *Planning Practice & Research*, 31(1), 1–22.

Easterly, W. (2009). How the millennium development goals are unfair to Africa. *World Development*, 37(1), 26–35.

ESPON (2017). Polycentric territorial structures and territorial cooperation policy brief. www.espon.eu/topics-policy/publications/policy-briefs/polycentric-territorial-structures-and-territorial (accessed 4 July 2018).

Evans, B., Elisei, P., Rosenfeld, O., Roll, G., Figueiredo, A., & Keiner, M. (2016). HABITAT III–Toward a new urban agenda. *Disp: The Planning Review*, 52(1), 86–91.

Fischer, T. B., Sykes, O., Gore, T., Marot, N., Golobič, M., Pinho, P., & Perdicoulis, A. (2015). Territorial impact assessment of European draft directives: The emergence of a new policy assessment instrument. *European Planning Studies*, 23(3), 433–451.

Griggs, D., Stafford-Smith, M., Gaffney, O., Rockström, J., Öhman, M.C., Shyamsundar, P., Steffen, W., Glaser, G., Kanie, N., & Noble, I. (2013). Policy: Sustainable development goals for people and planet. *Nature*, 495(7441), 305–307.

Hajer, M., Nilsson, M., Raworth, K., Bakker, P., Berkhout, F., de Boer, Y., & Kok, M. (2015). Beyond cockpit-ism: Four insights to enhance the transformative potential of the sustainable development goals. *Sustainability*, 7(2), 1651–1660.

Jordan, A., Wurzel, R. K., & Zito, A. R. (2003). 'New' instruments of environmental governance: Patterns and pathways of change. *Environmental Politics*, 12(1), 1–24.

Kaika, M. (2017). 'Don't call me resilient again!': The New Urban Agenda as immunology… or… what happens when communities refuse to be vaccinated with 'smart cities' and indicators. *Environment and Urbanization*, 29(1), 89–102.

Lambert, C. (2006). Community strategies and spatial planning in England: The challenges of integration. *Planning, Practice & Research*, 21(2), 245–255.

Lazarte, M. (2015). How to measure the performance of smart cities. www.iso.org/news/2015/10/Ref2001.html (accessed 22 Oct 2017).

Le Blanc, D. (2015). Towards integration at last? The sustainable development goals as a network of targets. *Sustainable Development*, 23(3), 176–187.

Lu, Y., Nakicenovic, N., Visbeck, M., & Stevance, A. S. (2015). Five priorities for the UN sustainable development goals. *Nature*, 520(7548), 432–433.

Medeiros, E. (2015). Territorial impact assessment and cross-border cooperation. *Regional Studies, Regional Science*, 2(1), 97–115.

Morphet, J. (2010). *Effective Practice in Spatial Planning*. Abingdon: Routledge.

Morphet, J. (2008). *Modern Local Government*. London: SAGE.

Morphet, J. (2013). *How Europe Shapes British Public Policy*. Bristol: Policy Press.

Morphet, J. (2017). Rescaling the suburban: New directions in the relationship between governance and infrastructure. *Local Economy*, 32(8), 803–817.

Morphet, J., & Hams, T. (1994). Responding to Rio: a local authority approach. *Journal of Environmental Planning and Management*, 37(4), 479–486.

Neuman, M., & Churchill, S. (2015). Measuring sustainability. *Town Planning Review*, 86(4), 457–482.

Nilsson, M., Griggs, D., & Visbeck, M. (2016). Map the interactions between sustainable development goals: Mans Nilsson, Dave Griggs and Martin Visbeck present a simple way of rating relationships between the targets to highlight priorities for integrated policy. *Nature*, 534(7607), 320–323.

O'Brien, P., & Pike, A. (2015). City deals, decentralisation and the governance of local infrastructure funding and financing in the UK. *National Institute Economic Review*, 233(1), R14–R26.

ODPM (2006). *Sustainable Communities: Building for the Future*. London: ODPM.

OECD (2015). *Local Economic Leadership*. Paris: OECD.

ONS (2017). *Annual Survey of Hours and Earnings: 2017 Provisional and 2016 Revised Results.* www.ons.gov.uk/employmentandlabourmarket/peopleinwork/earningsandworkinghours/bulletins/annualsurveyofhoursandearnings/2017provisionaland2016revisedresults (accessed 23 July 2017).

Parnell, S. (2016). Expectations of academic journals in crafting alternative global scholarship to drive a new urban agenda. *Urbanisation*, 1(1),1–5.

Sachs, J. D. (2012). From millennium development goals to sustainable development goals. *The Lancet*, 379(9832), 2206–2211.

Sachs, J. D., & McArthur, J. W. (2005). The millennium project: a plan for meeting the millennium development goals. *The Lancet*, 365(9456), 347.

Satterthwaite, D. (2016). A new urban agenda? *Environment and Urbanization*, 28(1): 3–12.

Schreiber, F., Fischer, K., Dellas, E., & Carius, A. (2016). *Designing the New Urban Agenda: Lessons from International Agreements*. Berlin: Adelphi.

Selman, P. (1998). Local Agenda 21: Substance or spin? *Journal of Environmental Planning and Management*, 41(5), 533–553.

Simon, D., Arfvidsson, H., Anand, G., Bazaz, A., Fenna, G., Foster, K., ... & Nyam-buga, C. (2016). Developing and testing the Urban Sustainable Development Goal's targets and indicators: A five-city study. *Environment and Urbanization*, 28(1), 49–63.

Stead, D. (2014). The rise of territorial governance in European policy. *European Planning Studies*, 22(7), 1368–1383.

Thakur, R. (2016). *The United Nations, Peace and Security: From Collective Security to the Responsibility to Protect*. Cambridge: Cambridge University Press.

Tuxworth, B. (1996). From environment to sustainability: Surveys and analysis of Local Agenda 21 process development in UK local authorities. *Local Environment*, 1(3), 277–297.

UN (2009). *Millennium Development Goals Report*. New York: UN. www.un.org/m illenniumgoals/ (accessed 4 July 2018).

UN (2016). New Urban Agenda Declaration on sustainable cities and human settlement for all. United Nations Conference on Housing and Sustainable Urban Development (Habitat III), Quito, 17–20 October. http://habitat3.org/the-new-urban-agenda/ (accessed 4 July 2018).

UN (2017). *Habitat III: New Urban Agenda*. New York: UN. http://habitat3.org/wp -content/uploads/NUA-English-With-Index-1.pdf (accessed 23 July 2017).

UN Habitat (2015). *The international guidelines on urban and territorial planning*. Nairobi, Kenya: UN Habitat.

UN Habitat (2016). *Monitoring framework, SDG Goal 11*.

Waage, J., Yap, C., Bel, S., Levy, C., Mace, G., Pegram, T., & Mayhew, S. (2015). Governing sustainable development goals: Interactions, infrastructures, and institutions. *The Lancet Global Health*, 3(5), e251–e252.

Watson, V. (2016). Locating planning in the New Urban Agenda of the urban sustainable development goal. *Planning Theory*, 15(4), 435–448.

Williams, P. M. (2002). Community strategies: mainstreaming sustainable development and strategic planning? *Sustainable Development*, 10(4), 197–205.

3 The Changing EU Context for Planning in the UK

Introduction

As the referendum on the UK's relationship with the EU in 2016 demonstrated, there is little understanding of the way in which the UK's EU membership has shaped, and continues to shape, British public policy, including that for planning. Although the UK's relationship with the EU will be changed by the Brexit referendum, it is also the case that the agreement to maintain full alignment of standards in Phase 1 of the negotiations between the UK and the EU (CEC 2017c) may mean that, in practical terms, the regulatory effects on planning practice may be minimal, although the access to legal means for the determination of the application of these standards to the European Court of Justice may be reduced. However, as this chapter discusses, there may be more significant changes in the operation of some principles and programmes that could have significant effects on planning legislation and delivery.

While the UK has been a member of the EU since 1 January 1973, it is hard to appreciate the ways in which this membership has influenced the context, legislation and practice of planning. While, as Evers and Tennekers (2016) have shown, it is not only in the UK where this lack of understanding of the EU's shaping role for planning has been recognised as a specific issue (Morphet 2013; Bulmer and Burch 2009; Haigh 1996). The context for planning provided by and through EU membership includes the ways in which the EU has evolved, takes decisions and where it acts on behalf of its member states in international treaties (Meunier 2005).

Yet these issues are fundamental in framing the practice of planning. The role of EU environmental legislation, which sets operational standards, is frequently mentioned as a key influence in determining UK planning practice (Knill and Lenschow 1998; Glasson et al. 2013; Lockwood 2013). However, these standards have been negotiated by the EU on behalf of its member states as part of a wider UK international commitment within treaties, both with the UN (Delreux 2014; Hedemann-Robinson 2015 Cowell 2017) and the World Trade Organization (WTO) in its trade and environment agreements (Daugbjerg and Swinbank 2015; Davies 2017). The WTO agreements also set the operating requirements for public procurement policies and these, together with other international agreements, will continue in operation, whatever the UK's continuing relationship with the EU (Morphet 2017).

This chapter reviews the way in which the UK's membership in the EU has shaped UK planning practice, both in setting policy and the application of standards. It reviews the main policy areas that the UK has pooled within EU decision making and discusses how these are shaped by the agreements that have been reached. Finally, it examines some of the potential effects of Brexit on UK planning practice.

How Does the EU Shape UK Planning Now?

Since 1973, the UK has participated in the development and agreement of all EU policy, including in those areas that have a major influence on planning, such as transport, energy, environment and cohesion policy. The European Commission (EC) has also taken a direct interest in planning through the preparation of the informal European Spatial Development Perspective (ESDP), which was adopted in Leipzig in 1999 (Faludi and Waterhout 2012; Duhr et al. 2010). This would have been a more formal approach if the UK government had not disputed the EC's powers to engage in planning policy. Following the adoption of the ESDP, which, despite its informal status, has been used to shape and inform policy in the UK (Shaw and Sykes 2003; GONE 2008; GOYH 2004), the EC was given wider powers over territorial policy in the Lisbon Treaty 2007 (CEC 2017a). There has been some discussion about what these powers may mean in practice and how they could be interpreted (Zonneveld and Waterhout 2005; Evers 2008; Medeiros 2016). The EC commissioned its own review (Barca 2009) and this remains the best basis on which to understand the scope and scale of territorial cohesion. In the EC review, Barca argues that there are strong theoretical, social and economic arguments for transferring policy to a place-based focus within the EU and that the use of the cohesion programme would be the best way to achieve this. Further, Barca argues that this place-based approach should be accompanied by changes in EU governance at all scales to reinforce the role of local knowledge and action within an overarching approach.

The EC is now beginning to exercise these new responsibilities for territorial cohesion in a range of ways including at macro regional and pan-EU scales which are discussed below. In parallel with the preparation of the ESDP, there were also attempts to bring together a more collective understanding of the different approaches to building and planning permits in member states as part of the implementation of the internal single market. A compendium of member state planning policies in the 1990s was compiled (CEC 2000) and has been updated to include the Accession states as they have joined the EU. This work has now been resumed (Nadin et al. 2016) and in the longer term there may be some convergence of planning and building permit regulation within the framework of the EU's Single Market.

How Does the EU Operate?

The EU works through several interlocking decision making processes that comprise the European Council of the member states, the European Parliament of directly elected MEPs, the EC, which is the civil service, and through the European Court of Justice, which upholds the decisions made and interprets the law (Nugent 2017). The EU is founded on a series of treaties, which are set within an international context and take precedence over domestic law in member states. The treaties, particularly those of Rome (1957), Maastricht (1992) and Lisbon (2007), identify where member states have pooled powers and sovereignty between them and these agreements are then developed into legislation and programmes of delivery. The EU legislation is cumulative and hence builds on the treaties over time. This differs from UK law, which is episodic and, under the British Constitution, domestic legislation can be set aside by any future Parliament (Morphet 2013). For some issues, the European Parliament legislates and there needs to be unanimity in voting, whereas for others, there need to be majorities made in ways that reflect the size and populations of member states.

The EU develops its legal and operational activities within a series of principles and programmes that derive from the interpretation of the cumulative treaties. These are set within seven-year programmes that are set to work within the elections for the European Parliament and the appointment of the President of the European Council and the head of the EC, together with the appointment of Commissioners, who have the lead responsibilities in different policy areas. The issues that frame the EU's activities are:

i. Principles

The EU operates through the adoption of several key principles, which are agreed in the foundational treaties. These define the scope for the operational agenda of the EC in its role in preparing policies, legislation and programmes. In terms of planning, the main principles that are of relevance are those of fairness, cohesion and subsidiarity. The EU also has the agreed responsibility of negotiation, implementation and measuring the compliance of EU member states to international treaty agreements to which individual member states are signatories. These include the environmental treaties with the UN and the trade and environment treaties with the WTO. The EC primarily manages these commitments through their absorption into EU legislation and policy programmes. A recent example is the adoption of the Urban Pact (2016) as a means of implementing UN policies for the New Urban Agenda (NUA). These responsibilities are run together in an integrated way, but it is important to recognise their provenance and the implications they have for policy change and continued commitments, should any member state leave the EU.

The principle of fairness shapes policy and delivery in several ways that influence planning practice across the EU. It provides the legal underpinning for differential policy and programmes for EU territory. There may be different approaches to peripheral, island or mountainous areas to ensure that they have the same access as other more central areas. The same applies to policies for rural areas with sparse populations or urban areas with higher than average levels of unemployment or poverty. Allied to this principle are those of economic, social and now territorial cohesion (Medeiros 2016). These principles are applied across the whole of the EU's area and are considered in terms of distance from the average levels of income, skills, worklessness or transport in comparison with other areas. This leads to specific programmes to redress these differences in ways that are appropriate to the culture, norms and values of these localities, as well as the member state government programmes.

From 1973 to 2013, these differences have been addressed through structural funds applied in separate programmes within each policy area (Becker et al. 2010; Bachtler and Turok 2013). Since 2013, these cohesion programmes have been put together with programmes for sustainability and urban mobility, research and development and rural areas (Bachtler and Mendez 2016). There has also been a requirement for sub-state rural areas to produce Community Led Local Development Plans (CLLDs) (CEC 2016), which provides a coordinated approach to spatial strategy and associated programmes to support their delivery. In the UK, these are local plans in England, Northern Ireland and Wales and community plans in Scotland (O'Brien et al. 2017).

At the strategic scale of city regions and functional economic areas (FEAs), the cohesion regulation has included the provision for Integrated Territorial Investment (ITI) strategies (CEC 2015). These are more like business plans and coordinate spatial issues and priorities with delivery programmes and projects. In the UK, the only ITI in existence is in Cornwall (CIOSLEP 2016) although others exist in other member states (van der Zwet et al. 2017). In the programme period 2021–2026, these are expected to be the dominant mode for the form of cohesion programmes. These plans are required to be set within government frameworks and provide a basis for investment.

ii.   Decision Making

To implement the powers in the treaties, the EC proposes work programmes that primarily operate in seven-year cycles, giving each member state the opportunity to hold a general election and reset policy to support their delivery (Goetz and Meyer-Sahling 2009). Within these programmes, the EC proposes legislation, spending and investment priorities and softer measures to support joint working that may not have a formal status. These might include associated areas of research, which are commissioned most often to pave the way for subsequent initiatives and to offer an inclusive approach in problem solving. The legislation that is included as part of these programmes can take 4–7 years to finalise and is subject to agreement by the Council of Ministers.

All EU legislation is anchored on specific treaty provisions and subsequent legal agreements, as the 'whereas' statements at the beginning of any regulation or directive will testify. Because this legislation is rooted in treaties, it can be regarded as cumulative and substantive at each change in the Commission's structure in every seven-year cycle. All this is in direct contrast with the five-year Parliamentary cycle in the UK, where Parliaments are not bound by decisions enshrined in legislation made by their predecessors. This legal framework has a significant effect on some of the post-Brexit arrangements for devolution that are currently empowered and guaranteed through EU treaty principles of subsidiarity, which cannot be secured in the future for more than a five-year Parliamentary period unless the UK has a written constitution.

iii.   Delivery

The EU functions through a system of multi-level governance (MLG) that integrates both vertical and horizonal relationships (Morphet 2013; Charbit and Romano 2017). In the vertical expression of MLG, this is operated within the principle of subsidiarity – that is, decisions are taken at the lowest level of governance appropriate. The principle of MLG operates within the EU and in member states. It underpins devolution and localism in the UK. There is considerable discussion about the function and role of MLG, with some theorists' suggesting that it is a formal mechanism for representing intergovernmentalism (Schakel et al. 2015), whereas others regard it as a means of achieving more integrationist agency within the EU (Hooghe and Marks 2001). Some suggest that MLG is almost an unexpected consequence of having to work across all the member states and find ways to engage with their sub-state governments (Stephenson 2013). However, MLG is possibly best understood as a policy option being pursued by the EU to improve its territorial strategies and integrate governance over a longer period (Morphet 2013).

The EU is also now incorporating this approach with the new dimension of territorial cohesion that was introduced in the Lisbon Treaty in 2007 (Bache 2007; Rumford 2006). Although initially considered to be a nebulous concept, the exposition of the role of territory within the EU has been set out by Barca (2009). However, is territorial governance different from MLG or is there some convergence going on? Stead (2014b) suggests that the focus on territorial governance is more about identifying boundaries and considering impacts than about policy design but this may be a national rather than EU view.

Horizontal and vertical integration come together through formal programmes that have particularly been developed through planning across macro regions in the EU when formal relationships for areas are agreed and include the vertical scale of government within themselves (European Parliament 2017). These agreements include strategic plans, priorities and delivery programmes and are adopted by the European Council and Parliament as well as the constituent governments within them. While the programmes incorporate bottom-up priorities, they also provide a means for pan-EU investment and programming to be delivered. These plans have now been agreed for the Baltic, the Adriatic, the Danube and the Alps regions (Metzger & Schmitt 2012; Stead 2014a). However, this central endorsement reinforces the principles of no new funding, no new structures and no new legislation and to obtain this support, these macrolevel agreements align and focus their programmes using existing budgets and instruments. This provides the EU with ways of coordinating and streamlining investment and achieving more from the investment that is made.

Another form of MLG contract with EU provenance that has been used across the UK is through the mechanism of city deals. These are territorial pacts and are part of the EU's economic programme, *Europe 2020* (Antonescu 2015). In these pacts, the issues of economic downturn that were an outcome of the 2008 world economic crisis are addressed at the local level. These city deals are contractual in their construction and involve both the local and central states' making commitments. While established to meet one form of EU policy initiative, city deals may also be a useful mechanism for developing single governments and programmes across FEAs. This is in preparation for an ITI approach across the EU. It is also interesting to note that, even faced with the uncertainty of Brexit, the UK is still adopting and implementing EU policy and preparing for the next programme period in what might be a risk mitigation strategy (Morphet 2018).

There have been critics of the relationship between MLG and territorial cohesion. Faludi (2013) has argued that these principles cannot work because they must operate within the principle of subsidiarity, whereas Davoudi (2005) states that they support economic rather than spatial objectives. While there was much consideration and criticism of the interrelationship between these concepts when they were introduced in the Lisbon Treaty, there are now opportunities to review how they are working in practice both across borders and within the states in the east of the EU, where such policy approaches appear to have been more helpful (Adams et al. 2012; Perkmann 2007; Crespy et al. 2007).

EU and Planning at Different Spatial Scales

The EU operates at a range of spatial scales that each have an influence and bearing on planning practice in the UK. In this section, each of them is considered in turn.

i.   EU-Wide

The ESDP was adopted in 1999 (Duhr et al. 2010; Faludi 2004). This was an informal plan, as the UK had disputed the EC's responsibilities in matters related to planning. Now that the territorial cohesion principle has been added to the foundational responsibilities of the EU, further work is commencing on taking forward an EU spatial and investment plan and programme. The work on considering a range of scenarios for the future of the EU has been undertaken (ESPON 2016) and a range of options has been suggested. These will be taken forward into the next EU programme period (2021–2027) and are likely to be linked to the investment plan for Europe launched in 2010 by the president of the EC and confirmed in its more wide-reaching role in his State of the Union speech in 2017 (Juncker 2017).

Some of the major EU-wide strategic planning activity that has a direct influence on UK planning at the national and local levels is through the Trans-European Networks, which are considered across the whole of the EU's territory but are implemented within member states and in specific localities.

ii.   Megaregional

The megaregional strategies were initially developed in *Europe 2000* (CEC 1991) and *Europe 2000+* (CEC 1994) and since then have been developing in soft forms that have been supported by EU INTERREG funding that was launched in 1992. In some parts of the EU, these megaregional areas have developed further and created plans, strategies and investment programmes that have been agreed by the member states and local authorities and the Council of Ministers and the European Parliament. The first megaregional strategy to be developed was that for the Baltic region and this has been followed by those for the Danube, the Adriatic and the Alps regions (CEC 2017b; European Parliament 2017). These vertical and horizontal contracts on joint programmes of action are agreed between all the constituent authorities as a means of supporting inclusive growth and spatial development.

iii.   City Regions and FEAs

The role of city regions, their mayors and their relationships to their wider peripheral areas has been growing in importance in EU policy, While the EU has always had an urban policy, which was very important in the UK in the later 1970s and early 1980s and which was delivered as the Urban Programme, the increasing understanding of the role of mayors and their economic contribution to FEAs has grown in importance since the early 1990s. This has occurred through the economic theories of Krugman and also through the Rio Earth Summit. As noted in Chapter 2, the UN has recently adopted the NUA, which has reinforced the role of urban areas and their contribution to achieving sustainable outcomes.

In the EU, the Covenant of Mayors has been established as a standing group and is particularly focussed on actions to address the climate and use of energy. The EU's response to the NUA has been the establishment of the Urban Agenda (UA), which is forming part of mainstream EU policy. The EU's UA is being developed through a series of partnerships, where issues are being reviewed with a view to mainstreaming them through the whole of the EU's operations. In terms of UK planning, the government has signed on to the NUA, so these requirements will also operate in the UK.

iv. Local Level

At the local level, the effect of EU legislation is most openly acknowledged through the application of environmental standards and the requirements that are contained within environmental impact assessments. As part of an assessment for the Dutch government, Evers and Tennekers (2016) reviewed how these regulations operate in practice at a local level. The application of these standards is generally provenanced in the specific EU legalisation and its application.

However, there are other ways in which EU practices influence local planning practice. These include the form of local and neighbourhood plans that are similar in style to the CLLD approach in the cohesion policy. Similarly, the National Planning Policy Framework (DCLG 2012; MHCLG 2018) requires that local plans in England work collaboratively with the strategic economic plan (SEP) and European Structural and Investment Fund (ESIF) plans prepared by local enterprise partnerships. There are also links to specific approaches to transport policy, including sustainable mobility and the implementation of specific projects for missing links and bottle necks such as those included in the Trans-European Network programmes. None of these influences are explicit, although appreciating their underlying presence and the context they create is frequently helpful in understanding the government's policy intentions (Morphet 2013).

What Are the Key EU Programmes that Relate to Planning?

There are several key policy areas that have been pooled within the EU by member states and that influence or have a direct relationship with planning. These are:

i. Energy

The EU has a range of pooled responsibilities for energy, which is one of its most long standing and developed programme areas. These responsibilities relate to the internal market and open access to private sector providers to the provision of supply as agreed by member states in through the WTO. There are also EU energy security-of-supply issues, which are being met through Trans-European Networks for Energy (TEN-E) grid, which operates much as the UK national grid does to ensure that supplies are available. The focus on energy management as part of a sustainability policy also has a link to more local cohesion programmes where there is a priority for local energy supply though a range of mechanisms, including combined heat and power, waste to energy, local nuclear facilities and energy management (House of Commons 2016). These issues have implications for planning, including building design and standards for energy reduction, location of services and facilities near to public transport and retrofitting existing buildings to minimise energy use.

ii Transport

EU transport policies, legislation and programmes operate on different spatial scales. At the strategic scale, these operate through the designation of Trans-European Networks – Transport (TEN-T). As part of the integration of the internal market and bringing together the territorial space of the EU, the trans-European transport policies have been in existence since 1997 and had a major re-set in 2013, when the overriding orientation of the routes across the EU shifted from East–West to North–South. However, some of the remaining East–West schemes and projects are still being completed. While the European Council adopts these routes, the EC is primarily engaged in improving their operation through support from specific projects that deal with any missing links or bottle necks. These TEN-Ts are defined as corridors rather than specific modes of transport. Some of the missing links can be upgraded via other transport modes within the corridor. Where new infrastructure is implemented to meet a gap, all three modes must be implemented. In the UK, there are examples of this in the A14 road in East Anglia, where the Cambridge-guided busway was a mode within the wider corridor, and on HS2, where additional modes of walking and cycling have been added into consideration.

While these major or core routes will have a life until 2030 or beyond to 2050, the EU has also decided to identify a second network within the core network framework through designated comprehensive networks. These also fit with the Organization for Economic Cooperation and Development's (OECD) approach to subnational infrastructure provision as a means of supporting regional economic growth (Allain-Dupré et al. 2017). Member states have been given until 2030 to propose those routes for designation although in practice, it is likely that work on identifying them will be completed before that date. Despite preparations for Brexit, the UK is still moving forward to identify TEN-T comprehensive corridors that are set out in proposal. Typical examples of comprehensive TEN-T corridors are CAMKOX – the National Infra-structure Commission's proposals for the new corridor between Oxford and Cambridge via Milton Keynes (NIC 2016) and the designated corridors identi-fied by Transport for the North (TfN 2017).

At a more local level, the EU is promoting urban mobility programmes through the European Local Transport Information Service (ELTIS) and these are primarily multi-mode, sustainable transport approaches for FEAs. These approaches focus on public transport, including buses, trams, trains, cycling and walking. They also include river transport. Each FEA in the EU has been invited to prepare a Sustainable Urban Mobility Plan (SUMP) and many UK local authorities have been pioneering this approach, including Bristol and Aberdeen. SUMPs are a key component of urban planning and in considering the relationship between urban areas and their peripheries.

iii.   Environment

A further major area where the EU has a key role for planning in the UK is through the environmental principles and standards that it has adopted. These must be used as part of any planning application where they are relevant, as well as in the provi-sion of good and services more generally. Much of the EU's environmental legisla-tion is derived from UN treaties and the EC acts as a means of interpreting these commitments into legislation and then the European Court of Justice (ECJ) acts as a mechanism for compliance. Any citizen can challenge a member state's compliance through the court after exhausting national remedies and this is regarded as a vital component of access to environmental justice for any locality or group.

In more recent UN agreements such as the Paris Climate Agreement (2016), the EU has been a participant and agreed terms on the part of all its member states. These are yet to be fully translated into delivery programmes but, like other places in the world, it is likely that city mayors will have a significant role in this delivery. Another dimension of the EU's environment programme has been achieved through its agricultural and food policies. Here, through the Common Agricultural Policy (CAP), there is a focus on sustainable land management and support for areas that might otherwise not be economically viable such as upland farming. At the same time, these programmes are also integral to managing the potential effects of climate change through upstream water management, forestation and development in flood plains. While many floods are caused by high rainfall, the extent to which any locality can manage them will depend on a wide catchment management plan.

The role of environmental legislation and its operational relationship with UK planning is best understood through environmental assessment directives and regulations and through specific standards for air and water quality and for waste and habitats (Glasson et al. 2013). The EU has the responsibility of formulating legislation and methods of testing compliance on behalf of all member states for obligations that they have entered into from their treaty agreements with the UN. While the EU has a role in these negotiations and represents the member states' views, each state must agree to them individually. In the UK, the various environmental assessment processes have frequently been misinterpreted in their delivery and the UK has had to pay fines and revise their regulations.

iv.   Cohesion

The principle of striving towards achieving economic and social cohesion is foundational in the EU trades and this has been the basis for the structural programmes of financial and other support in less developed areas of the EU, including the UK. In planning terms, the cohesion principle has supported funding for regeneration and skills and investment funding in specific locations where there is higher unemployment and lower pay rates in comparison with other parts of the EU. These have included Cornwall, West Wales, the Highlands and Islands and Northern Ireland. The structural funds programmes have now been widened to include all EU programmes at the local level, including rural development and agriculture, transport, research and development, skills and regeneration. In 2007 in the Lisbon treaty, the principle of territorial cohesion was added to economic and social cohesion and this now provides the EU with the opportunity to develop spatial plans and programmes in a more integrated way.

v.   Single Internal Market

The introduction of the single internal market within the EU in 1992 incuded the ability to operate across the whole of the EU's territory using the same regulations and with qualifications that were recognised everywhere. In the operation of planning systems, there are great areas of difference between member states, as the EU compendium of planning demonstrated when it was published in 1999. This issue was put on hold but since 2016, there has been a return to considering planning systems, led by the ESPON, with funding from the EU.

vi   Culture and Public Health

The EU also has other programmes that are important for planning, including those for culture and public health. The EU's programmes and support for heritage have started to be acknowledged for their scale and relevance (CEC 2017d) as assessments are made following the UK's Brexit referendum (Gardner and Harrison 2017; Hausler and Scott 2017)

vii   Housing

While housing has never been an EU policy competence, through the UA programmes a working group on affordable housing has been established. The role of housing in the UA has been reviewed by Colini (2016), who has taken a particularly British perspective on the implications of the relationship between housing and planning into consideration of the EU's potential role. This analysis also considers the rising costs of housing across the EU in relation to disposable income and the implications for shifting populations, migration and economic growth and their impact on housing demand. Colini also considers the shifting factors that are influencing housing supply in member states, including investment, and the effects that these may have on the EU overall.

The Effects of Brexit

While Brexit appears to be cast as an event, for those involved in planning, as with many other activities, it will be a process, some of which will be expected and understood at the outset, while other parts will be surprising and unexpected. For those engaged in planning in both its wider and more specific contexts, having some understanding of the likely changes and areas of challenge that could arise within a legal framework post Brexit is of utmost concern although difficult to predict.

What Will Be Retained after Brexit?

While UK treaty obligations with the WTO and UN will be major determinants of continuing legal frameworks for planning and environmental matters, there may be other pressures to maintain an approach that closely mirrors that used by the EU, both now and in the future. Here, the pressures for EU compliance will come through trade agreements and engagement with the single market. This issue could appear at several points in the negotiations. Firstly, access to a UK–EU trade agreement post Brexit may be reliant on acceptance of all the

EU's environmental regulations and the jurisdiction of the ECJ in compliance and disputes (CEC 2017c). This has already been mentioned as a way forward and would be like the position of members of the European Economic Area (EEA) – although in that case, members are required to take all EU legislation without any involvement in its negotiation or approval. If this compliance is not a general requirement of trade, then individual contracts for supply of goods and services may require that these standards be met. The withdrawal of the US from the Paris Climate Agreement may see this line reinforced. Secondly, there may be public pressure to maintain environmental standards. Research has shown that a high proportion of the electorate, whatever its stance on Brexit, wishes to see environmental standards remain unaltered in the future (Curtice 2017).

What else retained after Brexit will have an influence on planning? Although not bound by a treaty like the WTO and the UN, the UK is a member of the OECD and it is likely that this relationship will be strengthened in a post-Brexit world. The OECD was founded in the post-1945 settlement and remains fundamentally welfarist in its approach. While it is a soft power organisation, the OECD has a strong influence on education policy, as regular publication of the Programme for International Student Assessment (PISA) education league tables confirms. The OECD also reports on the economic performance of its members and their comparative competence in dealing with a range of regulatory and governance issues. These performance assessments also inform country judgements made by the International Monetary Fund (IMF) and other financial institutions.

One of the key policy areas where the OECD is heavily engaged and influential among its members is that of sub-state governance and fiscal federalism. Following on from the work of Nobel economist Paul Krugman, the OECD has undertaken more research that has identified a growth in national gross domestic product (GDP) where there is a link between the alignment of administrative and economic borders and strong democratic leadership over these areas (OECD 2015). In the UK, the delivery of these policies is through the creation of combined authorities with directly elected mayors. These approaches have also confirmed the need for integrated spatial plans for these areas, which underpin infrastructure investment within and between them. The mayors of the six new combined authorities in England, plus the Mayor of London, all have strategic planning powers, although each operates in separate ways. When we see the alignment between planning and investment in transport and energy, this begins to look very like the UK's obligations to the UN's NUA. So, despite Brexit, re-ordering responsibilities below state level, with planning at the heart of these processes, appears likely to continue.

What Will Be Lost after Brexit?

If many frameworks for environmental legislation and standards appear likely to remain post Brexit, what will be lost? The most obvious concerns will be about the role of the ECJ, although these must be tempered with be the commentary in the previous section about new trade agreements. Secondly, key institutional principles that will be lost are those of subsidiarity and fairness. Subsidiarity guarantees devolution and stays the government's hand on how it can centralise or retain powers that should be operated at other appropriate spatial scales. It has most resonance on issues such as devolution where, no longer based on treaty principles, all devolved powers will rest on the whim of five-year Parliaments unless the UK adopts a written constitution. There has been some assumption that devolved powers will remain the same or be increased post Brexit but in Chapter 4 of the Repeal Bill White Paper (HMG 2017), transport, agriculture and rural affairs and the environment are all policy areas that have been identified as ones where there could be a diminution of devolved powers.

The principle of fairness, set in the Treaty of Rome, has been used to support structural funds, differential investment programmes and the Barnett Formula, which supports the allocation of funds in Scotland, Wales and Northern Ireland. It will affect differential funding levels associated with growth deals, the current although soon-to-be-lost local government revenue support grant and funding by government agencies, including Homes England. If the UK wishes to retain this principle of fairness as a basis for redistribution across the UK, then either Parliament must adopt this principle – although, again, this will only last for five years – or the government will have to legislate specifically for each programme. This issue will affect local transport projects, which are supported through EU policies and legislation such as SUMPs, rural support packages and environmental interventions. At a more strategic scale, another major loss will be the Trans-European Networks (TEN-Ts) for transport modes and energy.

So far there has been no mention of the effects of Brexit on the designation of these networks nor the support funding that accompanies their design and implementation. Further, supplementary funding for these and other projects made available to the UK through the European Investment Bank and the Juncker Strategic Infrastructure Investment Fund will not be available. Also, as these routes are legally defined through regulations, there is no need to take the principle of development through the UK Parliament, although the National Policy Statements in the nationally significant infrastructure project (NSIP) regime provide an outward and visible connection. Without these EU regulations, each infrastructure scheme will have to be considered on its merits and return to a more traditional planning inquiry approach where the principle of development is tested. There is possibly some hope that the need to ensure good transport links between Ireland and the European mainland would support some specific scheme funding across the UK, as there is in Switzerland. However, the EC also has a priority for short sea shipping and this may be beneficial for transport connections to be maintained between Ireland and France, Spain and Portugal.

What else may be lost? The ending of free movement of labour means that arrangements for staff moving between countries and agreements on professional recognition may need to be changed. Other losses include access to the European Investment Bank, where the UK has been a very great user of services and where the UK loans book is one of the largest held by the bank. In diplomacy, the working together of all the EU embassies around the world to support common positions and mutual support will be lost. Finally, there will be a loss of rural subsidies that have been specifically negotiated between the EU and the WTO. Once the UK has left the EU, it will have to negotiate arrangements with the WTO, to which all 163 other members will need to agree, and these are very unlikely to include the rural subsidies, which will be lost.

What Will Be Foregone after Brexit?

While much of the focus will be on what will be lost or what will need to be renegotiated, what may be overlooked in Brexit discussions are those matters that are currently under discussion for adoption in 2021 in the next programme. The definition of the comprehensive transport networks across the EU, as mentioned earlier, will be one. A second important programme is the current development of a spatial investment plan for Europe to be adopted post 2030. This is bringing together the infrastructure plans and other major policy proposals for single funding and delivery programmes such as those already adopted for the mega regions.

The UK would have been part of the discussion in determining which areas would have investment priority and, based on experience, would probably have been very successful in securing investment programmes to support delivery. However, even the discussions about this approach are now excluding the UK on a practical basis. These discussions are also extending to heritage, tourism and cultural policy areas, into which, again, the UK would have expected to have a major input. The renewed focus on the ESDP and review of the planning systems, including regulations and policies in each member state, may support a plan and by 2030, the EU could be on its way to a common planning system across its territory. In the spatial planning sphere, the role of ITIs as spatially configured SEPs will be extended.

Finally, and not much spoken of, the six-monthly reviews of the UK's performance against four principal areas of defined weakness in the economy – planning, housing, infrastructure and youth skills – have had a stimulating effect on UK policy change. Without the EU's commentary and monitoring of the UK's actions, there may be fewer short-term measures but there will also be a loss of focus as other parts of the economy vie for attention, e.g. the automotive sector.

References

Adams, N., Cotella, G., & Nunes, R. (Eds.). (2012). *Territorial Development, Cohesion and Spatial Planning: Building on EU Enlargement.* London: Routledge.

Allain-Dupré, D., Hulbert, C., & Vincent, M. (2017). Subnational Infrastructure Investment in OECD Countries: Trends and Key Governance Levers. OECD Regional Development Working Papers, No. 2017/05, Paris: OECD Publishing.

Antonescu, D. (2015). Territorial pact in context of *Europe 2020. Procedia – Social and Behavioral Sciences*, 188, 282–289.

Bache, I. (2007). *Europeanization and Multilevel Governance: Cohesion Policy in the European Union and Britain.* Plymouth: Rowman & Littlefield Publishers.

Bachtler, J., & Mendez, C. (2016). *EU Cohesion Policy and European Integration: The Dynamics of EU Budget and Regional Policy Reform.* London: Routledge.

Bachtler, J., & Turok, I. (Eds.) (2013). *The Coherence of EU Regional Policy: Contrasting Perspectives on the Structural Funds.* London: Routledge.

Barca, F. (2009). *An Agenda for a Reformed Cohesion Policy: A Place-Based Approach to Meeting European Union Challenges and Expectation.* Brussels: CEC.

Becker, S. O., Egger, P. H., & Von Ehrlich, M. (2010). Going NUTS: The effect of EU structural funds on regional performance. *Journal of Public Economics*, 94(9), 578–590.

Bulmer, S., & Burch, M. (2009). *The Europeanisation of Whitehall.* Manchester: Manchester University Press.

CEC (1991). *Europe 2000: Outlook for the Development of the Community's Territory: A Preliminary Overview.* https://publications.europa.eu/en/publication-detail/-/publica tion/b1380f75-b5c2-4deb-94b4-49ab9a6c853b/language-en (accessed 4 July 2018).

CEC (1994). *Europe 2000+: Co-operation for European Territorial Development.* Luxembourg: Office for Official Publications of the European Communities. https://cordis. europa.eu/news/rcn/4496_en.html (accessed 4 July 2018).

CEC (2000). *The EU Compendium of Spatial Planning Systems and Policies.* Brussels: CEC.

CEC (2015). Scenarios for integrated territorial investments. http://ec.europa.eu/regiona l_policy/en/information/publications/reports/2015/scenarios-for-integrated-territoria l-investments (accessed 30 December 2017).

CEC (2016). European structural and investment funds: Community led local development (CLLD) guidance'. www.gov.uk/government/publications/european-structural-a nd-investment-funds-community-led-local-development (accessed 30 December 2017).

CEC (2017a). Territorial cohesion. http://ec.europa.eu/regional_policy/en/policy/what/ glossary/t/territorial-cohesion (accessed 4 July 2018).

CEC (2017b). Macro regional strategies. http://ec.europa.eu/regional_policy/en/policy/ cooperation/macro-regional-strategies/ (accessed 22 October 2017).

CEC (2017c). Joint report from the negotiators of the European Union and the United Kingdom Government on the progress during Phase 1 of negotiations under Article 50 TEU on the United Kingdom's orderly withdrawal from the EU. https://ec.europa.eu/ commission/sites/beta-political/files/joint_report.pdf (accessed 30 December 2017).

CEC (2017d) Mapping of cultural heritage actions in European Union policies, programmes and activities. http://ec.europa.eu/assets/eac/culture/library/reports/2014-heritage-mapp ing_en.pdf (accessed 30 December 2017).

Charbit, C., & Romano, O. (2017). Governing together: An international review of contracts across levels of government for regional development Regional Development. Working Paper 2017/04. Paris: OECD.

CIOSLEP (2016). Cornwall and Isles of Scilly integrated territorial investment strategy. www.cioslep.com/assets/file/Cornwall%20and%20IOS%20ITI%20Strategy.pdf (accessed 21 December 2017).

Colini, L. (2016). EU urban agenda: The challenge of 'affordable housing' in Europe. https://ec.europa.eu/futurium/en/housing/eu-urban-agenda-challenge-affordable-hou sing-europe-laura-colini-urbact-expert (accessed 30 December 2017).

Cowell, R. (2017). The EU referendum, planning and the environment: Where now for the UK? *Town Planning Review*, 88(2): 153–171.

Crespy, C., Heraud, J. A., & Perry, B. (2007). Multi-level governance, regions and science in France: Between competition and equality. *Regional Studies*, 41(8), 1069–1084.

Curtice, J. (2017). Factors influencing Brexit: The environment. Presentation to plenary. PSA Annual Conference, 10–12 April, Glasgow.

Daugbjerg, C., & Swinbank, A. (2015). Globalization and new policy concerns: The WTO and the EU's sustainability criteria for biofuels. *Journal of European Public Policy*, 22(3), 429–446.

Davies, P. G. (2017). *European Union Environmental Law: An Introduction to Key Selected Issues*. London: Taylor & Francis.

Davoudi, S. (2005). Understanding territorial cohesion. *Planning, Practice & Research*, 20(4), 433–441.

DCLG (2012). *National Planning Policy Framework*. London: DCLG.

Delreux, T. (2014). EU actorness, cohesiveness and effectiveness in environmental affairs. *Journal of European Public Policy*, 21(7), 1017–1032.

Dühr, S., Colomb, C., & Nadin, V. (2010). *European Spatial Planning and Territorial Cooperation*. Abingdon: Routledge.

ESPON (2016). Possible territorial futures applied research draft, final report. www.espon.eu/territorial-futures (accessed 4 July 2018).

European Parliament (2017). Implementation of macro-regional strategies. European Parliament Briefing document, September. Strasbourg: European Parliament. www.europarl.europa.eu/thinktank/en/document.html?reference=EPRS_BRI%282017%29608717 (accessed 23 July 2017).

Evers, D. (2008). Reflections on territorial cohesion and European spatial planning. *Tijdschrift voor economische en sociale geografie*, 99(3), 303–315.

Evers, D., & Tennekers, J. (2016). Europe exposed: Mapping the impacts of EU policies on spatial planning in the Netherlands. *European Planning Studies*, 24(10), 1747–1765.

Faludi, A. (2004). Spatial planning traditions in Europe: Their role in the ESDP process. *International Planning Studies*, 9(2–3), 155–172.

Faludi, A. (2013). Territorial cohesion and subsidiarity under the European Union treaties: A critique of the 'territorialism' underlying. *Regional Studies*, 47(9), 1594–1606.

Faludi, A., & Waterhout, B. (2012). *The Making of the European Spatial Development Perspective: No Masterplan*. London: Psychology Press.

Gardner, A., & Harrison, R. (2017). Brexit, archaeology and heritage: Reflections and agendas. *Papers from the Institute of Archaeology*, 27(1), p.Art. 24. doi:10.5334/pia-544.

Glasson, J., Therivel, R., & Chadwick, A. (2013). *Introduction to Environmental Impact Assessment*. London: Routledge.

Goetz, K. H., & Meyer-Sahling, J. H. (2009). Political time in the EU: dimensions, perspectives, theories. *Journal of European Public Policy*, 16(2), 180–201.

GONE (2008). *The North East of England Plan Regional Spatial Strategy to 2021*. London: DCLG

GOYH (2004). *Regional Spatial Strategy for Yorkshire and the Humber to 2016*. London: GOYH.

Haigh, N. (1996). Climate Change Policies and Politics in the European Community. In T. O'Riordan, & J. Jager (eds.), *Politics of Climate Change: A European Perspective*, (pp. 155–187). London: Routledge.

Hausler, K., & Scott, R. M. G. (2017). Outside the debate? The potential impact of Brexit for cultural heritage in the UK. *Art Antiquity & Law*, 22(2), 101–118.

Hedemann-Robinson, M. (2015). *Enforcement of European Union Environmental Law: Legal Issues and Challenges*. London: Routledge.

HMG (2017). *The Repeal Bill White Paper*. London: HMG.

Hooghe, L., & Marks, G. (2001). *Multi-Level Governance and European Integration.* Oxford: Rowman & Littlefield.

House of Commons (2016). The energy revolution and future challenges for UK energy and climate change policy. Third Report of Session 2016–2017, House of Commons Energy and Climate Change Committee, 13 October.

Juncker, J. C. (2017). State of the Union speech, 13 September. Brussels: CEC. https://ec. europa.eu/commission/priorities/state-union-speeches/state-union-2017_en (accessed 4 July 2018).

Knill, C., & Lenschow, A. (1998). Coping with Europe: The impact of British and German administrations on the implementation of EU environmental policy. *Journal of European Public Policy*, 5(4), 595–614.

Lockwood, M. (2013). The political sustainability of climate policy: The case of the UK Climate Change Act. *Global Environmental Change*, 23(5), 1339–1348.

Medeiros, E. (2016). Territorial cohesion: An EU concept. *European Journal of Spatial Development*, 60, 1–30.

Metzger, J., & Schmitt, P. (2012). When soft spaces harden: The EU strategy for the Baltic Sea Region. *Environment and Planning A*, 44(2), 263–280.

Meunier, S. (2005). *Trading Voices: The European Union in International Commercial Negotiations.* Oxford: Princeton University Press.

MHCLG (2018). Revised national planning policy framework. https://assets.publishing.ser vice.gov.uk/government/uploads/system/uploads/attachment_data/file/733637/National_ Planning_Policy_Framework_web_accessible_version.pdf (accessed 19 August 2018).

Morphet, J. (2013). *How Europe Shapes British Public Policy.* Bristol: Policy Press.

Morphet, J. (2017). *Beyond Brexit.* Bristol: Policy Press.

Morphet, J. (2018). Autopilot or risk mitigation? How Whitehall is continuing to deliver post Brexit EU policies. Presentation to panel. PSA Annual Conference, 26–28 March, Cardiff.

Nadin, V., Smas, L., Schmitt, P., & Cotella, G. (2016). *COMPASS: Comparative Analysis of Territorial Governance and Spatial Planning Systems in Europe.* Luxembourg: ESPON.

NIC (2016). The National Infrastructure Commission's interim report into the Cambridge – Milton Keynes – Oxford corridor. www.gov.uk/government/publications/ the-national-infrastructure-commissions-interim-report-into-the-cambridge-milton-key nes-oxford-corridor (accessed 21 December 2017).

Nugent, N. (2017). *The Government and Politics of the European Union* (8th ed.). Palgrave Basingstoke: Springer.

O'Brien, P., Sykes, O., & Shaw, D. (2017). 3 evolving conceptions of regional policy in Europe and their influence across different territorial scales. In I. Deas and S. Hinks (Eds.), *Territorial Policy and Governance: Alternative Paths* (pp. 57–74). London: Routledge.

OECD (2015). *Local Economic Leadership.* Paris: OECD.

Perkmann, M. (2007). Policy entrepreneurship and multilevel governance: A comparative study of European cross-border regions. *Environment and Planning C: Government and Policy*, 25(6), 861–879.

Rumford, C. (2006). Rethinking European spaces: Territory, borders, governance. *Comparative European Politics,* 4(2–3), 127.

Schakel, A. H., Hooghe, L., & Marks, G. (2015). Multilevel governance and the state. In *The Oxford Handbook of Transformations of the State,* (pp. 269–285). Oxford: Oxford University Press.

Shaw, D., & Sykes, O. (2003). Investigating the application of the European Spatial Development Perspective (ESDP) to regional planning in the United Kingdom. *Town Planning Review*, 74(1), 31–50.

Stead, D. (2014a). European integration and spatial rescaling in the Baltic region: Soft spaces, soft planning and soft security. *European Planning Studies*, 22(4), 680–693.

Stead, D. (2014b). The rise of territorial governance in European policy. *European Planning Studies*, 22(7), 1368–1383.

Stephenson, P. (2013). Twenty years of multi-level governance: 'Where does it come from? What is it? Where is it going?'. *Journal of European Public Policy*, 20(6), 817–837.

TfN (2017). 'Strategic Transport Plan position statement'. www.transportforthenorth.com/wp-content/uploads/TfN-Position-Statement22617.pdf (accessed 21 December 2017).

van der Zwet, A., Bachtler, J., Ferry, M., McMaster, I., & Miller, S. (2017). *Integrated Territorial and Urban Strategies: How Are ESIF Adding Value in 2014–2020? Final Report*. Brussels: CEC.

Zonneveld, W., & Waterhout, B. (2005). Visions on territorial cohesion. *Town Planning Review*, 76(1), 15–27.

Part II
Planning's Scalar Practices

4   National Infrastructure Planning

Introduction

While other countries within the EU and nations within the UK have a spatial plan for the whole of their territory, no such plan exists for the UK or England. Attempts have been made to construct a plan for England through the combination of policies from a range of government departments (Wong et al. 2012) but these do not provide an integrated approach to spatial policy, investment and environmental protection. There is no national spatial plan for England and while there are plans prepared by the National Infrastructure Commission (NIC) and the Industrial Strategy (DBEIS 2017), these are not spatially integrated or dynamic, unlike Scotland, Wales and Northern Ireland, where national plans are available at least for one if not more of these three dimensions. The Regional Strategies and their predecessors were abolished in England in 2010. While the Mayor of London has planning powers and produces a strategic plan, the new combined authorities with directly elected mayors have not yet prepared strategic spatial plans, although some have planning powers (Sandford 2017; Morphet 2017).

The approach to nationally significant infrastructure in England is also non-spatial. Infrastructure is an essential feature of economic, social and environmental well-being. While much infrastructure is required at the local level, frequently provided as part of wider local schemes for new development, the insertion of national infrastructure into any location can be a major challenge and potentially disruptive in its construction and subsequent operation. In the UK, there has been considerable criticism of the lack of infrastructure investment and the slow delivery of projects (NAO 2013; NAO 2016), which has led the government to focus more on the management of projects that are being delivered to support national interests. In this chapter, there is a consideration of the international context for the UK's performance and the need for infrastructure delivery together with an analysis of the system introduced in 2008, followed by an assessment of its subsequent operation.

International Context

The provision of major infrastructure in any country is a critical component of its economic, social and environmental wellbeing and planning is at the core of its delivery. The economic role of infrastructure is set out by international organisations such as the World Economic Forum (WEF), which includes an assessment of infrastructure provision and policy for each country in the world as part of its overall economy assessment. In international comparisons, the UK's position is 9th overall, but the WEF has given the UK an overall ranking of 24th for the climate for infrastructure provision (WEF 2016; Pisu et al. 2015), a much lower ranking than most of its economic competitors from the EU and wider. This ranking includes an assessment of the amount of investment made in infrastructure but also the legal, investment and policy environment for infrastructure in a country.

The Organization for Economic Cooperation and Development (OECD) has demonstrated the role of infrastructure in supporting economies and its work has extended to consider matters such as governance and integration between types of infrastructure (OECD 2017). It has also reviewed the implications for locations such as ports or cities. In its work, the OECD is also looking at the role of the labour force in being able to access employment and the diseconomies that can be generated by silo-based infrastructure investment (OECD 2011). The OECD also considers issues related to energy provision and the market as they affect the economies of its member states (Aspergis and Payne 2010). The World Trade Organization (WTO) has an integral role in the functioning of the markets for infrastructure, particularly where there is public policy and investment involved. Under the General Agreement on Government Procurement (GPA) (GATT 1979), public sector procurement must be open to private sector contractors, including contractors from other countries that have signed this WTO agreement.

The WEF, OECD and WTO have varied legal relationships to the UK government. The WTO agreement is an international treaty and the UK is bound by its provisions whilst it remains a signatory. The OECD is a membership organisation that does not bind its members to act in specific ways. However, the OECD exerts considerable soft power and influence on other international economic bodies such as the International Monetary Fund (IMF) and the World Bank, as well as international trading blocs such as the EU. The WEF is a group that is funded by the private sector and seeks to promote a better operating environment for the economy and its associated components. It undertakes research that is recognised in its field.

The social dimensions of infrastructure are critical in its operation and are why it remains a public service. The social dimension complements the economic role in the location of investment and the quality of service to different areas, e.g. broadband in rural areas (DCMS 2017), the issues of fuel poverty related frequently to construction issues in public housing (DECC 2016) and access to services, including public transport, and their linkages to public services such as health and education. Differential spatial access to public services is also an equity issue, which planning must consider when locating infrastructure investment at all scales (Castells and Solé-Ollé 2005; Sclar 2015).

The environmental dimension of infrastructure planning and delivery is linked to its economic role and this is recognised through the WTO trade and environment agreements (Bhaskar and Glyn 2014), although these are also subject to disputes and gaming in the management of assessment methods (Bigdeli, 2014; George 2014). This environmental relationship is also characterised through agreements made with the UN on climate change, development and sustainability, although some of these may be softer in their application (Kirton and Trebilcock, 2017). The environmental aspects of infrastructure include many dimensions, such as the regulation of infrastructure operation in use of fuels, pollution control, siting and safety and access to investment (Harper and Snowden 2017). While the economic aspects of infrastructure delivery have dominated consideration over a period of 30 years, the environmental dimensions are now playing an increasingly key role in infrastructure decision making. Assessments of the longer term effects of infrastructure investment, as well as those in their immediate operation, have now become more crucial. There are also more dominant concerns about climate change, the use of fossils fuels, their effects and their depletion, which also play an increasing role in decision making about infrastructure investment and resilience (Ibanez et al. 2016).

Major Infrastructure Delivery in the UK

Infrastructure delivery in the UK was primarily undertaken by the public sector after reforms undertaken by the post-war Labour government (1945–1951). This continued until the agreement to open public sector contacts and service delivery to the private sector through the General Agreement on Tariffs and Trade (GATT) GPA made by the Labour government in 1976, before the Thatcher era. Since then, the UK has been creating markets for its major public services that provide infrastructure, including water, energy, telecommunications and transport (Debande 2002; Raco 2016). These reforms have been characterised as deregulation or privatisation, but the government retains the ability to set standards for delivery. It can also open the market to providers or decide to retain core infrastructure services and networks as a universal supply. Each infrastructure type has a regulator to whom suppliers must apply and who controls investments levels in relation to pricing. The regulators also consider the provision of new supply for housing and repairs, replacement and maintenance for existing areas.

It is also the case that the use of the word 'privatisation' is inappropriate as the mechanism for competition. Within WTO agreements, public sector and state-owned bodies such as Energie de France (EDF), an energy company partly owned by the French government can bid for contracts to run services. However, during the Thatcher period, the overriding ideology was that the private sector would be more efficient than the public sector and there was perceived to be a focus on privatisation rather than competition. There was also a focus on achieving the highest price for the sale of public assets and services when alternative methods that allowed for quality and local providers were available. Through these processes, there was also a focus on lowest price rather than quality outcomes, although both approaches were permitted within WTO competition rules (Hermann and Flecker 2013). For some infrastructure services such as rail, the UK has adopted a different approach from other countries, in which it has separated the management of the track from the service providers. This has been problematic and over time many UK privatised services have been brought back into forms of state ownership before being placed back in the private sector (Bowman 2015; Wellings 2014; Grayling 2018).

The EU Policy and Legal Framework

Since 1973, the UK has been a member of the EU and as part of its membership, the UK pooled its sovereignty over infrastructure with other members. Over time, the role of infrastructure within the EU has grown. Initially this was through the effects of the WTO agreement on competition. The EU took responsibility for developing methods to deliver this system and to manage compliance, which it did on behalf of the WTO (Meunier 2005). The second major policy and legal development occurred through the creation of the single market in 1992, where the operation of infrastructure across borders between member states became an objective. This has included the development of energy grids for supply as well as energy markets for example (Clastres 2011; Helm 2014).

The third major period of development was following the political changes in Eastern Europe and application of Accession states to join the EU. Here there was a major challenge of integrating the east and the west of the EU, ensuing that goods and services could be supplied across the whole of its area – including the improvement of strategic infrastructure links by road, rail, water and air. The resulting approach was to designate Trans-European Networks – Transport (TEN-Ts) across the EU. These defined multimodal transport corridors. In the period from 1996 onwards, these were primarily east–west and the associated programmes identified locations where improvements were required to fill either missing links or to reduce bottle necks (Holl 2007). In 2013, TEN-Ts were revisited and in the light of the 2008 economic recession, these main corridors have been changed so that their primary focus is on a north–south axis (CEC 2013). In both cases, these corridor routes and associated improvement works have been included within EU regulations that have immediate legal effect once they are agreed through EU processes and do not require consideration or approval by member state parliaments. Each of these regulations takes many years to negotiate before its final agreement, a process undertaken by the European Commission (EC) and member states. This also means that once the final approval of the regulation, including the routes, has been agreed, each member state has had time to prepare its own domestic policy agenda to support their delivery (Morphet 2013).

At the same time as the EU strategic transport approach was being developed and implemented, complementary approaches on energy were evolving. These are through the Trans-European Networks for Energy (TEN-E) and latterly though the Energy Union, which are still being developed (Vickerman 1995; Kanellakis et al. 2013). This includes methods of ensuring supply, reduction of use and physical grids for energy transmission across the EU and into Norway, including the new link between Ireland and Northern France. Other policies and legislation have included airports and air travel, ports, broadband and the digital market and now an increasing focus on water supply markets.

The UK has been engaged throughout these processes. In terms of strategic infrastructure, the UK has implemented many improvements of services in corridors identified in the TEN-T regulation (CEC 1996), including the West Coast mainline improvement, London stations, Crossrail, the A14 and Cambridge guided busway and HS1 transport schemes. In a more recent package with focus on north–south links, routes including HS2, Crossrail 2 and the A1 have been identified as major programmes for delivery, although these will now be subject to the outcomes of the Brexit negotiations (Morphet 2017).

The EU, in its assessment of macroeconomic policy across the EU since the 2008 financial crisis, has identified infrastructure delivery as one the UK's major macroeconomic weaknesses, alongside its delivery of housing and planning (CEC 2017). Through six monthly monitoring events, this position has only marginally improved since this monitoring began in 2010, despite significant changes in the process and a range of announcements and initiatives. The government has introduced a Major Projects Authority, which merged with Infrastructure UK in 2016 to become the Infrastructure and Projects Authority. It has published a National Infrastructure Delivery Plan (HMG 2016), which has subsequently been updated, and established the NIC in 2015. However, these initiatives together with the innovative approach to the infrastructure planning system have not significantly improved the performance for the UK, as assessed by the wider international community, and this remains an acute issue.

2008 Planning Act

The progression of major infrastructure schemes as part of the EU regulations took some time to develop in the UK. There had been little or no investment in infrastructure since the UK's IMF crisis in 1976 and what was undertaken was increasingly the responsibility of regulated providers in the private sector. To move towards a delivery mode more consistent with the projects set out in the EU regulation, agreed in 1996, and an increased focus on infrastructure investment as part of the world economic assessment, the UK was slow in developing approaches to delivery. While the major consultancy industry had considerable experience in delivering infrastructure in the international context, there was less experience at home.

There was also a concern about how to move these projects forward through the regulatory system. Also, though the EU regulation (CEC 1996; CEC 2013) meant that there needed to be no parliamentary approval of the principle of development, there did need to be some acknowledgement and assessment of the schemes that were to be delivered in specific locations. The government introduced a range of mechanisms to seek to improve the speed of the system although none of these was implemented fully (Morphet and Clifford 2017a). Finally, following the Terminal 5 Inquiry at Heathrow, the government established a 'personality' review of the issues of delay, with some proposals. The review was chaired by Rod Eddington, formerly of British Airways, and while focusing primarily on airports, made specific recommendations about an innovative approach to the development and assessment of specific, nationally significant infrastructure schemes in England and Wales. This also incorporated many of the proposed changes that had accumulated since 1996 but established a different approach that was not intended to link with proposals to change the planning system but in effect recommended that this should be done (Eddington 2006).

The 2008 Planning Act that followed Eddington's review established a system for nationally significant infrastructure projects (NSIPs) that was to be managed by an independent body. Parliament was asked to consider and approve a range of national policy statements (NPSs) (PINS 2017) that would deal with specific infrastructure sectors and be put forward by the sponsoring government departments for that provision. These NPSs defined the capacity or scale limits of NSIP schemes that were required to use this system. Some projects could adopt this method although they might have a choice of other approaches such as the Transport and Works Act 1992, the Town and Country Planning Act system or through a hybrid bill procedure in Parliament.

The 2008 Act established an Independent Planning Commission (IPC) that would consider the proposed applications before their submission and then only accept them once they were satisfied that defined criteria were met. These included the environmental impact assessment, an impact statement provided by the local authority and meaningful consultation with the community (widely defined), and this had to be signed off by the local authority. Once submitted into the NSIP process, each stage was time-limited and all documents and processes were undertaken in the public domain. The acceptance stage took up to 28 days, the examination period took up to six months, the report-writing took three months and the decision making took three months. This allowed a project promoter to have certainty that their proposal would be determined within a one-year period from acceptance.

The IPC recruited a range of commissioners to undertake the examination of these applications and adopted a careful and precautionary approach to managing the processes. This IPC operated until 2010 when, following the general election, the Secretary of State for the Department of Communities and Local Government (DCLG) announced an intention to incorporate the IPC into the Planning Inspectorate National Service (PINS) and to change the responsibility for decision making from the IPC Commissioners to the relevant Secretaries of State who had prepared the NPS. This approach was to be conducted within the same time scale.

Between the introduction of the regime in 2008 and September 2016, there were 75 NSIP schemes submitted for development consent order (DCO) approval, of which 56 had been approved, 3 refused, 5 withdrawn and 11 were in progress (Morphet and Clifford 2017a). Overall, the approach to the NSIP process has been broadly welcomed by those who have used it. The promoters of NSIP schemes have recognised the value of the fixed timescale, bringing certainty as a primary feature. It is also considered to be more transparent than other processes, as all application documents are published, as are the transcripts and audio recordings of the examinations that are held in public.

Following the hearings and subsequent report, the decision to confer a DCO is made, which is a parliamentary process. Following this, any changes in the details of the DCO must go through material or non-material amendments processes. There had been no material amendments requested by 2017, but some non-material amendments had been submitted. While the remainder of the process has time limits set out in legislation, the non-material amendments have a recommended period of six weeks although some have taken ten months. This has influenced the practices of scheme promoters who, when receiving requests for changes by their delivery partner following the award of the DCO, have primarily preferred to implement the DCO as approved, even where this may cost more or be less innovative, rather than to make changes, as the process is uncertain.

In 2016, the National Infrastructure Planning Association (NIPA) commissioned some research to assess whether there was a major issue with this lack of flexibility and if there were ways that it could be overcome. NIPA wanted to review the perceived increase in the level of detail that was emerging in the practice of the system. This research found that the main focus of the NSIP promoters and their advisers was on the achievement of the DCO and that there had been an unintended consequence that this was becoming the end, rather than the delivery of the project as a whole. The research recommended, among other things, that there be a focus on delivery throughout, which would then ensure that flexibilities could be incorporated within the system (Clifford and Morphet 2017).

The planning of infrastructure investment in the UK has been impacted by devolution since 1999. Although there were variations between the four nations before devolution, this distinction has developed further since. In Northern Ireland, infrastructure services that were provided before the creation of the Irish state in 1922 now operate as single networks and since 1922, there remain special arrangements for their operation (ISNI 2011). In Scotland (Scottish Government 2015) and Wales (Welsh Government 2015), specific approaches to infrastructure delivery planning have been developed. In Scotland, this has been part of the strategic planning framework, which has been published in many versions since 2003. In Wales, spatial planning focused on the environmental and sustainable dimension of planning and the Welsh Assembly Government produced an infrastructure delivery plan in 2012, which was later accompanied by a separate planning system in 2016.

How Is the National Infrastructure Planning System Operating?

While the 2008 system for national infrastructure planning has operated efficiently, when the whole time frame for these nationally significant planning applications is considered, the 2008 system is not necessarily any quicker on average than the system that preceded it (Marshall and Cowell 2016). While the system reform was in response to the length of time taken for the Terminal 5 Planning Inquiry, this was atypical in terms of its length and complexity. The long timescale of the inquiry was also anticipated by the inquiry inspector before the inquiry opened. However, despite drawing attention to the likely length of time for the inquiry to the minster concerned, it went ahead and did take a long time.

The system for considering NSIPs within the 2008 Act is not one that is like other planning application processes. When a planning application is made, the rights of the land owner are potentially changed. This means that, under human rights legislation, the principle or argument for that development should be tested and proved. This is similarly the case when compulsory purchase orders (CPOs) are considered, as these deprive land owners of their property. The NSIP system uses the proxy of the NPS, approved by Parliament as the means through which a general level of consent is given for development through some indication of national need. However, the underlying legal basis for these remains in the EU regulations, through which the principle of development is established. Thus, the Planning Act 2008 created a secondary or 'detailed' planning consent stage but did not establish the primary need for the development. This means that the processes of consideration can be inquisitorial rather than adversarial, as would normally be the case in a planning application inquiry.

As the principle of development has been established though the NPS, the form of examination of the proposals is therefore concerned with its detailed delivery. This includes the impact of the form of the development on the local community. This is established through an impact statement prepared by the local authority (ies) where the proposal is geographically located. The local authority is also required to review the consultation undertaken by the project's promoter to ensure that adequate and meaningful public consultation has been undertaken. The preparation of the local authority's impact statement at the beginning of the process of consideration, at the pre-application stage, has meant that it is taken as a given in the acceptance of the scheme for consideration for the grant of a DCO, but this local assessment is not necessarily then examined for its implications during the active part of the examination process. The role of local authorities, although included within formal processes, is relatively marginalised and this has made the relationship between these authorities and applications difficult on occasion (Morphet and Clifford 2017a).

Another consequence of this secondary planning approach is that the system is primarily operated and led by lawyers and environmental consultants who have focussed on the NSIP process. While the 2008 Act system was designed to attempt to reduce promoter risks in application acceptance and time taken for decision, in some sectors, particularly energy, these risks are much higher. Here, the promoter of the scheme is required to obtain a DCO before they can bid for a licence for the scheme at the regular energy auctions. Further, while the Planning Act 2008 was expected to provide an almost automatic consent for any application that was approved for submission, three applications have been turned down on environmental grounds. These refusals were not because the facility was not needed but because its delivery was unacceptable in its specific design or location. Consequently, the costs and, in some cases, risks of submitting an NSIP application, including major costs for the pre-application stage, may be leading towards consent and this has underplayed the need to consider construction and delivery as the outcomes of the process (Clifford and Morphet 2017).

This has also led to a highly risk-averse approach – initially by the IPC but subsequently by legal and environmental advisers – that has been exacerbated by the incentivised fee structures offered by scheme promoters. As each examination will give rise to different issues given the nature of the proposal, specific location and means of delivery, there has been a risk minimisation approach adopted. This has incorporated all the issues raised at each previous examination in a cumulative way, in case these issues emerge later in the current examination. This is regardless of their potential relevance to the NSIP in hand.

Unlike a planning application, the DCO is drafted by the scheme promoter. Once approved, the DCO is made through a Parliamentary Order, which means that it is difficult to change. This means that if the design, methods of construction and operation of the project are not known at the time of the examination, then any agreements or commitment made at that point could fetter later considerations on the project's delivery, including technical advances and improved site use. These commitments may also include side agreements made with land owners and statutory consultees during the examination and these together may serve to undermine the ability of the subsequent constructers of the scheme to make any changes or improvements and may also serve to increase costs in delivery.

This is not the case for every scheme and some DCOs have been constructed in a hybrid way that allows the outline of the development to be considered within an environmental or Rochdale Envelope but, at the same time, the envelope approach provides a legal mechanism in which detailed elements of the project can be agreed as it is implemented. The envelope approach also identifies how the community is to be involved and more detailed agreements are to be discharged by specific local authorities or statutory consultees. This approach provides more flexibility in practice for the delivery of the project.

Community engagement on any NSIP is an essential feature for the acceptance of the application for a DCO into the formal examination process. However, after this initial engagement, the community can find it difficult to engage with the process as the project progresses through the examination system and then into operational delivery (Clifford and Morphet 2017; Rydin et al. 2018; Morphet and Clifford 2017b). Communities have sometimes found it difficult to engage where there is no final design at this application stage. Communities may not be represented at the examination and in some cases, examiners may explore specific issues that, in their view, communities have overlooked. Further, once the project progresses into the construction phase, it is often difficult for communities to engage with the process and active communication can break down (Morphet and Clifford 2017b). This can be overcome by the establishment of a core project management function for the life of the project and the appointment of an individual to be a main contact during the delivery process.

One key issue is the ways in which community and public engagement are made. This is primarily undertaken using meetings, newsletters and surveys. The promoter must demonstrate how they have responded to any community comments in the development and design of their scheme. In France, there is a process of public debate before a national infrastructure project is considered and then the findings are followed through the delivery of the process La Commission nationale du débat public (CNDP) (Marshall 2016; Davies and Slade 2017). In this approach, there is an independent auditor who is appointed and undertakes a community-based inquiry/debate into the scheme. The auditor remains after this report process to ensure that the promoters implement what has been agreed. In other schemes in the UK and outside the NSIP, such as HS1, an independent person is appointed for the community to use to seek information or to make complaints or queries about contractor behaviour on site. Both approaches could usefully be adopted within the NSIP system in England.

There are also other interests that find it difficult to engage in the NSIP process, including land owners. This is primarily because there is a confusion between this system and that used for planning applications, where the principle of the development and the need for land is established through the process. Land owners expect the process to be adversarial and to have the opportunity to argue about the loss or temporary use of their land during construction as part of the examination process (Clifford and Morphet 2017).

The prime pressure of the six-month examination period is stress caused to the participants. It has also pressurised participants to agree side deals at the margins of the examination. These deals on land or ways of working exclude the community and may lead promoters to accept a short-term agreement at the price of a longer term disbenefit to the implementation of the project. Statutory consultees must respond to the NSIP as submitted and have done so in mixed ways. Some have developed a streamlined approach and some agencies have been working together to improve their efficiency and effectiveness. Other organizations and consultees have waited until there is greater scheme detail before they have engaged. This might be quite late into the examination process, when other matters have already been agreed.

Emerging English Policy on National Infrastructure Delivery and Management

There are two key approaches to infrastructure delivery emerging in England, which have yet to be fully developed into operation. The first is the creation of the NIC, which was initially set up to be an independent body to consider all infrastructure planning and decision making. The approach taken by the NIC included both the definition of the comprehensive networks and the vertical multi-scalar contract approach. The NIC also considered the integrated approach with spatial development, announcing early that it would be concerned with these issues. However, following the referendum on the UK's membership in the EU, there was a hiatus in the institutional development of the NIC, following which it lost its independent status and emerged as an agency owned by the government through the Treasury. This was a significant response to Brexit and, while the work of the NIC has not changed, its independent powers have been curtailed. Rather than being a means of responding to and delivering policy and legislation agreed by the UK in the EU, the NIC has started to focus on the policy of the OECD (NIC 2017). As the EU and OECD have been working together in these issues, the policies are very similar. However, the UK's membership in the OECD is not bound by treaties and following Brexit, these UK–OECD relationships may become more important, but not binding.

Brexit will have another major impact on the UK's national infrastructure delivery system. Firstly, the schemes that the UK wishes to pursue will need to be taken through Parliament from the outset, as they will not be included within EU regulations. While government departments can revise their NPSs, the schemes will need to be identified in more detail and the NPSs may need to be changed into national planning policy statements. Brexit will also have an influence on the degree of devolution offered to Scotland, Wales and Northern Ireland. In the future, the reference to national infrastructure might encompass the whole state, rather than each nation.

A second area that will need to be considered in national infrastructure delivery will be the issues of supply and the energy market. The UK may be able to maintain formal supply links with the EU, not least as there are an already several pipelines in place and under development, e.g. between Ireland, the UK and Norway. The provisions of replacement nuclear power stations at Hinkley Point and in Cumbria may be affected, depending on the customs union arrangements that the UK has with the EU, and may affect supply. However, the UK remains bound by the WTO agreements on competition and this will remain the same. The maintenance of links with the EU for supply will have implications for the application of EU environmental regulations and, potentially, the role of the ECJ to determine any disputes. The role and application of EIA may well remain unchanged, again, to ensure the UK complies with its international obligations, including those to the UN and the WTO and as part of a longer term trade deal.

Conclusion

While the UK has changed its national infrastructure planning system in the period since 2008, this has not been marked by a significant improvement in performance. One issue is that all national infrastructure projects are set within a political context of government that means that they may be delayed or reviewed after each general election. There is no cross-party approach to delivering projects across the life of parliaments, as occurs in other countries. Further, the management of national infrastructure planning is not transparent, and issues are not available for wider public debate. While there have been institutional reforms in government for the management of these processes, it is uncertain whether they will achieve any improvements in performance and outcomes of national infrastructure delivery.

References

Aspergis, N., & Payne, J. E. (2010). Renewable energy consumption and economic growth: Evidence from a panel of OECD countries. *Energy Policy*, 38(1), 656–660.

Bhaskar, V., & Glyn, A. (2014). *The North, the South and the Environment*. Abingdon: Routledge.

Bigdeli, S. Z. (2014). Clash of rationalities: Revisiting the trade and environment debate in light of WTO disputes over green industrial policy. *Trade, Law and Development*, 6, 177.

Bowman, A. (2015). An illusion of success: The consequences of British rail privatisation. *Accounting Forum*, 39(1), 51–63.

Castells, A., & Solé-Ollé, A. (2005). The regional allocation of infrastructure investment: The role of equity, efficiency and political factors. *European Economic Review*, 49(5), 1165–1205.

CEC (1996). *Decision No 1692/96/EC of the European Parliament and of the Council of 23 July 1996 on Community Guidelines for the Development of the Trans-European Transport Network*. Brussels: CEC.

CEC (2013). *Regulation (EU) No 1315/2013 of the European Parliament and of the Council of 11 December 2013 on Union Guidelines for the Development of the Trans-European Transport Network and Repealing Decision No 661/2010/ EU Text with EEA Relevance*. Brussels: CEC.

CEC (2017). *Europe 2020* national reform programmes: UK. https://ec.europa.eu/info/2017-european-semester-national-reform-programmes-and-stability-convergence-programmes_en#united-kingdom (accessed 22 December 2017).

Clastres, C. (2011). Smart grids: Another step towards competition, energy security and climate change objectives. *Energy Policy*, 39(9), 5399–5408.

Clifford, B., & Morphet, J. (2017). *Infrastructure Delivery: The DCO Process in Context Technical Report*. London: NIPA.

Davies, N., & Slade, D. (2017). *How to Design an Infrastructure Strategy for the UK*. London: IfG.

DBEIS (2017). Industrial strategy. www.gov.uk/government/policies/industrial-strategy (accessed 4 July 2018).

DCMS (2017). High speed broadband to become a legal right Universal Service Obligation will deliver high speed broadband across the UK. Press notice, 20 December.

Debande, O. (2002). Private financing of transport infrastructure: an assessment of the UK experience. *Journal of Transport Economics and Policy*, 36(3), 355–387.

DECC (2016). *Annual Fuel Poverty Report Statistics 2016*. London: DECC.

Eddington, R. (2006). *The Eddington Transport Study – The Case for Action: Sir Rod Eddington's Advice to Government*. London: HMT.

GATT (1979). *General Agreement on Government Procurement*. Geneva: GATT.

George, C. (2014). Environment and regional trade agreements: Emerging trends and policy drivers. OECD Trade and Environment Working Papers, No. 2014/02. Paris: OECD. https://doi.org/10.1787/5jz0v4q45g6h-en (accessed 4 July 2018).

Grayling, C. (2018). East Coast Rail update. Statement to Parliament, 16 May. www.gov.uk/government/speeches/east-coast-rail-update (accessed 4 July 2018).

Harper, C., & Snowden, M. (2017). *Environment and Society: Human Perspectives on Environmental Issues*. Abingdon: Taylor & Francis.

Helm, D. (2014). The European framework for energy and climate policies. *Energy Policy*, 64, 29–35.

Hermann, C., & Flecker, J. (Eds.). (2013). *Privatization of Public Services: Impacts for Employment, Working Conditions, and Service Quality in Europe.* London: Routledge.

HMG (2016). *National Infrastructure Delivery Plan 2016–2021.* London: HMG.

Holl, A. (2007). Twenty years of accessibility improvements: The case of the Spanish motorway building programme. *Journal of Transport Geography,* 15(4), 286–297.

Ibanez, E., Lavrenz, S., Gkritza, K., Mejia-Giraldo, D. A., Krishnan, V., McCalley, J. D., & Somani, A. K. (2016). Resilience and robustness in long-term planning of the national energy and transportation system. *International Journal of Critical Infrastructures,* 12(1–2), 82–103.

ISNI (2011). *Investment Strategy for Northern Ireland 2011–2021.* Belfast: ISNI.

Kanellakis, M., Martinopoulos, G., & Zachariadis, T. (2013). European energy policy: A review. *Energy Policy,* 62, 1020–1030.

Kirton, J. J., & Trebilcock, M. J. (2017). *Hard Choices, Soft Law: Voluntary Standards in Global Trade, Environment and Social Governance.* Abingdon: Routledge.

Marshall, T. (2016). Learning from France: Using public deliberation to tackle infrastructure planning issues. *International Planning Studies,* 21(4), 329–347.

Marshall, T., & Cowell, R. (2016). Infrastructure, planning and the command of time. *Environment and Planning C: Government and Policy,* 34(8), 1843–1866.

Meunier, S. (2005). *Trading Voices: The European Union in International Commercial Negotiations.* Princeton: Princeton University Press.

Morphet, J. (2013). *How Europe Shapes British Public Policy.* Bristol: Policy Press.

Morphet, J. (2017). Combined authorities–The next big thing? *Town and Country Planning,* March, 96–103.

Morphet, J., & Clifford, B. (2017a). *Infrastructure Delivery: The DCO Process in Context.* London: NIPA.

Morphet, J., & Clifford, B. (2017b). The national infrastructure planning regime – the role of local authorities and communities. *Town and Country Planning,* August, 296–302.

NAO (2013). *Over-Optimism in Government Projects.* London: NAO.

NAO (2016). *Delivering Major Projects in Government: A Briefing for the Committee of Public Accounts.* London: NAO.

NIC (2017). Strategic infrastructure planning international best practice. www.gov.uk/government/publications/strategic-infrastructure-planning-international-best-practice–2 (accessed 22 December 2017).

OECD (2011). *Strategic Transport Infrastructure Needs to 2030.* Paris: OECD.

OECD (2017). *Getting Infrastructure Right Framework for Better Governance.* Paris: OECD.

PINS (2017). National infrastructure planning national policy statements. https://infrastructure.planninginspectorate.gov.uk/legislation-and-advice/national-policy-statements/ (accessed 22 December 2017).

Pisu, M., Pels, B., & Bottini, N. (2015). Improving infrastructure in the United Kingdom. Economic Department Working Paper No. 1244. Paris: OECD.

Raco, M. (2016). Mass privatisation and the changing nature of governance in the UK. In M. Bevir and R.A. W. Rhodes (Eds.), *Rethinking Governance: Ruling, Rationalities and Resistance* (pp. 50–69) London: Routledge.

Rydin, Y., Natarajan, L., Lee, M., & Lock, S. (2018). Artefacts, the gaze and sensory experience: Mediating local environments in the planning regulation of major renewable energy infrastructure in England and Wales. In M. Kurath, M. Marskamp, J. Paulos, J. Ruegg (Eds.), *Relational Planning* (pp. 51–74). Cham: Palgrave Macmillan.

Sandford, M. (2017). Combined authorities. House of Commons Briefing Paper No. 06649, 4 July 2017. London: House of Commons Library.

Sclar, E. (2015). The political economics of investment Utopia: Public–private partnerships for urban infrastructure finance. *Journal of Economic Policy Reform*, 18(1), 1–15.

Scottish Government (2015). *Infrastructure Investment Plan*. Edinburgh: Scottish Government.

Vickerman, R. (1995). Location, accessibility and regional development: The appraisal of trans-European networks. *Transport Policy*, 2(4), 225–234.

WEF (2016). *Global Competitiveness Report*. Geneva: WEF.

Wellings, R. (2014). The privatisation of the UK railway industry: An experiment in railway structure. *Economic Affairs*, 34(2), 255–266.

Welsh Government (2015). *Infrastructure Investment Plan*. Cardiff: WG.

Wong, C., Baker, M., Hincks, S., Schulze-Baing, A., & Webb, B. (2012). A map for England: Spatial expression of government policies and programmes. Final report, Royal Town Planning Institute. Manchester: Centre for Urban Policy Studies University of Manchester. www.rtpi.org.uk/media/11202/map_for_england_final_report__2012_.pdf (accessed 5 July 2018).

5 Strategic Planning in England

Introduction

The role and practices of strategic planning in the UK have changed over time and are strongly located within the governance and culture of each UK nation. This chapter will consider the development and challenges of the practice and delivery of strategic planning in England, while later chapters will consider how these fit within the planning systems of Scotland, Wales and Northern Ireland. Strategic planning in England has always exhibited a tension in the disputed dominance between economic and spatial considerations. That tension was strong in the 1930s and 1960s, and remains the same now (Glasson and Marshall 2007). However, until the Local Democracy, Economic Development and Construction Act 2009, the management and ownership of strategic planning, using both administrative and functional economic area (FEA) boundaries, has primarily been in the hands of the government.

Although in the period of the Labour government (1997–2010) there were increasing attempts to demonstrate some democratic involvement and accountability (Morphet 2017a) in the processes of strategic planning, they remained captured by central government. This centralised dominance included a focus on housing development, which was increasingly associated with economic growth (HMT 2007). In 2000, the London government was devolved to a directly elected mayor with an assembly with a scrutiny, rather than an operational decision making, function. Following the 2009 Act and the 2016 Cities and Devolution Act, the combined authorities (CAs), each with a directly elected mayor, were established and have since started to be implemented in several primarily, but not exclusively, urban areas in England (Sandford 2017).

The focus on spatial governance and democratic accountability has provided a mixed picture of the responsibility for strategic planning on these newly formed CAs with directly elected mayors. Each CA has been established using a Parliamentary Order, so that vary in relation to their responsibilities and duties. The pattern of responsibilities in each area is to some extent related to the acceptance of specific powers to the local authorities sitting within each new authority area (Morphet 2017b). In London, the mayor is responsible for preparing a strategic plan and has responsibilities for Transport for London and regeneration, together with some aspects of health and housing. Using these powers together, the Mayor of London can prepare a plan that combines strategic planning with its delivery. The methodology for the London Plan is based on the 1991 Planning Act and does not include spatial planning delivery requirements, setting it at odds with the planning powers of the London Borough, which prepares spatial plans for the whole of its local authority areas under the 2004 Planning and Compulsory Purchase Act. The London Borough plans include a spatial planning delivery focus. This has meant that the London Plan has had to retrofit its requirements for infrastructure delivery outside the plan (MoL 2016).

Outside London, the planning powers of the directly elected mayors are more mixed and there is little consensus of what strategic planning may comprise (Allmendinger et al. 2016). The first wave of mayors of CAs were elected in 2017 and while they had a range of powers at the outset, there is an expectation that these will be increased and filled in over time. It is also possible to see that, within the 'bespoke' powers of each mayor, there is considerable commonality of the powers they have (Morphet 2017b). Further, there has been little or no discussion about how such strategic plans should be constructed and delivered, apart from a focus on housing (DCLG 2017). This is complicated by discussions and uncertainties over Brexit, as the EU approach to strategic planning is being developed into an active form for the period from 2021 onwards (ESPON 2017: Krukowska and Lackowska 2017; European Parliament 2015). Despite uncertainties, this approach to strategic planning for the EU may provide a model that is followed in the UK, including England.

Why and How Is Strategic Planning Emerging?

Although there are strong antecedents of strategic planning for places and local economies in the UK and elsewhere, there has been a more recent surge in trends, given the increasing role of the new economic geography. Krugman demonstrated that trade within states, between FEAs, can be as important for national gross domestic product (GDP) as trade between nations (Krugman 1991; 2011). This approach has become a key focus of policy and delivery in many states and the driving force of the Organization for Economic Cooperation and Development's (OECD) local economic development policy. This approach has been further enhanced since the OECD found that, where there is strong democratic governance aligned with FEA boundaries, such as directly elected mayors, this can further enhance GDP (OECD 2015; 2017). Since then, there have been a growing number of sub-state governance reorganisations and changes in OECD members across the world, including the EU (Mitchell and Watts 2010).

In the EU, there has been joint work with the OECD, which has agreed on a common approach to and definition of FEAs (Dijkstra and Poelman 2012). This has been taken forward within the EU through the Covenant of Mayors and through the Urban Pact (CEC 2016a) and Urban Agenda (2016b). The European Parliament has also considered the role of cities within the structures in EU institutional decision making (Heinelt 2017) following the adoption of the

Urban Pact in 2016. What this study found was that cities across the EU were heterogenous in their powers, being able to make both horizontal agreements with neighbouring authorities and vertical agreements between governments that are operational at different scales of the state. While the principle of subsidiarity assists in supporting the increasing role and powers of cities in their governance and control over funds for delivery, it does not help in reverse – that is, in defining a role in decision making within EU institutions. Heinelt (2018) stated that it is difficult to define ways in which cities could be included within the institutional structures of the EU. Nevertheless, given their role in dealing with climate change, economic growth and migration, cities should be regarded as policy makers rather than policy takers. One way that has been identified in this study is through the more systematic use of the Integrated Territorial Investment (ITI) strategies that were include within the cohesion regulations, as an option for member states to use (CEC 2013a). These institutional forms across the whole of the EU could reinforce the scale of governance and the control over devolved expenditure but also provide a means for establishing a relationship for policy input directly with the European Commission (EC).

What Are Functional Economic Areas?

FEAS emerged as a concept in the 1960s (Fox and Kumar 1965; Berry 1966). FEAs are primarily defined by the journey to work patterns in sub-state areas and identify cultural and economic ties and help to express the differences within states. In taking forward the concept in England, the government initially chose to use the term 'Functional Economic Market Area' (FEMA) (DCLG 2010). While the emphasis given to FEMA was on the labour market and economic definitions, there was also a strong relationship with the provision of housing to serve these markets. The government used these concepts to base the introduction of Local Enterprise Partnerships (LEPs) in 2010. While LEPs are underpinned by some local governance, they are not democratic bodies or subject to the code of conduct in public life, despite their management of government and EU funds.

The role of LEPs in encouraging local authorities into operational FEAs and as preparatory to the creation of CAs is significant but seldom understood. LEPs assisted in longer term building of sub-state identity and association before these FEAs could be effective units of government (Coombes 2014). However, the process of rescaling the state was undertaken through 'nudge' rather than institutional rescaling, as occurred with local governments in 1974 and in the early 1990s (Lowndes and McCaughie 2013). This method fits within the application of the principle of subsidiarity rather than centralism (Pemberton and Morphet 2014).

The Disruptive Reform of Strategic Planning in England

Whilst the new sub-regional arrangements in England have been associated with the Coalition government since 2010, the Labour Government was also undertaking a similar programme of reform immediately before this. The Sub-National

Economic Development and Regeneration Review for England (HMT 2007) led to the rescaling between the former regional and emergent sub-regional levels. Contractual relationships at the sub-regional level were created through Multi-Area Agreements (MAAs) between 2008 and 2010. The Local Democracy, Economic Development and Construction Act 2009 abolished Regional Spatial Strategies (RSSs), replacing them with Regional Strategies, and reformed political processes for strategic governance. Regional planning teams were already being wound up by the time of the 2010 general election.

When the Coalition government announced (again) the abolition of Regional Strategies soon after the general election in 2010, there was an assumption that the processes and institutions that supported strategic planning in England had been swept away in a tide of localism (Bafarasat and Baker 2016). At the same time, local authorities were invited to form LEPs for FEAs, creating new sub-regions across England (Morphet and Pemberton 2013). The initial assumption, made by many local authorities, that LEPs would only be recognised by the government in areas of economic stress was short-lived. In practice, the pressure was in the other direction, as local authorities reluctant to join LEPs soon found.

Initially LEPs were criticised as soft or fuzzy spaces with indeterminate accountabilities. They were formed as non-accountable, business-led organisations with self-appointed boards. Their role was not to replace the regional development agencies that were abolished by the Labour government in 2009, but rather to develop local priorities for the EU and local growth plans and programmes (Pike et al. 2015). They initially had no strategic planning role. Local authorities were members of the LEPs but did not control them. The central organisations of LEPs were kept minimal through small funding allocations although a national network was quickly established to share information and experience. Each LEP had a senior civil servant who acted as its liaison with central government.

As the LEPs developed their roles, focussing on transport and skills, the issue of democratic accountability remained a concern for local authorities. Although planning appeared to be off the LEP agenda, housing soon emerged as an element of economic infrastructure, as part of their strategic economic plans (SEPs) (DBIS 2013) and programmes, including indications of volume and location. The National Planning Policy Framework (DCLG 2012) identified the need for local authorities to work collaboratively with LEPs in the preparation for and delivery of their plans although LEPs had no formal role within the English planning system. However, in 2017, following the election of mayors in the newly formed CAs, the indicative quantity of housing included in the SEPs, without any basis in planning, were indicated as the targets within each area.

The government commissioned a review of the governance of LEPs (Ney 2017; MHCLG 2018) in recognition of the £12bn in public funding, for which LEPs were responsible. This review recommended immediate governance changes for LEPs. These included the clarification of the role of the local authority finance officer, through which LEP finance is passed but for which there is no responsibility or accountability. Secondly, there was a recommendation that all members of LEPs and their staff should be subject to a code of conduct in public life. In the review, there were examples where LEP board members were receiving funds for contracted delivery from within the organisation, which is contrary to public codes of conduct (HMG 1995).

Since their formation, LEPs have been developing horizontal integration between neighbouring localities. The government has also developed City Deals that devolve powers to local authorities and boost their role in democratic leadership of these new sub-regions. City Deals act as vertical contracts between central and local governments, which commit both to achieving defined targets, including for infrastructure, housing delivery and training (O'Brien and Pike 2015; Clayton and McGough 2015). City Deals areas may include more than one local authority if the FEA boundaries suggest that this is appropriate.

Although LEPs are included as part of the City Deal stakeholder group, City Deals are contracts between democratically accountable bodies. City Deals bring with them incentives through funding, freedoms and flexibilities for the local authorities concerned. Reviewing the range of these freedoms and flexibilities provides a means of assessing the likely expanded future scope of local authorities within the state. These include more powers for skills and training delivery, transport, housing and single integrated investment pots across local and central governments (Sandford 2017).

An emerging response by local authorities to the institutional indeterminacy of LEPs has been to shift towards the creation of CAs. These were enabled by the 2009 Local Democracy, Economic Development and Construction Act and extended through the Cities and Local Government Devolution Act 2016. CAs provide underpinning for groups of local authorities working together using Parliamentary Orders. Local authorities can also use the powers in the 1972 Local Government Act s123 to work together but any local authority can decide to leave such a grouping following a resolution of their own council. Each CA is established through a bespoke Parliamentary Order. The use of this legal framework to create the CA means that it is more likely that local authorities will remain inside these groupings and seek to resolve any differences internally. In both CAs and joint committees, local authorities agree to pool each of their specific powers in mutually agreed areas such as transport. The decisions on these issues can then only be made by all the local authorities together and are binding on all members. Further, local authorities can only vote once on these issues within the CA, rather than twice within the CA and in their own council.

CAs were initially considered as an approach for a few local authorities but have been pursued actively by groups of local authorities throughout England (Townsend 2017). This interest has been partly driven by the scale of devolution that the government has so far been prepared to deliver to the 'model' CA, Greater Manchester. Proposals here include the devolution of the whole of the National Health Service (NHS) England budget of £6bn from 2016. Proposals for Manchester include the devolution of the whole of the NHS England budget of £6bn from 2016 and will be added to the £2bn of devolved funds already agreed. In London, the Mayor received health powers in the 2017 Budget (London Health Board 2017), which includes access to the use of revenues from NHS asset sales to reinvest in London's health care. There will also be closer working between health and social care functions in the NHS and London Boroughs.

These devolved responsibilities make CAs attractive to many other local authorities trying to solve financial conundrums, including balancing priorities for personal health and care services and investing in economic growth. However, even these devolved budgets are said to only reflect one third of central government spending in Greater Manchester. More devolution will be required to move the UK to EU averages of devolved funding and the directly elected mayors have called for this (MoL 2017).

While there has been considerable attention paid to reshaping the sub-state economic governance space comprising LEPs, CAs and City Deals, each with individual local authorities within them, the development of strategic planning has progressed less. Whilst these new institutions are working together in interlocking arrangements and overlapping memberships, it is the CA that is likely to emerge as the overarching governance structure within which the LEPs and City Deals will sit. Further, the creation of local Economic Prosperity Boards (EPBs), a so-far unused provision in the Local Democracy, Economic Development and Construction Act 2009, could take on the economic development functions. These functions are currently held by LEPs that have no legal or democratic basis. Like City Deals, CAs are also developing their own agenda for strategic infrastructure and managing transport systems. Groups of CAs are also starting to work together to achieve major infrastructure investment, including the North of England and the Midlands Engine (ME 2017).

Since 2010, planning has been focused on the local, including the new neighbourhood planning system introduced in 2011. Although the planning system introduced in 2004 included strategic planning through RSSs, these were quickly captured by central government agendas and dominated by new housing provision (Baker and Wong 2013; Boddy and Hickman 2013). The pressure to prepare local plans within a constantly moving and potentially destabilising central government framework has continued. Local authority planners have had their attention focused towards, and perhaps distracted by, the local and neighbourhood, rather than strategic, scales (Brownill 2017).

In the parallel governance space, LEPs have published SEPs and European Structural and Investment Fund (ESIF) programmes in 2013. (DCLG et al. 2017) SEPs and ESIFs have been prepared within frameworks of government guidance given by central government. The SEP guidance, (DBIS 2013) focused LEPs on their bidding role for central government growth funds. They are also intended to act as integration and delivery plans for other funding from a variety of sources, including bonds, the private sector, the local authority's own resources (including assets), housing associations, other government funding for transport and further education as well as EU funding.

SEPs and ESIFs have been developed outside the planning system in England and are untested by the government's Planning Inspectorate. Yet al.though prepared by unaccountable bodies, their priorities and programmes are spatial.

Further, the priorities and programmes in SEPs are emerging as key issues to be considered in examinations of local plans and planning appeals without any overt identification of their status (Johnston and Blenkinsopp 2017). However, more recently, the delivery of housing has been appearing in specific growth deals (Ward 2017) and duties to deliver housing have been placed on directly elected mayors in CAs (Morphet 2017b).

Although the process of establishing LEPs has been regarded as an English initiative, it is possible to see parallels in the other nations of the UK. The Scottish strategic development plan (SDP) system was introduced in the 2006 Planning, etc. Scotland Act. This created sub-regional planning areas around Dundee, Edinburgh, Glasgow and Aberdeen. Unlike the LEPs, these SDP areas are placed under boards that are cross-sectoral and led by local authorities. In 2014, a City Deal was agreed by the UK government and Glasgow.

In Wales, the Wales Spatial Plan (2004) created six sub-regions with their own boards, each led by an Assembly Member. Unlike the SDPs in Scotland, these boards have never developed into strategic planning or programming bodies. Instead, Wales has adopted city regions and the City Deal approach as in England, with three designated cities in Cardiff-Newport, Swansea and North Wales. These are similar place-based contracts between central government, the Welsh Government, local authorities and stakeholders.

In Northern Ireland, the Regional Development Strategy (RDS) (2002) established key sub-regions and the strategic approach has been taken through the reform of local government, implemented in 2015. All these sub-regional arrangements in the UK nations have been a long time in development and stretch back to the implementation of the devolution process in 1999.

The Role of the EU in Strategic Planning

How has the landscape for strategic planning changed during the 2014-2020 period? Are there any underlying principles that help identify the future direction of travel, particularly for this new sub-regional level? What seems clear is that the objections to a lack of accountability in the LEPs (Ney 2017) will be overcome by the democratic leadership of the CAs as they are established. It also seems likely that there will be a policy reset for strategic plans for these CAs, integrating them into the wider planning framework, and that these strategic plans will be undertaken in ways that are similar to but different from current local planning methodologies, with a greater focus on delivery. The contractual relationships for cities are likely to be extended into more rural areas. In the emerging contractual arrangements, each governance scale will work with the others as appropriate to support and deliver projects, not least as the devolved funds increase as a proportion of the whole available.

These futures are predictable – at least until 2020. How do we know this? The answer lies in the submerged policies and legislation, agreed by the UK within the EU, that underpin them (Morphet 2017a). The negotiation and implementation of EU Regulation (1303/2013), which was finally agreed in

December 2013 and became effective from 1 January 2014, sets out the objectives, institutions, funding and methodologies for this sub-state integrated planning system for the period 2014–2020. The role of this regulation and its application have also been reviewed by the European Parliament (Pucher et al. 2015).

Although implemented in 2014, this regulation has been in discussion and negotiation since at least 2000. When the ESDP was published in 1999 by an informal Ministerial Council of the EU, some concluded that this marked the end of any attempt to develop a spatial policy for Europe (Faludi 2004). The informal approach to preparing the ESDP had been adopted following some uncertainty about the role of the EC in territorial and spatial policy when work started in 1993. This concern was raised primarily by the UK government. However, whilst the work on the ESDP proceeded to publication in 1999, the EC developed a legal solution that would remove this uncertainty (Faludi 2005) and its application appears to be as much a policy stance as a means of producing specific outcomes (Abrahams 2014). To overcome this disputed power of policy initiation for spatial matters, the EC decided to insert a new power to give them the initiative on territorial matters within the EU's existing core principles for social and economic cohesion. This would be achieved through the means of the next available EU treaty negotiation.

The treaty negotiations that started in 2001 took longer than anticipated and were not agreed until 2007, as the Lisbon Treaty, implemented in 2009. From this point, territorial cohesion became an objective and principle of the EU. The EU's cohesion policies are implemented through seven-year programmes that set out the priorities and the funding programmes that support their delivery at the sub-state level, including structural funds. The Lisbon Treaty was signed in 2007, making it too late to be implemented through the 2006–2013 programme but it did allow more preparation to be made before the start of the next programme for 2014–2020.

The longer period of policy development started with the Barca Report (Barca 2009). This set out a future for EU cohesion policies to be spatial, integrated and contractual across all governance scales. This approach reflected the completion of the application of the principle of subsidiarity to sub-state levels also in the Lisbon Treaty. This principle was also reflected in the use of the term 'territory' – 'territorialisation' in French is equivalent to 'devolution' in English.

Whilst the new approach to territorial cohesion was conceived at a time of economic growth, the global economic crisis in 2007 meant that the EU reviewed its own approach to managing its economic policies. In 2010, *Europe 2020* was adopted, which set out the priorities for this period, concentrating on infrastructure, energy and reforms of the single market. Implementation of this policy programme was agreed through a growth and stability pact, which set out the specific reform programmes that would be required for each member state to reach these 2020 objectives. In the UK, the priorities set were reforms in infrastructure, planning, housing and youth training policies. These overall objectives and the specific reform programme for each member state were also to be carried forward in the new cohesion regulation and to be incorporated within the specific delivery objectives.

The inclusion of territory into the cohesion principle launched many different approaches. It has shifted the EU's territorial interests from places that were lagging behind the EU's social and economic averages. Cohesion programmes were formerly focussed on areas where these conditions predominated (usually identified by their eligibility for structural funds) and cross-border areas. The addition of the principle of territorial cohesion has extended cohesion objectives and policies to all the EU's geography, in an edge-to-edge, rather than a targeted spatial, approach.

Territorial cohesion has also started to change the focus of EU policies and programmes (Medeiros 2016). These have traditionally been organised on a sectoral basis, reflected through the internal structures of the EC Directorates General (DG) and Commissioners. Each DG operates defined programmes, but these have not been aligned with each other. Territorial cohesion has meant a reconsideration of these programmes and their relationships with each other as they are delivered together in a spatial context. This has started to generate change across the EC's institutions, policies and programmes towards integration. The focus of policies and programmes has started to shift from sector to place.

These reforms have been implemented in many ways. Firstly, from 2015, EU Commissioners have been given a wider range of roles. Portfolios have been changed and some Commissioners have roles in overarching EU policy integration and delivery. Cohesion regulation 1013/2013 is another element of this implementation strategy and, unlike a directive, must be implemented by each member state as-written. Another key component of integration is that between budgets. In the past, cohesion programmes have been a means of focussing EU funding. The innovative approach is concerned with how public-sector funds are used across the whole of the EU's geography. This includes funding from central and local government and utilities, which are defined as public bodies within EU legislation. A further approach to integrating a territorial focus has been to consider this across scales of governance. Where projects are commissioned, they frequently require agreements between different democratic organisations. This multi-government, contractual approach is expected to be extended from this agreement for vertical alignment of commitments to projects to horizontal agreements across boundaries and borders.

Following the adoption of the cohesion regulation in December 2013, each member state was required to submit a Partnership Agreement by April 2014 (CEC 2014). This was to set out how they intended to implement the regulation. Once submitted, the Partnership Agreements were assessed by the EC for their alignment and compliance with EU legislation, including the implementation of policies to support *Europe 2020*. The Partnership Agreements were approved before implementation in 2015.

The strategy and content for individual Partnership Agreements were set out in Regulation 1303/2013, where it states that 'Member States shall...ensure complementarity between Union policies and instruments and national, regional and local interventions' (CEC 2013b Annexe 1 4.1). Partnership Agreements are to include:

- An analysis of the Member State's or region's characteristics, development potential and capacity, particularly in relation to the key challenges identified in the Union strategy for smart, sustainable and inclusive growth, the National Reform Programmes;
- An assessment of the major challenges to be addressed by the region or Member State, the identification of the bottlenecks and missing links, innovation gaps, including the lack of planning and implementation capacity that inhibit the long-term potential for growth and jobs. This shall form the basis for the identification of the possible fields and activities for policy prioritisation, intervention and concentration;
- Identification of steps to achieve improved coordination across different territorial levels, taking account of the appropriate territorial scale and context for policy design... and sources of funding to deliver an integrated approach linking the Union strategy for smart, sustainable and inclusive growth with regional and local actors.

CEC 2013b Annexe 1 p414

The regulation (Article 15.2) sets out how these integrated approaches are to be combined at the local level. This makes the link to two institutional frameworks –ITI strategies and programmes for the strategic level and Community Led Local Development (CLLD) partnerships at the local scale – that can be included within ITI programmes. Whilst CLLD programmes are entirely local, ITIs are developed between the state and the FEA or sub-region.

ITIs represent a new form of strategic planning and the regulation includes a set of thematic objectives that must be addressed in an integrated way (Article 36). They provide a means of prioritisation using criteria-based assessment of plan and programme outcomes using the defined objectives as follows:

1. strengthening research, technological development and innovation;
2. enhancing access to, and use and quality of, ICT;
3. enhancing the competitiveness of SMEs, of the agricultural, fishery and aquaculture sectors;
4. supporting the shift towards a low-carbon economy in all sectors;
5. promoting climate change adaptation, risk prevention and management;
6. preserving and protecting the environment and promoting resource efficiency;
7. promoting sustainable transport and removing bottlenecks in key network infrastructures;
8. promoting sustainable and quality employment and supporting labour mobility;
9. promoting social inclusion, combating poverty and any discrimination;
10. investing in education, training and vocational training for skills and lifelong learning;

11. enhancing institutional capacity of public authorities and stakeholders and efficient public administration.

CEC 2013b Article 9

In terms of strategic planning methodology, the approach identified for preparing an ITI is systematic. The regulation sets out the key elements of the ITI, which are:

- a designated territory and an integrated territorial development strategy;
- a package of actions to be implemented; and
- governance arrangements to manage the ITI.

ITI can be adopted for a major urban area, a sub-region or across sub-regions or borders. They are contracts between central and sub-regional scales of governance. In terms of governance, ITIs are the responsibility of democratically accountable bodies although some or all of the management can be delegated to other bodies. In the English case, this would place CAs in the governance role and they may delegate their responsibilities in all or in part to LEPs or EPBs.

The second element of delivery is through a local development strategy prepared within the CLLD provisions of the regulation and subsequent guidance. In the past CLLD have only been used in rural locations but they are now available everywhere. As the EC stresses, CLLD must be prepared from the bottom up. CLLD can form part of the ITI, which may be prepared from the bottom up or from the top down. Article 33 states that a CLLD strategy shall contain at least the following elements:

a   the definition of the area and population covered by the strategy;
b   an analysis of the development needs and potential of the area, including an analysis of strengths, weaknesses, opportunities and threats;
c   a description of the strategy and its objectives...measurable targets for outputs or results;
d   a description of the community involvement process in the development of the strategy;
e   an action plan demonstrating how objectives are translated into actions;
f   a description of the management and monitoring arrangements of the strategy;
g   the financial plan for the strategy.

How are ITI and CLLD applied in the UK? The draft Partnership Agreement submitted by the government in April 2014 was finally approved in October 2014. In the initial submission, the UK indicated that it had no intention of using ITI whilst CLLD would only be used in rural areas. UK government departments were identified as the Managing Authorities and delivery was to be through LEPs. The version approved by the EC differs from this. There is a positive statement that there would be an ITI for

Cornwall and that ITI could be used elsewhere if local authorities wished. This marked a major shift away from LEPs and opened the way to devolved and integrated programmes to be developed and delivered. This suggests that there may be a need to review the form and content of SEPs to bring them into clear alignment with the objectives set out in the regulation and the UK's 2020 reform programme.

The EC has undertaken research to assess how ITI and urban strategies are adding value in their use of cohesion funds (van der Zwet et al. 2017). This study, which includes the examination of the Cornwall and Isles of Scilly ITI in England, have shown that these strategies have been successful in focussing on place-based policies that have been integrated and innovative. However, the research found that CLLD was not a frequently used component in the construction of the ITI and this was identified as being an issue of both local relevance and capacity. The research has shown that these strategies have been particularly effective in developing the programmes and governance of FEAs. Tensions were found between the sectoral and spatial programmes and taking an integrated approach was found to be particularly challenging. In terms of the governance of these strategies, this research found that it was most common for them to be developed by new bodies that incorporated vertical and horizontal arrangements. Finally, the report recommended that 'the initial experience indicates that the Commission should consider applying the principles of a place-based approach to a larger part of the post-2020 programmes and interventions' (van der Zwet et al. 2017 para 7.9.2).

Strategic Planning in England after 2020

Where might strategic planning go in the period beyond 2020? As most of Europe is discussing the delivery of the 2014–2020 programme, the EC is now started working on the programme for 2021–2027. Already there have been some significant moves in spatial planning. The first has been through the linked spatial planning policy agendas adopted by the Italian, Latvian, Luxembourg and Dutch EU Presidencies (2014–2016). Each has chosen to focus on a different spatial scale – in Italy, it was FEAs; in Latvia, smaller polycentric communities and for Luxembourg, there will be a major initiative to start discussions on a Territorial Vision 2050 for Europe to be completed by 2020. This appears to be a major review and replacement of the ESDP and this time it will go beyond the informal status of its predecessor. It will also be a significant component of cohesion policy post 2020.

Whatever the UK's relationship with the EU following the Brexit referendum in 2016, the UK will need to firm up its own priorities and objectives for its spatial strategy for the future. The UK has been identified as the only EU member without a strategic spatial plan for the state. Therefore, these discussions on Europe's Territorial Vision 2050 may be difficult. The government could rely on the strategic NPSs for infrastructure (PINS 2017) but these are not spatial. The UK infrastructure plan (HMT 2016) remains a grouping of sectoral plans that do not make much reference to each other and do not work as an integrated whole and industrial strategy (DBEIS 2017) is sectoral with specific spatial implications but not an integrated approach.

Unlike the ESDP, the new territorial approach is likely to have a key role in identifying locations for investment in infrastructure. This has started with the Juncker Investment Plan for Europe established by the president of the EC in 2014 (CEC 2017). Within an emerging EU long-term policy and investment process that is privileging the spatial, a state strategy that is sector-led may be at a disadvantage. The core TEN-T network, also revised and agreed in December 2013, is to be supplemented by an in-filling comprehensive network by 2030. The locations of these routes, nodes and hubs could have a significant effect on growth in the longer term. The current discussion on TEN-E as part of the EU's Energy Union strategy will have a significant effect on the location and type of investment.

At the local level, CLLD will be a key component in the ITI for communities ranging between 10,000 and 150,000 in population. There is guidance on the methods of preparation of their local development strategies, which includes an eight-step approach to address the EU-wide objectives within a locally led setting. In England, for example, these could include neighbourhood plans. But where do local development plans made under the 2004 Act fit in? Are they an imperilled species? The focus on CAs, ITI and CLLD suggests that these will be the new and predominant scales. The increasing destabilisation of the local planning system together with increasing ministerial criticism means that they may be the casualties of these strategic and neighbourhood approaches. ITI and CLLD strategies are plans developed through business planning methods focused on investment and delivery. These strategies are accompanied by delivery programmes for the budgets allocated through the spatial plans, like an extended version of the infrastructure delivery plans that most local authorities already have.

So, the future appears to lie in democratically accountable strategic and neighbourhood plans already in legislation and set within a spatial plan for the UK and the EU. In England, strategic planning may become a CA function, or at least operate at this scale. Spatial planning, with its emphasis on delivery, may not have been lost in 2010 but may emerge stronger and more powerful than before. In many ways, this reflects a return to the intention of the 1947 Planning Act. Planning is not just policy and regulation but is fundamentally concerned with delivery based on social, economic and environmental principles. There were mistakes in implementing the 1947 Act, including delay, blight and an over-centralised approach to the redevelopment of urban areas. However, a greater role for local authorities as patient developers for housing, commercial and other infrastructure fits well with practices in other countries. Rather than its demise, all this might herald a bright future for strategic spatial planning.

References

Abrahams, G. (2014). What 'is' territorial cohesion? What does it 'do'? Essentialist versus pragmatic approaches to using concepts. *European Planning Studies*, 22(10), 2134–2155.

Allmendinger, P., Haughton, G., & Shepherd, E. (2016). Where is planning to be found? Material practices and the multiple spaces of planning. *Environment and Planning C: Government and Policy*, 34(1), 38–51.

Bafarasat, A. Z., & Baker, M. (2016). Strategic spatial planning under regime governance and localism: Experiences from the North West of England. *Town Planning Review*, 87(6), 681–703.

Baker, M., & Wong, C. (2013). The delusion of strategic spatial planning: What's left after the Labour government's English regional experiment? *Planning Practice & Research*, 28(1), 83–103.

Barca, F. (2009) *The Barca Report: An Agenda for a Reformed Cohesion Policy*. Brussels: CEC. http://ec.europa.eu/regional_policy/archive/policy/future/barca_en.htm (accessed 23 July 2018).

Berry, B. J. (1966). Reflections on the functional economic areas. In *Research and Education for Regional and Area Development*, (pp. 56–64). Ames, IA: Center for Agricultural and Economic Development, Iowa State University.

Boddy, M., & Hickman, H. (2013). The demise of strategic planning? The impact of the abolition of regional spatial strategy in a growth region. *Town Planning Review*, 84(6), 743–768.

Brownill, S. (2017). Neighbourhood planning and the purposes and practices of localism. In S. Brownill and Q. Bradley *(Eds.), Localism and Neighbourhood Planning: Power to the People?* (pp. 19–38). Bristol: Policy Press.

CEC (2013). Regulation (EU) No 1301/2013 of the European Parliament and of the Council of 17 December 2013 on the European Regional Development Fund and on specific provisions concerning the investment for growth and jobs goal and repealing Regulation (EC) No 1080/2006. www.jobsandgrowthni.gov.uk/regulations/regulation-title-2 (accessed 5 July 2018).

CEC (2013). CEC Regulation 1301/2013. *Official Journal of the European Union L347*, 56, 20 December.

CEC (2014). Summary of the partnership agreement for United Kingdom, October. https://ec.europa.eu/info/sites/info/files/partnership-agreement-united-kingdom-summary-oct2014_en.pdf (accessed 31 December 2017).

CEC (2016a). The pact of Amsterdam: Urban agenda for the EU. www.eea.europa.eu/themes/sustainability-transitions/urban-environment/links/eu-strategies-and-policies/the-pact-of-amsterdam-urban (accessed 22 December 2017).

CEC (2016b). Urban agenda for the EU. https://ec.europa.eu/futurium/en/urban-agenda (accessed 22 December 2017).

CEC (2017). Investment plan for Europe: The Juncker plan. https://ec.europa.eu/commission/priorities/jobs-growth-and-investment/investment-plan-europe-juncker-plan_en (accessed 31 December 2017).

Clayton, N., & McGough, L. (2015). *City Deals and Skills*. London: UK Commission for Employment.

Coombes, M. (2014). From city-region concept to boundaries for governance: The English case. *Urban Studies*, 51(11), 2426–2443.

DBEIS (2017). *Industrial Strategy*. London: DBEIS.

DBIS (2013). Growth deals: Initial guidance for local enterprise partnerships. www.gov.uk/government/publications/growth-deals-initial-guidance-for-local-enterprise-partnerships (accessed 22 December 2017).

DCLG (2010). *Functional Economic Market Areas*. London: DCLG.

DCLG (2010). *National Planning Policy Framework*. London: Department of Communities and Local Government. https://assets.publishing.service.gov.uk/government/uploads/system/uploads/attachment_data/file/6077/2116950.pdf (accessed 5 July 2018).

DCLG (2017). *Planning for the Right Homes in the Right Places: Consultation Proposals*. London: DCLG.

DCLG, DEFRA, DWP, & DBEIS (2017). Guidance England 2014 to 2020 European structural and investment funds. www.gov.uk/guidance/england-2014-to-2020-european-structural-and-investment-funds (accessed 31 December 2017).

Dijkstra, & Poelman, H. (2012). *Cities in Europe: The New OECD-EU Definition*. Brussels: CEC.

European Parliament (2015). *Tools to Support the Territorial and Urban Dimension in Cohesion Policy: Integrated Territorial Investment (ITI) and Community-Led Local Development (CLLD) Briefing Research for REGI Committee*. Strasbourg: EP. www.europarl.europa.eu/RegData/etudes/BRIE/2015/563391/IPOL_BRI(2015)563391_EN.pdf.

ESPON (2017). ReSSI regional strategies for sustainable and inclusive territorial development: Regional interplay and EU dialogue. Targeted analysis draft. Final report. Luxembourg: ESPON.

Faludi, A. (2004). Spatial planning traditions in Europe: Their role in the ESDP process. *International Planning Studies*, 9(2–3), 155–172.

Faludi, A. (2005). Territorial cohesion: An unidentified political objective: Introduction to the special issue. *Town Planning Review*, 76(1), 1–13.

Fox, K. A., & Kumar, T. K. (1965). The functional economic area: Delineation and implications for economic analysis and policy. *Papers in Regional Science*, 15(1), 57–85.

Glasson, J., & Marshall, T. (2007). *Regional Planning*. London: Routledge.

Heinelt, H., (2017). *The Role of Cities in the Institutional Framework of the European Union*. Strasbourg: European Parliament.

Heinelt, H. (2018). *European Union Environment Policy and New Forms of Governance: A Study of the Implementation of the Environmental Impact Assessment Directive and the Eco-management and Audit Scheme Regulation in Three Member States*. London: Routledge.

HMG (1995). The 7 principles of public life. www.gov.uk/government/publications/the-7-principles-of-public-life (accessed 31 December 2017).

HMT (2007). *Sub-National Economic Development and Regeneration Review*. London: HMT.

HMT (2016). National infrastructure delivery plan 2016–2021. www.gov.uk/government/publications/national-infrastructure-delivery-plan-2016-to-2021 (accessed 31 December 2017).

Johnston, L., & Blenkinsopp, J. (2017). Challenges for civil society involvement in civic entrepreneurship: A case study of local enterprise partnerships. *Public Money & Management*, 37(2), 89–96.

London Health Board (2017). Health and care devolution: What it means for London. www.london.gov.uk/sites/default/files/what_health_devolution_means_for_london_2017.pdf (accessed 31 December 2017).

Lowndes, V., & McCaughie, K. (2013). Weathering the perfect storm? Austerity and institutional resilience in local government. *Policy & Politics*, 41(4), 533–549.

Krugman, P. (1991). Increasing returns and economic geography. *Journal of Political Economy*, 99(3), 483–499.

Krugman, P. (2011). The new economic geography, now middle-aged. *Regional Studies*, 45(1), 1–7.

Krukowska, J., & Lackowska, M. (2017). Metropolitan colours of Europeanization: Institutionalization of integrated territorial investment structures in the context of past cooperation in metropolitan regions. *Raumforschung und Raumordnung (Spatial Research and Planning)*, 5(3), 275–289.

MoL (2015). *London Infrastructure Plan 2050 Update*. London: Mayor of London.

MoL (2017). Mayors unite to call for major devolution to city regions, Mayor of London press release statement, 1 November. www.london.gov.uk/press-releases/mayoral/mayors-unite-to-call-for-major-devolution-to-citie (accessed 5 July 2018).

ME (2017). Midlands Engine vision for growth. www.midlandsengine.org/wp-content/uploads/Midlands-Engine-Vision-for-Growth.pdf (accessed 22 December 2017).

Medeiros, E. (2016). Territorial cohesion: An EU concept. *European Journal of Spatial Development*, 60, 1–30.

Pucher, J., Naylon, I., & Tödtling-Schönhofer, H. (2015). Review of the adopted partnership agreements research for REGI Committee. www.europarl.europa.eu/RegData/etudes/STUD/2015/563393/IPOL_STU(2015)563393_EN.pdf (accessed 31 December 2017).

MHCLG (2018). Revised national planning policy framework. https://assets.publishing.service.gov.uk/government/uploads/system/uploads/attachment_data/file/733637/National_Planning_Policy_Framework_web_accessible_version.pdf (accessed 19 August 2018).

Mitchell, W., & Watts, M. (2010). Identifying functional regions in Australia using hierarchical aggregation techniques. *Geographical Research*, 48(1), 24–41.

Morphet, J. (2017a). Sub-regional strategic spatial planning: The use of statecraft and scalecraft in delivering the English model. *Town Planning Review*, 88(6), 665–682.

Morphet, J. (2017b). Combined authorities: The next big thing? *Town and Country Planning*, March, 96–103

Morphet, J., & Pemberton, S. (2013). 'Regions out—sub-regions in': Can sub-regional planning break the mould? The view from England'. *Planning Practice & Research*, 28(4), 384–399.

Ney, M. (2017). *Review of Public Assurance for LEPs*. London: DCLG.

O'Brien, P., & Pike, A. (2015). City deals, decentralisation and the governance of local infrastructure funding and financing in the UK. *National Institute Economic Review*, 233(1), R14–R26.

OECD (2015). *Local Economic Leadership*. Paris: OECD.

OECD (2017). *Governing the City*. Paris: OECD.

Pemberton, S., & Morphet, J. (2014). The rescaling of economic governance: Insights into the transitional territories of England. *Urban Studies*, 51(11), 2354–2370.

Pike, A., Marlow, D., McCarthy, A., O'Brien, P., & Tomaney, J. (2015). Local institutions and local economic development: The local enterprise partnerships in England, 2010–. *Cambridge Journal of Regions, Economy and Society*, 8(2), 185–204.

PINS (2017). National planning policy statements. https://infrastructure.planninginspectorate.gov.uk/legislation-and-advice/national-policy-statements/ (accessed 31 December 2017).

Townsend, A. (2017). Combined authorities – where next? *Town and Country Planning*, September, 343–353.

Sandford, M. (2017). Combined authorities. House of Commons Library Briefing Papers No. 6649, 4 July. London: House of Commons Library.

van der Zwet, A., Bachtler, J.Ferry, M., McMaster, I., & Miller, S. (2017). Integrated territorial and urban strategies: How are ESIF adding value in 2014–2020? Final Report. Brussels: CEC.

Ward, M. (2017). Local growth deals. House of Commons Library Briefing Papers No. 7120, 22 November.London: House of Commons Library.

6 Local Planning and Housing

Introduction

Local plans are the way in which local authorities in England identify the social, economic and environmental priorities that will be delivered through spatial policies and programmes. Some of these will be though projects that are delivered directly by the local authorities, while others will be promoted by other public bodies and the private and voluntary sectors. These projects will be progressed through the planning system in the form of planning applications. These will be determined through the lens of policies and proposals in local plans and their interpretation. Applications for development of sites may be made by any individual, regardless of whether they have a legal interest in the land. Applicants for planning permission may have no intention to directly deliver the project for which planning permission is sought. In England in 2017, over 50 per cent of planning permissions for major housing development were obtained by land agents, representing owners rather than developers (McPhillips 2017).

The process and practice of developing a local plan and then adopting it so that it has a legal status are defined by legislation that is tempered by government guidance (DCLG 2012; MHCLG 2018; PINS 2016) and then tested by case law and decisions that can give precedent to any specific interpretation. It is the responsibility of every local authority in England to prepare a local plan. However, since local plans were introduced in 1970, there has never been a point when all local authorities have had an adopted local plan at the same time. This may be for a range of reasons, including the frequent changes in legislation and guidance issued by central government. Local plans can be delayed by local political difficulties associated with the need to identify land for housing or roads. Further, the interpretation of the legislation can also delay plan making and adoption. The principles of spatial planning were introduced in the 2004 Planning and Compulsory Purchase Act in England. (Morphet 2011) While local plans are prepared to guide development, they also frame the location for new development within an assessment of local and wider strategic needs, although they have frequently been regarded as a means to retain the status quo as far as possible. They have also been used to contain sprawl and achieve sustainable development (Millward 2006).

This chapter will consider changes in the local planning system and practice since the introduction of the National Planning Policy Framework (NPPF) (DCLG 2012) and Planning Guidance (PINS 2016) and their effects on the preparation of plans and the delivery of planning regulation. It considers the role of Community Infrastructure Levy (CIL) and other mechanisms for developer contributions. It will also discuss the focus of planning to provide housing through a range of means, including new settlements, financial incentives and the use of new local investment powers included in the 2011 Localism Act. The chapter will also discuss the role of the private sector in planning, its influence in shaping policy and its effects on delivery.

Local Plans in Context

Local plans are at the heart of planning decision making in England. Any planning application, other than those defined by the 2008 Planning Act for Nationally Significant Infrastructure Projects (NSIPs) (see Chapter 4), will be made to the local authority, which will have to determine whether the application is in conformity with any national policy and standards and if it fits within the local plan policy. Where there are neighbourhood plans (NPs), these might identify more detailed approaches, but they are also set within the vertical alignment of policies and plans set by the strategic and local plans. The NP also must be in conformity with the local plan (see Chapter 7). The system being used in England relies on the 2004 Planning and Compulsory Purchase Act, while subsequent legislation, regulations and guidance have identified how this legislation should be used and interpreted.

When local plans were reformulated in 2004, they were set within the context of Regional Spatial Strategies (RSSs) also included in the same legislation. The RSSs identified major housing and other land use designations and were used to identify strategic housing targets and then hand these down for the constituent local authorities. In this approach, local politicians adopted the allocated housing numbers, but they could shift the blame for this on the RSS and central government. The RSSs also considered other land uses and locations for major environmental, cultural, social and economic infrastructure. While the RSS was intended to be the strategic regional plan, other government departments quickly added their own plans for economic development, transport and the environment and culture although they did not have the same legal force in decision making for planning applications as the RSS (Baker et al. 2010).

In 2009, the then-Labour government passed legislation that abolished the RSS and the other regional plans from other departments, with a view to introducing a single regional strategy to incorporate these plans and policies in an integrated way. However, shortly after these changes were to be implemented, the general election in 2010 led to a change in government. The incoming Coalition government was guided in its approach to planning policies by two policy papers that had been prepared by the Conservatives Party in opposition. *Open source planning* (Conservative Party 2010) was set on a foundation laid by *Control shift*, an earlier, more strategic approach to local authorities, their organisation and how planning might fit within this (Conservative Party 2009). When the Conservatives came into Coalition government, they abolished all regional strategies and replaced them with Local Enterprise Partnerships (LEPs). These were non-democratic coalitions of businesses but also served to nudge local authorities to work together in FEAs (Bentley et al. 2010; Pemberton and Morphet 2014).

Regardless of the quality of and process in achieving these RSSs, local authorities were concerned about the lack of strategic context for their own plan making. Added to this, there were perceived to be difficulties in implementing the system introduced in 2004 and, despite numerous initiatives, it was not possible to speed up the process (RTPI 2007). At the same time, there were problems raised by the absence of a target for the number of homes to be provided, which had previously been contained in the RSS. This left the individual local authorities to determine the number of homes to be provided in their local plan. The government required that the housing requirements should be determined using common methodologies. However, this led to many local political issues in the allocation of housing sites, causing delay in the preparation of local plans. This delay in local plan preparation was also frustrating for the government. In the period since 2004, local plans have become transformed by their almost total focus on housing provision, to the detriment of their wider role.

What Is Spatial Planning?

The introduction of spatial planning comprised some specific features that were largely misunderstood at the time (Shaw and Lord 2007) and, it is argued, changed the role and purpose of planning in practice. This caused uncertainty (Gunn and Hillier 2014), which was compounded by the earlier failures of plans submitted into the examination system (Marshall 2009). The government undertook a specific inquiry into these issues, which attempted to identify what the issues were, and then a later study (RTPI 2007) determined that the main cause was a misunderstanding of the function and role of spatial planning and its direct link to the responsibility for delivery. There were also other features that it incorporated, including an inquisitorial rather than adversarial role in the process of adoption, and these are discussed further in this chapter.

Local Planning Practice since 2011

While local plans are still made within the legal framework of the Planning and Compensation Act 2004, the use of the term 'local development frameworks' (LDFs) to describe them was dropped in the 2011 Localism Act. This was first set out in the form of the NPPF and then in the reform of planning policy guidance, which was reduced from numerous documents to a single online version, which, it was argued, could be more easily be kept up-to-date.

The NPPF (DCLG 2012) was introduced as guidance following the 2011 Localism Act and switched the policy framework context from local to national, as LDFs returned to become local plans. The NPPF was initially offered for consultation before its adoption (Davoudi 2011) and in its conception replaced much of the guidance that had hitherto existed. The NPPF comprised sections on the promotion of town centres, the rural economy, infrastructure delivery for all services and social and community facilities, climate change and the historic environment. However, the main thrust of the NPPF was to reorient the local plan toward the delivery of housing, rather than taking a view across all localities and land uses in the local plan, in a turn that was more neo-liberal than had hitherto been the case (Raco 2014; Cheshire et al. 2012).

The NPPF had influence on house builder practices (Karadimitriou 2013). In the approach outlined in the NPPF, each local authority was expected to revise or prepare their local plan afresh so that it would be in conformity with the housing provision. The NPPF included requirements for objectively assessed need (OAN) for housing, with a presumption in favour of development unless there were specific reasons why this could not be the case. It was stated in the NPPF that development that accorded with the local plan should be identified quickly so that it could be implemented. Subsequently, although there was evidence that planning consents for housing were being delivered both more rapidly and in greater volume, there was less evidence that developers were increasing their implementation of housing development in an equally rapid way (Grayston 2017).

Rather than address the practices of the development industry, the government-established Local Plans Expert Group (LPEG) was formed and this called again for planning reforms in delivery of housing planning permissions (DCLG 2016). This was another attempt to speed up the process of housing delivery through plan making. LPEG attributed failures to build housing at the speed required by government to a range of factors, including the difficulty of agreeing ways of demonstrating housing needs, the challenges in working across boundaries in housing market areas and the political will to build housing. LPEG recommended that there should be a single approach to assessing OAN that could be applied across all local authorities and which local plans would be required to meet in designating land for development. The LPEG recommendations were accompanied by another report on the functioning of the CIL, again from the perspective of the housing developers (Peace 2017), although this was released at the same time as a housing white paper, *Fixing our broken housing market* (DCLG 2017a), that took a far wider view of all the components in the delivery of housing, rather than focusing on the issue of planning permissions, which had hitherto been the case.

In retrospect, the LPEG report may have been the high-water mark of the focus of private sector housing developer criticisms of the planning system in providing planning permissions for housing. Rather than focus on local authorities planning functions, the report also considered the ways in which housing developers operated and how wider sources of housing supply could be encouraged. The white paper recognised that developer behaviour was a major factor in the failure to build housing on consented sites or only to build them very slowly, in line with sales, when development was underway. It also considered ways in which other providers of housing could be encouraged to enter the market including financial institution providing build to let at market rents, housing associations and local authorities. Where housing developers were slow in their use of planning consents, the white paper suggested other approaches including a review of developer practices of land holding and the role of local authorities in progressing permitted housing developments though their wider powers such as those for compulsory purchase orders.

Following the publication of the housing white paper, the government called a general election and the Housing Minster, Gavin Barwell, who had sponsored the initiative lost his seat. Usually, white papers are abandoned following an election and policy development starts again but, in this case, the government continued with progressing its proposals. Further, Gavin Barwell was appointed to lead the Prime Minister's team and progress the proposals contained in the white paper at arm's length. The first initiative was to publish a consultation paper, *Planning for the right homes in the right places*, published as a consultation paper (DCLG 2017b). In this, the government proposed a common method of assessing OAN that used a multiplier of housing price and income in each local authority to determine the housing numbers to be included in the local plan. Using this method, the OAN demonstrated that increases in housing numbers would be required in local authorities in much of the South of England and much lower numbers, if any increase at all, for local authorities further north. This was a very unpopular approach, not only from the South but also the North, where local authorities wished to build housing as part of their economic regeneration policies.

It subsequently emerged that there were no formal powers requiring local authorities to adopt this method of calculating OAN and that they would have to continue to justify their calculation method through the local plan process. A further housing supply issue arose from this consultation paper, as it emerged that the OAN was for market housing and did not include assessments for housing for those with specific requirements such as for social and affordable rent and for older people and those with disabilities.

In the 2017 budget, the government provided more funding for housing developers through the Help to Buy scheme. The government increased its subsidy for housing to £44bn although as much as 75 per cent was focussed on Help to Buy initiatives. There was subsequent public objection to the level of profits this was generating for housing developers (Rovnick and Williams 2017). Following the budget, the government announced a review into the failure of developers to implement existing planning consents for housing in the light of consents' being available for over 600,000 homes at the end of 2017 (Letwin 2018).

However, by 2017, it had emerged that while local authorities had responded to the government's pressures to provide more planning permission for housing, even if there had not been an equal response from developers. The number of housing completions increased in 2017 to 317,000 and this was initially viewed as a positive response from housebuilders. It later transpired that the government definition of housing completions had changed to include not only new-build properties, but also the conversion of large homes into smaller flats and the conversion of offices to residential use. There has also been an increase in local authorities' building homes through wholly owned housing companies (Hackett 2017). So the increase of housing demonstrated did not reflect an increase in developer-provided new-builds, but an increase in other means.

While housing developers are in business to build homes, there is no legal requirement on them to do so, even where they own land with extant planning permissions for housing. They are, rather, bound by their duty to provide a return to their shareholders. This can be achieved in several ways, including building fewer houses on larger plots. Many local authority politicians have taken the political criticism from their constituents for approving planning permission for major housing developments, only to find that the developments, together with their promised planning contributions for social infrastructure, have not been delivered. Instead, housing developers have frequently sought to renegotiate their contributions following the achievement of planning consent, based on requests to re-examine viability appraisals for development. Some local authorities have sought to claw back any developer profits subsequently achieved by using 'overage' clauses in their planning agreements, which ensures that developers pay more to local authorities if they achieve a higher sales price than the viability assessment indicated.

These developer practices have meant that many local authority politicians have become frustrated. They believe that their political bravery in the face of a hostile electorate has not been met by an equal approach by the developers. At the same time, housing developers have appeared to have the ear of the government and have been consistently complaining about planning processes and local authority performance. In response, the local authorities have started to directly provide houses in a more systematic way. This has occurred through a variety of mechanisms, including building on smaller plots, building as a registered housing provider, using the housing revenue account of the local authority, and through establishing wholly owned housing companies. In research undertaken by Morphet and Clifford (2017), the motivations for local authorities providing housing again have been examined, as well as the ways in which local authorities are funding this development, have been examined.

Since 1980, local authorities have been restricted in their ability to build social housing through government legal and financial controls. However, in the 2011 Localism Act, local authorities have been granted more powers to establish housing companies and to develop housing using their general funds. This housing may be for sale, affordable or market rent and can include some social rented properties. When examining the motivations of local authorities engaging in housing provision, both in more traditional and more innovative ways, the main motivation indicated was the need to provide housing in the local authority area, with the second reason cited as meeting homelessness. The third motivation was the need to generate income for the council to run other services, not least as the government's Revenue Support Grant for local authorities is removed in 2020. Following these reasons, local authorities were also providing housing to deal with planning-stalled sites and unimplemented consents. The research found that this housing development has primarily been funded through internal sources of land and capital. However, many local authorities are taking loans from the public works loans board and the private sector, including hedge funds.

Alongside local authorities, there are other new providers delivering housing. These include financial institutions that are seeking investment to serve their pension fund clients such as Legal and General. Here, the institutions are building housing for market rent, which provides index-linked revenue to meet their needs. These providers, like housing associations, are also engaging in modern methods of construction, using modular, factory-built components or dwellings to provide housing more quickly.

What appears to be the case is that the planning system is now understood not to be the main obstacle to building more homes, but rather the need to find willing developers and providers who will build the homes for which they have planning consent. Housing developers have frequently argued that the sites available in the five-year land supply identified in local plans are not viable for development and that they need land in more attractive locations on which to build market housing. They will frequently attempt to access these sites, not identified in the local plans, through the mechanism of planning appeals. However, this also suggests that there has been a conflation of the role of the five-year land supply for housing and the land required to meet the needs of the local private sector housing market. Housing need is greater than can be met by the market, so it is unsurprising that some housing sites may not be viable for market sale but may be appropriate for other forms of housing, such as that for older people or for social and affordable rent. Local plans also need to address other issues, including retrofitting existing housing to meet environmental objectives together with economic growth and place making.

What Are the Key Issues in Local Planning?

Delivery

Local plans prepared before 2004 were concerned with a plan-led approach, where the expectation was that plans made by the local authority would be implemented by others. The 2004 Planning and Compulsory Purchase Act changed this expectation, so that local authorities preparing and adopting plans were increasingly expected to be directly engaged in delivering them. This meant that local plans had to identify how they were to be implemented and delivered (Morphet 2011). The mechanism for assessing the deliverability of the local plan was the introduction of tests of soundness against which each plan was to be examined. This included an assessment of the resources required to deliver the plan, with a particular focus on infrastructure.

After 2004, all local plans needed to demonstrate that the provision of infra-structure to support the plan's delivery had been adequately examined and that there were commitments from providers and those responsible to support the plan with projects and/or resources. This was a departure for local plans and the pro-cess of engaging directly with infrastructure providers was a new element of plan preparation. The results of these deliberations and commitments were generally contained within an infrastructure delivery plan (IDP). In 2007, no local plan had an IDP, in comparison with all sound plans examined and adopted in 2017.

Some local authorities engaged planning consultants to prepare their IDPs although the majority were prepared by local plans teams. The process requires establishing relationships with infrastructure providers, whether they were within the local authority or outside. This can be particularly difficult, as some local authority departments have not been in the practice of engaging in dialo-gue about their requirements. Outside the local authority, public utilities are private companies set within the context of regulators and require con-fidentiality for their investment proposals. Some local authorities have met each infrastructure provider separately, while others hold regular meetings and briefings, which have allowed providers to share information with the local authority and each other.

The form of the IDP has generally been as a separate evidence report for the local plan, although some local authorities have included the IDP within the local plan. The IDP usually comprises some narrative about each type of infrastructure, accompanied by a schedule of each project that is in the pipeline. These projects must be included within the sponsoring organisation's own financial capital pro-gramme and cannot include 'wish list' projects. The schedule can be organised by date of delivery, type of infrastructure, location of the project or by thematic groupings. The IDP is meant to be detailed for the first five years of the plan and can continue beyond this if projects extend into the next period. The IDP can be updated regularly as new projects are added, as agreed by their owners.

From a nil base in 2007, IDPs are now part of the local plan process and are considered by the inspector as part of the examination of the local plan. How-ever, some local authorities do not yet understand how an IDP should be put together and are required by the inspector to prepare a new IDP while the examination of the plan is halted or they are required to prepare one immedi-ately after the local plan has been adopted. The most frequent concerns expressed in these processes include a range of issues. Some IDPs comprise descriptions of local infrastructure providers and how they operate but do not include any specific schemes in an IDP schedule. A second problem is where consultants have assumed a 'predict and provide' model for infrastructure requirements based on new developments rather than on locating the specific infrastructure projects in the context of existing capacity and condition. These frequently extend over a prolonged period of time and lead to expectations of large infrastructure costs that are not related to the reality of investment. A third issue is where the projects included in the IDP schedule are assumed to be fully funded through developer contributions and have not taken account of existing budgets and programmes already committed to by the local authority and other infrastructure providers. This approach leads to unrealistic viability assessments and can stall development.

Inquisitorial Rather than Adversarial Examination Processes

Until 2004, the process of adoption of any local plan involved an adversarial style of examination. This meant that all those who wished to make representations on the proposals included or omitted from the local plan could do so through a quasi-legal hearing. Frequently, land owners and other interests were represented by barristers. There were concerns about the inequitable nature of the process, with those less able to finance legal representation being less successful in making their cases (Bruton and Nicholson 2013). Following this Examination in Public (EiP), as this hearing process is called, the independently appointed planning inspector would weigh up the balance of the arguments and set them in the context of the general approaches in the plan and report, following which the local authority would make modifications to the plan.

After 2004, the method of examination changed to one that was inquisitorial. In this approach, which has attracted little research or attention, the independent inspector examines the local plan against the tests of soundness and then determines which issues need to be considered through further processes. This may be by requesting further work or through an examination by this independent person. This examination does not delve into the whole of the plan but focuses on specific issues where the inspector considers that the local plan has not sufficiently addressed an issue, where the tests of soundness have not been met or where there is some doubt over whether the proposal set out can be delivered. The tests of soundness are shown in Box 6.1.

Box 6.1 Local Plans: Tests of Soundness to Be Applied in the Examination by an Independent person (EIP)

- **Positively prepared** – the plan should be prepared based on a strategy which seeks to meet objectively assessed development and infrastructure requirements, including unmet requirements from neighbouring authorities where it is reasonable to do so and consistent with achieving sustainable development;
- **Justified** – the plan should be the most appropriate strategy, when considered against the reasonable alternatives, based on proportionate evidence;
- **Effective** – the plan should be deliverable over its period and based on effective joint working on cross-boundary strategic priorities; and
- **Consistent with national policy** – the plan should enable the delivery of sustainable development in accordance with the policies in the Framework.Source: NPPF 2012 para 182.

This inquisitorial approach was also later used for NSIPs in the 2008 Planning Act, where the principle of development for the project had already been agreed through EU regulations. Is there any parallel with the inquisitorial approach introduced for local plans in the 2004 Planning and Compulsory Purchase Act? While the local plan is examined in an inquisitorial way, any planning application that is determined within its policies is still examined through an adversarial model. The 2004 Act had been preceded by a planning green paper (DTLR 2001), where the concept of a local development framework was introduced to frame the local plan, with a stated. In this, the concept of a local development framework was introduced to frame the local plan, with a stated intention of not detailing policies for every site. In the green paper, it was proposed to shift from the adversarial to the inquisitorial system although there was a misleading 'fudge' used in adopting the same acronym for both processes – the Examination in Public (EiP) for the adversarial model and the Examination by an Independent Person (EIP) for the inquisitorial model.

This switch in approach was one of the factors that might, in retrospect, be seen to have destabilised the local plans system. All parties to the system – the local authorities, communities and land owners/developers – found it difficult to understand which roles they should play. Those who still wanted their 'day in court' to consider specific planning issues on sites in an adversarial way were left without this opportunity if the examining inspector found no issues to debate in the plan's proposals. Secondly, the local authority was left to comply with specific tests of soundness, some of which were misunderstood and misapplied. Thirdly, some local authorities simply did not understand the changes that were being implemented.

Why was this change from an adversarial to an inquisitorial process made? The most obvious reason to consider is that local plan examinations were taking too long. While the examination process was seen to be part of the problem, there were also issues about the scale and number of policies in each plan – sometimes there were over 200, which meant that there were many opportunities to raise objection to the plan. A second reason was that taking such an approach meant that those from the community who wished to engage in the process were frequently excluded because they could not afford to appoint a barrister to present their case in a way that could be heard equally. Another issue for many community groups was the quasi-judicial atmosphere that predominated in these processes.

Another reason that may have been informing the decision to make this switch was the use of administrative law. Finally, the change may have been made in preparation for changes thought to be emerging through the EU, where the context for planning was moving to a more spatial or territorial cohesion approach that is emerging within EU regulations.

Duty to Cooperate

While there was some initial strategic framework for the local plan through the RSS, there was also a requirement to use the duty to cooperate that was introduced in 2007 (Morphet 2009; Baker and Wong 2013). There is some suggestion that this duty was introduced by the Coalition government following their election in 2010 (Allmendinger and Haughton 2014; Boddy and Hickman 2013) but it was in operation before. The duty, set out again in the Localism Act 2011, is an important means of encouraging local plans to relate to each other (Wong et al. 2015) and take account of the wider housing market area (Rozzee 2014). This has been defined in the guidance and through the tests of soundness but has been frequently difficult to achieve. It is said that a duty to cooperate is not a duty to agree (Morphet 2009).

Differences between adjoining local authorities or groups in housing market areas may mean that some local authorities have been pressured to take more housing or specific types of developments that are politically unpopular (Hamiduddin and Gallent 2012). Further, there have been claims by adjoining authorities that the duty to cooperate has not been sufficiently fulfilled, meaning that there may be insufficient infrastructure available to support new development, including for roads, schools or other facilities. This approach has now been further developed into a requirement for adjoining local authorities to prepare a statement of common ground – that is, where they agree and where they do not. There have also been concerns that the duty to cooperate does not provide an overall strategic approach that could adequately replace the RSS (Haughton et al. 2013) and that it undermines the economic and spatial strategies of the regions that were left without a strategic planning framework.

The pressure to build housing has been seen to be politically difficult. However, since 2013, when it was agreed that local authorities in England would lose their revenue support grant from the government (an annual payment that has assisted in providing services and is allocated according to some tests of need), local authorities have been incentivised to approve more new housing though the payment of a New Homes Bonus by the government. Local authorities in locations that have traditionally been against growth have started to develop a more engaged approach to housing delivery. Some local authorities, such as Aylesbury Vale, have decided that they want to be financially independent. They have sought to achieve this through a range of measures, including holding a lottery, providing subscription services and providing housing. Other local authorities have established wholly owned housing companies to build more housing, primarily for rent, to enable them to have a longer term reliable income (Morphet and Clifford 2017). Others have started to assemble a property portfolio across commercial land uses for the same reasons.

Viability

The role of viability was introduced as an operational concept in the NPPF (2012) and it applies both to plans and decision making about individual planning applications. In the NPPF, the government stated that 'plans should be deliverable and that the sites and scale of development identified in the plan should not be subject to such a scale of obligations and policy burdens that their ability to be developed viably is threatened'. The inclusion of a test of viability, that is, ensuring that proposals in the plan and the supporting infra-structure can be delivered in reasonable way, has increasingly been extended to be used to assess the development contributions made on any site for housing (Gurran and Whitehead 2011). Where sites are previously developed, brownfield land, the costs of development may be higher than on greenfield sites although these brownfield sites may already be supplied with infrastructure and services, which would be an additional cost on greenfield locations. However, these infrastructure and utility costs are generally not borne by the developers but through the charges for utility service that all users make in their tariffs for energy and water. Thus, society pays for the development of greenfield sites. However, government policy also reminds planners that the use of brownfield sites before greenfield sites is national policy and, as such, the difference in viability between two competing sites should be considered when decisions are taken (Bramley and Watkins 2014).

There are no standard methodologies for viability testing of a development or plan. The government advises that the gross development value should be calculated using comparables for the area and, on a housing site, relative to the gross sales or rentals expected to be achieved by the development. The costs of the development should also be taken into consideration, including building costs and any remediation, infrastructure and planning requirements together with the costs of financing the development. In practice, these costs vary, and many calculations are not open-book or transparent although some local authorities may require this. Further, there is also a requirement to include the cost of the land and a developer's profit.

There have been two guides published on methods of calculating viability. The approach of development surveyors (RICS 2012) has been in the form of a guidance note and focuses primarily on the site, although it does address the wider issues of viability testing for the whole of a local plan. The second approach is undertaken by a group that included the Local Government Asso-ciation and wider public interests led by Sir John Harman, formerly chair of the Environment Agency (NHBC 2012). There, the focus is on the local plan and includes a step-by-step guide to a methodology.

In some locations, the role of viability assessments has been seen to reduce the quantity of affordable housing available in the plan. Local authorities have come to see the five-year land supply as land for private housing and not for all types of housing. In London, the Mayor has published supplementary planning guidance on the use of viability testing in housing (MoL 2017), in which his policy is for half of new homes built in London to be affordable. The MoL has also offered a fast-track approach that would d allow developers to proceed without a viability assessment and negotiation if over 35 per cent of housing provided is affordable. However, the MoL can only offer this approach and apply this policy on sites where he has a formal interest, that is of over 150 units.

In practice, many applicants for planning permission negotiate an agreement for the contribution that the development can make to the area through plan-ning obligations or CIL (Grayston 2017). However, after consent has been obtained, they may argue that the development is no longer viable and that contributions should be recalculated downwards and this is common. They may also argue that as the site cannot be delivered as it is not viable, then other sites outside those defined in the local plan's five-year land supply should be consented to meet local housing need. These sites are more likely to be on greenfield land and on the periphery of settlements and may be determined on appeal. These approaches have led to considerable pressure on housing delivery using developer contribution methods (Morrison and Burgess 2014).

Why Don't Local Authorities Adopt Local Plans?

There are many reasons why local authorities do not adopt local plans, as shown in Box 6.2.

Box 6.2 Why Don't Local Authorities Adopt Local Plans?

- The process takes too long.
- The system changes frequently and officers are risk-averse in pursuing current options, in case another version comes along.
- Conservative local authorities took advice from the shadow Secretary of State, in 2008, that there was no need to pursue a plan and they find it difficult to start again.
- The political fixes that are made to get the plan to submission point become unstuck when faced with examination and then the plans are either delayed or found unsound.
- The political majority in the local authority changes at some point in the preparation.
- The political issues are too difficult and it is easier to blame the Secretary of State for planning decisions that are made on appeal.
- The local authority doesn't have sufficient financial resources to appoint staff.Source: Author.

While the government has proposed intervention in those local authorities that have not made sufficient progress with their local plan, this continues to provide a political blame shift from local politicians to central government. Given Conservative politicians in government have continued to press local authorities for local pan completion since 2010, there appears to be very little dialogue with the authorities that are not making progress about understanding the blockages and how these might be overcome. There have also been no specific incentives for those local authorities that are under control of the same political party as the government. Much of the government's pressure to complete local plans has been top-down and has taken a developer's perspective without much appreciation of the local political issues. Planning needs a stable political period to progress, yet in some local authorities, there are council elections three years in every four and it is hard to make progress in these cases. There have been pressures to prepare joint local plans but, again, these can fail at political hurdles. If government is keen to have a full set of local plans for local authorities in England, then it must be clearer about the political and financial benefits and incentives for local authorities to adopt their local plan.

Conclusions

Were these changes in local planning England a response to neo-liberal pressures, as some have suggested (Waterhout et al. 2013)? The introduction of spatial planning in 2004, which supports the delivery role, has returned planning in England to its original form as set out in the Town and Country Planning Act 1947. However, the subsequent changes in the practice of this legislation, interpreted the Localism Act 2011 and the NPPF (2012, 2018), have provided an overriding focus on housing delivery, whether through the introduction of neighbourhood planning or viability testing. The three governments since 2010 have also supported housing through non-planning finance measures for private housebuilders through help to buy schemes. This funding has been neo-liberal in its focus and could have been used for other housing needs such as social rent and accommodation of older people that remain challenges in provision. While the planning system has been pressurised to find more housing sites to meet local need, there is now a wider recognition that housing provision is not being held back by the planning system but by developers and their build out rates (DCLG 2017a; Letwin 2018). However, where planning could be more active is in the designation of sites for non-market housing as part of its total allocation within local plans. At the same time, local authorities are now developing housing through wholly owned housing companies and seeking to make up local shortfalls through more direct means (Morphet and Clifford 2017).

References

Allmendinger, P., & Haughton, G. (2014). Post-political regimes in English planning. In J. Metzger, P. Allmendinger, & S. Oosterlynck (Eds.), *Planning Against the Political: Democratic Deficits in European Territorial Governance* (pp. 29–51). Abingdon: Taylor & Francis.

Baker, M., Hincks, S., & Sherriff, G. (2010). Getting involved in plan making: Participation and stakeholder involvement in local and regional spatial strategies in England. *Environment and Planning C: Government and Policy*, 28(4), 574–594.

Baker, M., & Wong, C. (2013). The delusion of strategic spatial planning: What's left after the Labour government's English regional experiment? *Planning Practice & Research*, 28(1), 83–103.

Bentley, G., Bailey, D., & Shutt, J. (2010). From RDAs to LEPs: A new localism? Case examples of West Midlands and Yorkshire. *Local Economy*, 25(7), 535–557.

Boddy, M., & Hickman, H. (2013). The demise of strategic planning? The impact of the abolition of Regional Spatial Strategy in a growth region. *Town Planning Review*, 84 (6), 743–768.

Bramley, G., & Watkins, D. (2014). 'Measure twice, cut once': Revisiting the strength and impact of local planning regulation of housing development in England. *Environment and Planning B: Planning and Design*, 41(5), 863–884.

Bruton, M., & Nicholson, D. (2013). *Local Planning in Practice*. Abingdon: Routledge.

Cheshire, P., Leunig, T., Nathan, M., & Overman, H. (2012). *Links between Planning and Economic Performance: Evidence Note for LSE Growth Commission*. London: LSE Growth Commission and Institute for Government.

Conservative Party (2008). Conservative Party open source planning green paper. Policy Green Paper no 14 2010. www.cgms.co.uk/bulletin/Conservative%20Party%20Planning%20Paper.pdf (accessed 5 July 2018).

Conservative Party (2009). Control shift returning power to local communities. Policy Green Paper no 9. London: The Conservative Party.

Conservative Party (2010). *Open Source Planning*. London: The Conservative Party.

Davoudi, S. (2011). Localism and the reform of the planning system in England. *disP – The Planning Review*, 47(187), 92–94.

DCLG (2012). *National Planning Policy Framework*. London: DCLG.

DCLG (2016). Local plans expert group: Report to the Secretary of State. www.gov.uk/government/publications/local-plans-expert-group-report-to-the-secretary-of-state (accessed 31 December 2017).

DCLG (2017a). *Fixing Our Broken Housing Market*. London: DCLG.

DCLG (2017b). Planning for the right homes in the right places: Consultation proposals. www.gov.uk/government/consultations/planning-for-the-right-homes-in-the-right-places-consultation-proposals (accessed 31 December 2017).

DTLR (2001). Delivering fundamental change. Planning Green Paper. London: DTLR.

GraystonR. (2017). *Slipping Through the Loophole*. London: Shelter.

Gunn, S., & Hillier, J. (2014). When uncertainty is interpreted as risk: An analysis of tensions relating to spatial planning reform in England. *Planning Practice and Research*, 29(1), 56–74.

Gurran, N., & Whitehead, C. (2011). Planning and affordable housing in Australia and the UK: A comparative perspective. *Housing Studies*, 26(7–8), 1193–1214.

HackettP. (2017). *Delivering the Renaissance in Council-Built Homes: The Rise of Local Housing Companies*. London: Smith Institute.

Hamiduddin, I., & Gallent, N. (2012). Limits to growth: The challenge of housing delivery in England's 'under-bounded' districts. *Planning Practice & Research*, 27(5), 513–530.

Haughton, G., Allmendinger, P., & Oosterlynck, S. (2013). Spaces of neoliberal experimentation: Soft spaces, post politics, and neoliberal governmentality. *Environment and Planning A*, 45(1), 217–234.

Karadimitriou, N. (2013). Planning policy, sustainability and housebuilder practices: The move into (and out of?) the redevelopment of previously developed land. *Progress in Planning*, 82, 1–41.

Letwin, O. (2018). Independent review of build out: Draft analysis. www.gov.uk/government/publications/independent-review-of-build-out-draft-analysis (accessed 19 August 2018).

Marshall, T. (2009). Planning and new labour in the UK. *Planning, Practice & Research*, 24(1), 1–9.

McPhilips, M. (2017). 'Phantom Homes': Planning Permissions, Completions and Profits. Research Briefing. London: Shelter. https://england.shelter.org.uk/professional_resources/policy_and_research/policy_library/policy_library_folder/research_phantom_homes_-_planning_permissions,_completions_and_profits (accessed 5 July 2018).

MHCLG (2018). Revised national planning policy framework. https://assets.publishing.ser vice.gov.uk/government/uploads/system/uploads/attachment_data/file/733637/National_ Planning_Policy_Framework_web_accessible_version.pdf (accessed 19 August 2018).

Millward, H. (2006). Urban containment strategies: A case-study appraisal of plans and policies in Japanese, British, and Canadian cities. *Land Use Policy*, 23(4), 473–485.

MoL (2017). *Affordable Housing and Viability Supplementary Planning Guidance (SPG)*. London: Mayor of London.

Morphet, J. (2009). Local integrated spatial planning: The changing role in England. *Town Planning Review*, 80(4–5), 393–414.

Morphet, J. (2011). *Effective Practice in Spatial Planning*. Abingdon: Routledge.

Morphet, J., & Clifford, B. (2017). *Local Authority Direct Provision of Housing*. London: NPF and RTPI. http://rtpi.org.uk/media/2619006/Local-authority-direct-p rovision-of-housing.pdf (accessed 5 July 2018).

Morrison, N., & Burgess, G. (2014). Inclusionary housing policy in England: The impact of the downturn on the delivery of affordable housing through Section 106. *Journal of Housing and the Built Environment*, 29(3), 423–438.

Nadin, V. (2007). The emergence of the spatial planning approach in England. *Planning, Practice & Research*, 22(1), 43–62.

NHBC (2012). *Viability Testing Local Plans: Advice for Planning Practitioners*. London: NHBC.

NLP (2012). Viability: A planner's perspective, RTPI presentation. www.rtpi.org.uk/m edia/531663/viability_presentation.pdf (accessed 3 December 2017).

Peace, L. (2017). Community infrastructure levy review: Report to government. www. gov.uk/government/publications/community-infrastructure-levy-review-report-to-go vernment (accessed 31 December 2017).

Pemberton, S., & Morphet, J. (2014). The rescaling of economic governance: Insights into the transitional territories of England. *Urban Studies*, 51(11), 2354–2370.

PINS (2016). Planning practice guidance. www.gov.uk/government/collections/planning-p ractice-guidance (accessed 31 December 2017).

Raco, M. (2014). The post-politics of sustainability planning: Privatisation and the demise of democratic government. In J. Wilson and E. Swyndgedouw (Eds.), *Post Political* (pp. 25–47). Edinburgh: Edinburgh University Press.

RICS (2012). *Financial Viability in Planning* (1st ed.). London: RICS. www.rics.org/uk/ knowledge/professional-guidance/guidance-notes/financial-viability-in-planning-1st-edi tion/ (accessed 5 July 2018).

Rovnick, N., & Williams, A. (2017). Persimmon chairman resigns over £100m CEO bonus, 15 December. www.ft.com/content/c9f88bf8-e175-11e7-8f9f-de1c2175f5ce (accessed 31 December 2017).

Rozzee, L. (2014). A new vision for planning: There must be a better way? *Planning Theory & Practice*, 15(1), 124–138.

RTPI (2007). *Effective Practice in Spatial Planning*. London: RTPI.

Shaw, D., & Lord, A. (2007). The cultural turn? Culture change and what it means for spatial planning in England. *Planning, Practice & Research*, 22(1), 63–78.

Waterhout, B., Othengrafen, F., & Sykes, O. (2013). Neo-liberalization processes and spatial planning in France, Germany, and the Netherlands: An exploration. *Planning Practice & Research*, 28(1), 141–159.

Wong, C., Baker, M., Webb, B., Hincks, S., & Schulze-Baeing, A. (2015). Mapping policies and programmes: the use of GIS to communicate spatial relationships in England. *Environment and Planning B: Planning and Design*, 42(6), 1020–1039.

7   Neighbourhood Plans

Introduction

Neighbourhood plans were introduced in England in 2011 through the Localism Act and so became part of mainstream planning practice. Before this, many localities prepared parish plans frequently and on an informal basis. The introduction of neighbourhood plans was part of a discourse on improving local empowerment and a bottom-up approach to decision making (Brownill and Bradley 2017) but in practice was a means of overcoming local objections to housing (Smith 2016). The government took the view that, if local communities had some control over the location of housing in their area and received some of the financial benefits deriving from developers' contributions, they would consider these housing sites in a more positive light.

This chapter considers the development of neighbourhood plans in practice, including a discussion of some of the key issues that arise from their preparation, including the resources required, the nature and type of consultation, whether these neighbourhood plans have speeded up the delivery of housing and how the infrastructure contributions that have been made available to neighbourhood plan areas are likely to be spent. However, there is also a wider issue about the nature of the coverage of neighbourhood plans – with some local authorities having many in their areas and others having few or none. There are also issues covering the nature of the relationship between neighbourhood planning areas and parishes, which have legal powers to run services and can raise a precept on the local council tax to do so. Finally, there is some consideration of whether there will be a fuller use of neighbourhood plans in the future.

The Introduction of Neighbourhood Planning

Context and Antecedents

Before neighbourhood planning was introduced in the 2011 Localism Act, there were informal parish plans, which were frequently prepared for rural parishes. They were frequently intended to provide a contribution to the evidence for local plans that were made for the wider area. However, the plans were often not used in evidence, for a number of reasons. This may have been because the democratic nature of the group making the plan or the use of appropriate public consultation methods did not meet the legal tests for inclusion in the local plan (Gallent et al. 2008). These parish plans came in many forms, including village design statements and wider versions situated in LA21 plans. In the rural white paper *Our countryside – the future – a fair deal for rural England* (Defra 2000), it was proposed that all rural parishes should prepare a plan (Owen 2002). However, there was no following consideration of methodologies or proposals to set these plans within the statutory planning system. Increasingly, parish plans were regarded as a bridge between bottom-up, community based approaches and the more formal process that are used to adopt a local plan (Owen and Moseley 2003) and Bishop (2010) demonstrates how parish plans performed this role. As the statutory planning system was reformed through the 2004 Planning and Compulsory Purchase Act, there were moves to find ways in which parish plans could be developed to contribute to local plans through providing both evidence and consultation (Gallent et al. 2008).

At the same time as the proposals for parish plans were being developed, there was a parallel initiative being introduced by government, which increased the powers of parish councils in rural areas (Woods 1998). This was part of the then-government's introduction of new localism through devolving powers to neighbourhoods (Jones 2007). There was also a focus on neighbourhoods, where intervention was required, but parish plans were primarily concerned with the way in which issues of rural housing could be addressed through planning means, rather than wider social-economic approaches. There were also government-led neighbourhood pathfinders and development company approaches in urban areas but these were seen to be primarily middle class and, like neighbourhood plans after 2011, primarily concerned with issues in relation to housing provision (Bailey and Pill 2011). While these parallel developments between parish plans and parish powers were not specifically linked, the process of bringing them closer together within a widened approach to neighbourhood planning was taken in the introduction of neighbourhood planning in the Localism Act 2011.

Localism Act 2011

In the Localism Act 2011 the spatial scale of neighbourhood plan was introduced, comprising of three components:

- Neighbourhood development plans (NDPs);
- Neighbourhood development orders;
- Community rights to build orders

Through this legislation, NDPs can be progressed by a parish or town council, a neighbourhood forum or a community group. The parish or town council has a freestanding legal status, which also provides other powers on a raft of legislative arrangements. These are predominantly designated in rural areas but the potential for urban parishes has been explored since the 2011 Act and some have been designated such as Queen's Park in London (Seager 2016). A neighbourhood forum must be a group approved by the local authority. The neighbourhood forum must have a minimum of 21 people who live or work in the area and/or can be locally elected councillors for all or part of the area under consideration. One of the significant issues that has arisen since the introduction of NDP powers is that some local authorities have taken a considerable time to determine if the neighbourhood forum is the appropriate group for the area (Bradley 2015).

Once the group has formed and a plan has been made, then it is subjected to an independent examination to determine whether it is in conformity with national and local planning policies. Following this, the NDP is subject to a referendum in the area, after which, if there is a majority for the plan, the NDP is declared as having been 'made'. The local authority then has a legal duty to bring it into force and, once in this position, it has the same legal status as the local plan. The NDP can be 'made' or adopted prior to the local plan for the area. Where there is a made plan, the parish council or neighbourhood forum is eligible for 25 per cent of the Community Infrastructure Levy (CIL) for the area, derived from developments that the NDP supports, if there is a CIL charging scheme in place. Where there is no NDP, the community is eligible to receive 15 per cent of the contributions.

Some local authorities have provided guidance to neighbourhood fora and parish councils about how to prepare an NDP. The Metropolitan Borough of Calderdale (2013) suggested that using a neighbourhood development order (NDO) would be an effective way of ensuring that the NDP is delivered. This focus on delivery is also supported by a suggested monitoring framework. In Herefordshire, the local authority has provided a range of detailed guidance notes, including one on implementation and monitoring (HCC 2015). This approach also provides a useful check for those making the NDP that the proposals are the ones that will deliver the outcomes that the community wants. It also includes an indicative schedule that NDPs could use to build up the delivery requirements. In Broadland, the local authority has provided guidance on the process of preparing the NDP but stops short of its implementation.

There has also been a focus on local design guidance in NDPs. This has occurred through general advice that has been provided by organizations such as the Design Council (2013), English Heritage (2014) and Historic England (2017). While there is a focus on the role of design within NDPs, with a concern for visual appearance, there are also considerations of codes for sustainable design to improve health and wellbeing, where retrofitting existing places is as important as the design of new development (Barton and Grant 2015).

When neighbourhood plans were introduced into the Localism Bill (2010), much of the rhetoric was about local communities' taking control of their local areas. ResPublica (Kaszynska et al. 2012 p4) suggested that the Localism Act would represent a big shift in power away from central and local governments and that this was the message that should be heard.

The passage of the Localism Act marked a significant transfer of power away from Whitehall into the hands of local authorities and local communities. This devolution of decision-making and promotion of civic activism will provide greater opportunities for communities to mobilise local resources and through new neighbourhood planning powers, help re-shape our towns and cities from the bottom-up.

(p 4)

In many ways, the initial launch of neighbourhood planning suggested that the preparation and adoption of an NDP would lead to the potential to prevent local change and new development. While this general view was promoted, the subtext of all the ministerial speeches about the role of NDPs suggested that they were to be used as tools of local growth, which would be incentivised through access of communities to both CIL funding and New Homes Bonuses that would be provided to neighbourhood planning (NP) groups to spend on local infrastructure.

While the general statements about the role of NDPs suggested that communities would be free to determine what they wanted in an area – 'decide what you want then tell us' – the local authority is required to agree the area for the NDP and then, if necessary, choose between the groups to take the plan forward. The local authority also must certify the conformity of NDPs with national and local planning policies, generating a potential series of conflicts between neighbourhood planning areas and the local authorities if there is any disagreement.

The promise of a substantial proportion of the CIL and New Homes Bonuses going to NDP areas that take more development is seen to be a substantial incentive to groups although there also needs to be some mechanism for prioritising local development and then delivering it. However, if the NDP is not in an area that has strong market viability, then there may be no CIL and in a down turn, there will be less CIL if it is renegotiated after planning consent has been given. While the New Home Bonus, which is passed to local authorities for new housing was mentioned as a possible source of funding to deliver the NDP, there was no agreement that it should be passed to NDP groups.

In areas where there are parish councils, they are expected to be responsible for the NDP but elsewhere, a group must form to take on this task. In some locations, there have been rival groups and the local authority has been required to select between them. There may also be issues in relation to the private sector's role in the NDP process, not least where there may be one or two large landowners with control of most of the development, and there may be pressures locally to support development in some specific locations (Brownill 2017a).

One of the major issues in preparing neighbourhood plans has been the extent to which local communities can provide resources to undertake the task (Brownill 2017b). Local authorities are expected to provide the support funding and professional assistance but this has been problematic, not least when planning services in local authorities have lost more staff in comparison with other departments since the recession in 2010 (Parker 2017). The government has given independent consultancies some funding to provide support and this has been in addition to that given to local authorities. There have also been concerns that the financial and professional resources spent on NDPs at the local level have been to the detriment of local plan preparation, which the government is also keen to advance. It was also estimated from the outset that the cost of an NDP could be as much as £250,000.

Much of the language around the methodology for local plans suggested that it would be easy and that if the neighbourhood agreed then the council would be required to provide support. The formal processes for NDPs must be compliant with local plans and require a formal hearing. If there are failures in the NDP preparation process, then the plan may not be able to be made. The process is outlined in Box 7.1. The process also must include local councillors and is not a means of bypassing council decision making or creating a mandate for the council when determining a planning application on the NDP area. Further, the private sector may find the process inhibits development and may oppose decisions made in the NDP. There are also issues of process and prematurity. An NDP can be prepared prior to a local plan's being adopted but this may give rise to some tensions around respective priorities and sites to be included in the local plan.

Box 7.1 Processes for Adopting a Neighbourhood Plan

1 Defining the neighbourhood;
2 Applying to be a neighbourhood forum;
3 Undertaking pre-application consultation/assessment;
4 Local authority's duty to support;
5 Submit draft plan/order for independent examination;
6 Local authority validation check;
7 Independent examination;
8 Examiner's report;
9 Referendum on (modified) plan/order;
10 Adoption by local authority – part of development plan.

Neighbourhood Planning Act 2017

The Neighbourhood Planning Act 2017 clarified some of the issues that had been occurring in practice and through appeals on specific planning applications caught between the temporal choreography of neighbourhood and local plans. A local authority must now have regard to an NDP that has been examined by an independent person post-examination but is not yet 'made' in a formal sense. This regard is in the form of a material consideration when determining planning applications. Secondly, once an NDP plan has been successful in being supported in a referendum, it must become part of the development plan. In these changes and clarifications, the NDP has started to have an influential role on the local plan and the way in which local planning decisions are made. even though they must be considered within the local plan framework.

Neighbourhood Planning in Practice

Since the introduction of NDPs, how quickly have they been taken up in practice and what issues have emerged?

Operation

NDPs are part of a vertical alignment of plans for any locality. While being promoted by the government, they provide a means through which communities can exert control over development in their areas, as part of a vertical alignment of plans for any locality that must agree. While these plans have to be part of the basis of decision making through the determination of planning applications for development, the changing focus on the local authority's responsibility for delivery of the plan also means that NDPs can be regarded in part as programmes for delivery. This might occur through the income that the neighbourhood forum receives through CIL, but may also be a mechanism to guide other investment, including the local authority's own capital programme priorities. ResPublica proposed that there should also be a specific neighbourhood contract as has emerged through city deals but, as yet, this has not been implemented (Dobson 2013).

Take-Up

While the take-up of neighbourhood planning has been significant, with 1,906 NDPs commenced by October 2016 (Parker and Salter 2017) and with over 400 successful neighbourhood planning referenda, there are criticisms of the differential use of neighbourhood planning in various parts of England (Parker 2017). These include concerns about the role that local authorities are playing in defining and guiding plans and concerns that NDPs are progressing in areas with populations in higher socio-economic groups. These groups are said to be motivated to use the NDP as a means of gaining greater control over new development and having access to financial resources to promote their views.

The process of preparing an NDP takes time and in some locations, the plans are being led by retired professionals (Gallent and Robinson 2012; Derounian 2016a), whereas elsewhere, local communities do not have access to the same kind of expertise and experience (Gunn et al. 2015). Of those NDPs that have been pursued, more have been promoted in the South East and South West, with the parish council model being the predominantly chosen route over neighbourhood fora, although some urban areas, such as Leeds, had 35 active neighbourhood planning fora by 2016 (Parker and Salter 2017).

Normative Practices

While neighbourhood plans have been described as a mechanism for including more local people in decision-making, there have also been those who have argued that they are processes of encouraging greater support for local housebuilding using CIL and other resource diversions (Parker and Salter 2016). However, there are also differences in practice on the part of the local authority, including the resources and commitment provided to the NDP process (Brookfield 2017).

A second issue is that, in practice, despite where the NDPs start, the community's priorities, objectives and preferences are placed within a normative framework. The community must adopt this framework to be successful through the process (Derounian 2016b; Lord et al. 2017). This is primarily through the need for the plan to be in conformity with the local plans and secondly for all plans to adopt new housing targets though identifying local sites. The reward for such an approach includes CIL funding but also some control over where development is located and the removal of more random outcomes that might be generated through the planning appeal process in response to developers' speculative applications. The processes of neighbourhood plan making are inevitably concerned with convergence of differential views about place and development in the defined communities, in a form of bounded collaboration (Parker et al. 2015). The neighbourhood referenda have supported the NDPs although in some cases, the majority has been just over the 50 per cent required (Joyce 2016).

There are different scales of local authority support, some using NDPs to promote agendas and others seeing them as a removal or diversion of resources. There can also be tensions between local councillors and the neighbourhood forum, not least as councillors have a directly elected mandate and the neighbourhood forum can be self-appointed. Councillors may also consider that the neighbourhood forum has been established in response or opposition to their positions on local issues (Sturzaker and Gordon 2017).

Process and Progress

The take-up of NDPs has been high initially but the number of NDPs that have been taken to referenda is much smaller (Parker 2017). The instigation of NDPs in neighbourhood forum areas was primarily from individuals or existing community groups. Parker et al. (2015) also found that, in 35 per cent of the cases overall, it was indicated that the local authority had acted to initiate neighbourhood planning.

Containment of Views

While much of the political rhetoric of neighbourhood planning, both in its initial inception in 2011 and now, has been focussed on local community decision making, with nudged and incentivised acceptance of housing development, Pill and Bailey (2012) also argue that NDPs are a means of achieving containment of differing views. However, it is also the case that although there might be individuals who are skilled or retired professionals engaging in NDPs, they have to seek some coalescence in views for the wider community members and groups that may exist in their areas (Bradley 2015). This may be the case in both urban and rural areas.

Contestation

While NDPs have been supported by the government, they have also been tested by the market. As Joyce (2016) states, private sector developers have a love–hate relationship with NDPs, with some working with the parish council or neighbourhood forum, while others take the NDP to judicial review, even overturning the local plan in the process. Further, although many plans have been started, not all plans have been completed, either because the process has been abandoned by the promoting group or the evidence has not proved strong enough when faced with inspection.

Are NDPs Able to Deliver for Their Areas?

All NDPs, once made, are required to monitor their progress in delivery although some, such as the one in Stratfield Mortimer in West Berkshire, state that, as the parish council is not the planning authority, it cannot take any specific action to implement the NDP. This is unlike other areas, where parish councils and neighbourhood fora have started, as part of their process of preparing an NDP, to develop their own delivery plans for the implementation of their priorities and proposals. In some cases, this is a general statement of how the NDP will be delivered, such as in the example shown in Table 7.1.

Some NDPs have prepared a separate report on how their proposals will be delivered. In Bembridge, on the Isle of Wight, the NDP is accompanied by a delivery strategy and action plan (Bembridge 2014), which are focussed on the way in which the CIL and S106 funding that will be available to the NDP area will be spent. Here, the delivery plan is taken as part of the parish council's wider function and budget and is an example of an integrated approach. In Freshwater, also on the Isle of Wight, the NDP covers two parishes although the majority of development is likely to be in only one. Here, the careful monitoring of infrastructure investment for the whole area has been identified as a delivery priority.

Table 7.1 NDP Approach to Delivery

(a) Private sector investment in the Parish through new development will be crucial; we must be open to development which, in turn, must be sensitive to the very special environment of both the AONB and National Park in which the Parish sits.

(b) The statuary planning process will direct and control private developer and investor interest in the Parish in the context of the Neighbourhood Plan and the wider Local Authorities and National Planning Policy Framework.

(c) Investment in, and management of, public services, assets and other measures to support local services and vitality and viability for the villages within the Parish.

(d) The voluntary and community sector will have a strong role to play particularly in terms of local community infrastructure, events and village life.

Source: Buckland Monachorum Devon NDP nd p40 para 7.2.

In Thame, the NDP delivery strategy (Thame Town Council 2012) was prepared by the town council and includes an indication of which organisation is responsible for delivery. It identifies which infrastructure is required for specific sites and the types of infrastructure and requirements for developments overall. In this approach, the NDP delivery plan is attempting not only to prioritise the expenditure of any resources made available to it, but also to lock the local authority and others into NDP priorities for their area through a process of reverse engineering. Other neighbourhood fora have taken on specific mechanisms to promote the delivery of their NDPs. In Kirdford, in West Sussex, the neighbourhood forum has established the Kirdford Parish Community Land Trust (KP-CLT), which is an independent not-for-profit society. The role of the KP-CLT is to deliver 17 community projects that have been identified in the NDP and that have are on a schedule that includes details of the project, when it should be delivered and how the project will be managed long-term.

In Feock (Feock 2018), in Cornwall, a wider approach to delivery has been taken, based on a systematic review of all policies contained within the NDP. This is also set out in a thematic schedule, with delivery of environmental, seascape, historic, housing, economy and movement projects grouped together. The schedule sets out how the specific proposals are to be secured and monitored together with partners and what actions are required to deliver them. The delivery strategy also includes placemaking objectives for village hearts and gateways.

Do Neighbourhood Plans Deliver Housing More Quickly?

While NDPs are focussed on housing delivery, there can be a complex relationship between the NDP and the local plan, particularly where they are not in synchronicity. The NDP can have a view about housing sites in their area that may differ from the local plan and may take precedence if the local plan has not been adopted. This has caused issues and challenges from private sector land agents and developers (Bradley et al. 2017). Bradley and Sparling (2017) suggest that devolution of power is an unusual alignment between liberalisation and planning through the housing market.

The government has undertaken some research to review whether the presence of an NDP has a key influence on the speed of delivery of housing (DCLG 2015; Panesar 2016). In this research, it has been found that those local authorities with NDPs are likely to have identified 10 per cent more housing units than those without NDPs. However, as these reports demonstrate, the adoption of higher numbers for housing in the NDPs have not led to a speedier build-out and some of the case studies indicate that permitted developments have yet to commence construction and, in every case considered, the completion levels were low. This research does not identify any underlying causes for this slow build-out of permitted dwellings. However, it seems likely that having an NDP does not, as yet, increase the speed of delivery, even if it increases the numbers of dwellings permitted.

What Future for Neighbourhood Development Plans?

Are NDPs a neo-liberal tool to encourage nudged compliance to housing development and reduce opposition to local plans through the incorporation of likely objectors? There is evidence that they are more likely to be taken up in locations with more development pressures in the South East and South West of England (Parker and Salter 2017). There appears to be no evidence that housing sites within NDP areas are being built out more rapidly than they might be elsewhere. Further, as neo-liberal tools, they attract the use of resources which, in turn, could be drawing resources away from local plan making. Local authorities also have a responsibility to meet the needs of the whole of their areas and the NDP processes can act as a drain and diversion from more mainstream support to the communities in need in the whole local authority area (Griggs and Roberts 2012).

NDPs can be a mechanism for reducing or removing conflict through incentivisation and nudging people into compliance although Wills (2016) argues that people feel more positive about the outcomes and processes when taking an active part. However, NDPs and neighbourhood fora may be a means of overcoming social fragmentation and increasing cohesion (Kearns and Forrest 2000) through the development of common values and civic culture. There may be a differential set of opportunities appearing across the country as take-up varies, as some local authorities have many NDPs and others none. In this variation, Davoudi and Cowie (2013) argue that there are issues of legitimacy.

While some neighbourhood plans appear to have engaged in delivery of their priority outcomes, others have taken a more passive approach. While the leadership of neighbourhood fora might suggest that there is more control of local decision making (Durose and Lowndes 2010), the process is legalistic and includes a requirement for vertical compliance with the local plan. Does the process of preparing and implementing an NDP provide a more localised form of decision making for communities? In some ways, the processes offer more social control (Putnam 2001) although Bailey (2017) argues that they may unleash a new form of spatial planning.

Alternatively, NDPs may be regarded as a neo-liberal approach to plan making (Pugalis and Townsend 2013; Wills 2016). With their vertical alignment with other spatial scales, NDPs may be tools of MLG. NDPs may be also be regarded as a neo-liberal approach to plan making while Parker et al. (2015) argue that NDPs are being re-scripted to conform with local plans, although this process may not meet the initial expectations of those who established the process.

The development of NDPs at a small scale may also represent opportunities missed in creating healthy places (Pfeiffer and Cloutier 2016). In supporting walking and safe environments rather than being focused primarily on new housing provision, NDPs could have wider benefits. Further, the focus on the new development may be to the detriment of existing places in communities. Further, the focus on the new development may be to the detriment of existing places in the communities.

Thus, the processes of neighbourhood planning exist within a range of issues for planning, which have yet to be resolved. Many areas that have prepared NDPs are wealthier than the average and may rely on existing community organisational architecture (Sturzaker and Shaw 2015). While preparation of NDPs may start with a protectionist or oppositional stance to new development, are these communities incorporated into the process or do they stall when there is an appreciation of the normative principles that underlie them? NDPs may also be formed in opposition to local politicians, but the processes clearly demonstrate that the local authority needs to provide technical, professional and financial resources to support parish councils and neighbourhood fora. There are also discrepancies in the powers between neighbourhood fora and parish councils and this can be evidenced through the confidence of some parish councils in taking forward priorities and projects for their areas using legal forms that are supported by previous activities and experience. It will be interesting to note whether the newly formed neighbourhood fora decide to seek parish council powers and if the process of creating NDPs is a step forward in reinforcing the community tier in multi-level governance.

References

Bailey, N. (2017). Housing at the neighbourhood level: A review of the initial approaches to neighbourhood development plans under the Localism Act 2011 in England. *Journal of Urbanism: International Research on Placemaking and Urban Sustainability*, 10 (1), 1–14.

Bailey, N., & Pill, M. (2011). The continuing popularity of the neighbourhood and neighbourhood governance in the transition from the 'big state' to the 'big society' paradigm. *Environment and Planning C: Government and Policy*, 29(5), 927–942.

Bailey, N., & Pill, M. (2015). Can the state empower communities through localism? An evaluation of recent approaches to neighbourhood governance in England. *Environment and Planning C: Government and Policy*, 33(2), 289–304.

Barton, H., & Grant, M. (2015). Retrofitting suburbia for health. In H. Barton, S. Thompson, S. Burgess, & M. Grant (Eds.), *The Routledge Handbook of Planning for Health and Well-Being: Shaping a Sustainable and Healthy Future* (pp. 225–238). Abingdon: Routledge.

Bembridge (2014). *Bembridge Neighbourhood Development Plan 2014*. www.iwight. com/azservices/documents/2879-Made-Bembridge-NDP.pdf (accessed 5 July 2018).

Bishop, J. (2010). From parish plans to localism in England: Straight track or long and winding road? *Planning Practice & Research*, 25(5), 611–624.

Bradley, Q. (2015). The political identities of neighbourhood planning in England. *Space and Polity*, 19(2), 97–109.

Bradley, Q., Burnett, A., & Sparling, W. (2017). Neighbourhood planning and the spatial practices of localism. In *Localism and Neighbourhood Planning: Power to the People?* (pp. 57–74). Bristol: Policy Press.

Bradley, Q., & Sparling, W. (2017). The impact of neighbourhood planning and localism on house-building in England. *Housing, Theory and Society*, 34(1), 106–118.

Brookfield, K. (2017). Getting involved in plan-making: Participation in neighbourhood planning in England. *Environment and Planning C: Politics and Space*, 35(3), 397–416.

Brown, G., & Chin, S. Y. W. (2013). Assessing the effectiveness of public participation in neighbourhood planning, *Planning Practice and Research*, 28(5) 563–588.

Brownill, S. (2017a). Assembling neighbourhoods: Topologies of power and the reshaping of planning. In S. Brownill, & Q. Bradley (Eds.), *Localism and Neighbourhood Planning: Power to the People?* (pp. 145–162). Bristol: Policy Press.

Brownill, S. (2017b). Neighbourhood planning purposes and the practices of localism. In S. Brownill, & Q. Bradley (Eds.), *Localism and Neighbourhood Planning: Power to the People?* (pp. 19–38). Bristol: Policy Press.

Brownill, S., & Bradley, Q. (2017). Introduction. In S. Brownill, & Q. Bradley (Eds.), *Localism and Neighbourhood Planning: Power to the People?* (pp. 1–15). Bristol: Policy Press.

Buckland Monachorum Devon NDP (nd). The neighbourhood plan for the parish of Buckland Monachorum. https://bucklandmonachorumplan.co.uk/images/Plan-dec-2017/NP-Vers-5.1-Nov-17–min.pdf (accessed 16 July 2018).

Davoudi, S., & Cowie, P. (2013). Are English neighbourhood forums democratically legitimate? *Planning Theory & Practice*, 14(4), 562–566.

DCLG (2015). *Neighbourhood Planning Progress on Housing Delivery*. London: DCLG. https://mycommunity.org.uk/wp-content/uploads/2016/08/Neighbourhood-planning_-progress-on-housing-delivery-.pdf (accessed 7 December 2017).

Derounian, J. (2016a). This green and neglected land: How the National Planning Policy Framework fails to meet the needs of communities. Blog entry, British Politics and Policy at LSE, 9 June. http://eprints.lse.ac.uk/71440/ (accessed 5 July 2018).

Derounian, J. (2016b). It's neighbourhood planning, Jim… But not as we know it. *Town and Country Planning*, 85(3), 142–144.

Design Council (2013). *Design in Neighbourhood Planning: How Can We Help You?* London: Design Council.

Dobson, J. (2013). *Responsible Recovery: A Social Contract for Local Growth*. London: ResPublica.

Durose, C., & Lowndes, V. (2010). Neighbourhood governance: Contested rationales within a multi-level setting – A study of Manchester. *Local Government Studies*, 36 (3), 341–359.

English Heritage (2014). Neighbourhood planning and the historic environment. https://historicengland.org.uk/advice/planning/plan-making/improve-your-neighbourhood/ (accessed 5 July 2018).

Feock (2018). *Feock Neighbourhood Development Plan 2018*. www.cornwall.gov.uk/environment-and-planning/planning/neighbourhood-planning/neighbourhood-planning-in-cornwall/tab-placeholder/a-i/feock-neighbourhood-development-plan/ (accessed 5 July 2018).

Gallent, N. (2013). Re-connecting 'people and planning': parish plans and the English localism agenda. *Town Planning Review*, 84(3), 371–396.

Gallent, N., Morphet, J., & Tewdwr-Jones, M. (2008). Parish plans and the spatial planning approach in England. *Town Planning Review*, 79(1), 1–29.

Gallent, N., & Robinson, S. (2012). *Neighbourhood Planning: Communities, Networks and Governance*. Bristol: Policy Press.

Griggs, S., & Roberts, M. (2012). From neighbourhood governance to neighbourhood management: A 'roll-out' neoliberal design for devolved governance in the United Kingdom? *Local Government Studies*, 38(2), 183–210.

Gunn, S., Brooks, E., & Vigar, G. (2015). The community's capacity to plan: The disproportionate requirements of the new English neighbourhood planning initiative. In

S. Davoudi and A. Madanipour (Eds.), *Reconsidering Localism* (pp. 147–167). London: Routledge.

HCC (2015). Neighbourhood planning guidance note 11: Implementation and monitoring. www.herefordshire.gov.uk/downloads/file/3702/guidance_note_11_implementation_and_monitoring (accessed 5 July 2018).

Historic England (2017). Neighbourhood planning advice. https://historicengland.org.uk/advice/planning/plan-making/improve-your-neighbourhood/ (accessed 8 December 2017).

Jones, A. (2007). New wine in old bottles? England's parish and town councils and new labour's neighbourhood experiment. *Local Economy*, 22(3), 227–242.

Joyce, S. (2016). Neighbourhood plans: Five years on, Strutt and Parker. www.struttandparker.com/knowledge-and-research/neighbourhood-plans-five-years-on (accessed 8 December 2017).

Kaszynska, P., Parkinson, J., & Fox, W. (2012). Re-thinking neighbourhood planning: From consultation to collaboration. Green paper. London: ResPublica.

Kearns, A., & Forrest, R. (2000). Social cohesion and multilevel urban governance. *Urban Studies*, 37(5–6), 995–1017.

Kokx, A., & Van Kempen, R. (2010). Dutch urban governance: Multi-level or multi-scalar? *European Urban and Regional Studies*, 17(4), 355–369.

Locality (2016). Design in neighbourhood planning design with council. https://mycommunity.org.uk/wp-content/uploads/2016/09/Design-in-Neighbourhood-Planning_FINAL220216-1.pdf (accessed 8 December 2017).

Lord, A., Mair, M., Sturzaker, J., & Jones, P. (2017). 'The planners' dream goes wrong?' Questioning citizen-centred planning. *Local Government Studies*, 43(3), 344–363.

Lowndes, V., & Sullivan, H. (2008). How low can you go? Rationales and challenges for neighbourhood governance. *Public Administration*, 86(1), 53–74.

Miquel, M. P., Cabeza, M. G., & Anglada, S. E. (2013). Theorizing multi-level governance in social innovation dynamics. In F. Moulaert et al. (Eds.), *International Handbook of Social Innovation* (pp. 155–168) Cheltenham: Edward Elgar.

Owen, S. (2002). From village design statements to parish plans: Some pointers towards community decision making in the planning system in England. *Planning Practice and Research*, 17(1), 81–89.

Owen, S., & Moseley, M. (2003). Putting parish plans in their place: Relationships between community-based initiatives and development planning in English villages. *Town Planning Review*, 74(4), 445–471.

Panesar, S. (2016). *Neighbourhood Planning: Progress on Housing Delivery* (October 2016 edition). London: DCLG.

Parker, G. (2017). The uneven geographies of neighbourhood planning in England. In S. Brownill, & Q. Bradley (Eds.), *Localism and Neighbourhood Planning* (pp. 75–92). Bristol: Policy Press.

Parker, G., Lynn, T., & Wargent, M. (2015). Sticking to the script? The co-production of neighbourhood planning in England. *Town Planning Review*, 86(5), 519–536.

Parker, G., & Salter, K. (2016). Five years of neighbourhood planning. A review of take-up and distribution. *Town and Country Planning*, 85(5), 175–184.

Parker, G., & Salter, K. (2017). Taking stock of neighbourhood planning in England 2011–2016. *Planning Practice and Research*, 32(4), 478–490. www.tandfonline.com/doi/full/10.1080/02697459.2017.1378983.

Pfeiffer, D., & Cloutier, S. (2016). Planning for happy neighborhoods. *Journal of the American Planning Association*, 82(3), 267–279.

Pill, M., & Bailey, N. (2012). Community empowerment or a strategy of containment? Evaluating neighbourhood governance in the City of Westminster. *Local Government Studies*, 38(6), 731–751.

Pugalis, L., & Townsend, A. (2013). Rescaling of planning and its interface with economic development. *Planning Practice & Research*, 28(1), 104–121.

Putnam, R. D. (2001). *Bowling Alone: The Collapse and Revival of American Community*. New York: Simon and Schuster.

Seager, C. (2016). Parish councils suit city dwellers too, not just rural Britain. *The Guardian*, 11 May. www.theguardian.com/public-leaders-network/2016/may/11/urban-parish-councils-city-dwellers-control-local-issues (accessed 8 December 2017).

Smith, L. (2016). Neighbourhood planning, SN 05838, 11 July. London: House of Commons Library. https://researchbriefings.parliament.uk/ResearchBriefing/Summary/SN05838 (accessed 6 July 2018).

Sturzaker, J., & Gordon, M. (2017). Democratic tensions in decentralised planning: Rhetoric, legislation and reality in England. *Environment and Planning C: Politics and Space*, 35(7), 1324–1339.

Sturzaker, J., & Shaw, D. (2015). Localism in practice: lessons from a pioneer neighbourhood plan in England. *Town Planning Review*, 86(5), 587–609.

Thame Town Council (2012). Thame neighbourhood plan delivery strategy. www.southoxon.gov.uk/sites/default/files/Delivery%20Strategy_0.pdf (accessed 16 July 2018).

Wills, J. (2016). Emerging geographies of English localism: The case of neighbourhood planning. *Political Geography*, 53, 43–53.

Woods, M. (1998). Advocating rurality? The repositioning of rural local government. *Journal of Rural Studies*, 14(1), 13–26.

8   Planning in Scotland

Introduction

The development of the planning system in Scotland following devolution in 1999 has been a deliberate process of both modernising the system and ensuring that it addresses distinct Scottish issues (Allmendinger, 2001, 2006; Lloyd and Purves, 2009). Until 2017, it was more concerned with establishing a strategic scale of planning at both national and sub-regional levels than with focussing on reform at the local level – unlike the other UK nations. Scotland's continuing debate about separateness has influenced these approaches, particularly in pursuing economic objectives. Scotland's approach to national planning, particularly for key infrastructure and the management of rural areas, has been distinctive and pioneering in the UK context, linking the environment and the national infrastructure priorities with the planning system from the outset in the National Planning Framework (NPF) (2004). A new spatial hierarchy for planning was introduced in the planning white paper *Modernising the planning system*, (2005), including national and strategic scales. This has been primarily focussed on creating an investment programme that can deliver infrastructure for economic success but can also work within the EU's frameworks. The economic focus has also been apparent in the second layer of this planning policy, through strategic planning areas that have focussed on four city regions – Edinburgh, Glasgow, Dundee and Aberdeen – and subsequently through City Deals introduced new city policy (Scottish Government 2016).

What was the planning context before devolution? In the 1973 Act, Scotland's area was divided into a two-tier local authority system with large regions and local authorities set within them (Wannop 2014). This system continued until 1996. Strategic planning and transport were key responsibilities of the upper-level strategic councils. As Lloyd (1997) demonstrates, there has always been a strong strategic focus in planning for and within Scotland. During the 1973–1996 period, there were many national planning guidelines covering issues such as petrochemical development, skiing and technology, in addition to more familiar guidance for housing, industry and major retail locations, which was refreshed in 1981, at a time when three-quarters of Scotland was covered by structure plans. Lloyd continues by arguing that national planning policy in

Scotland, delivered through guidance, has always been assertive. It is also possible to see a pro-active pattern in the development and adoption of guidance, which has been maintained over time. This approach continued beyond local government reorganisation in Scotland in 1996, when two-tier local government was abolished, and unitary local authorities were established (Wilson and Game 2011). The reform of the planning system did not emerge until after the implementation of devolution in Scotland in 1999 and in many ways the character of the NPF in its two iterations and the associated planning guidance has continued this approach.

This chapter reviews the approaches to planning in Scotland that have been put into practice in this period, many of them innovative, and then the more recent planning reforms proposed in 2017. These include the merger of spatial and community plans and a revised approach to strategic plans. The chapter will also review the role of City Deals in Scotland and how they have been used to focus a potentially re-centralising agenda of emerging governance for FEAs.

Planning for the Nation

The development of the planning system in Scotland following devolution built upon an essentially different system that was already in existence. Planning in Scotland reflected both a different legal system and legal rights for land ownership (Adams 2015). The newly devolved government built on that basis but also wanted to have a distinct approach from other UK nations. When the Scottish Executive published its first NPF in 2004, it had a strong economic focus (Lloyd and Purves, 2009) that differed from the spatial planning route being taken in England and the sustainability focus in Wales, both of which were being implemented contemporaneously. It is also important to note that, while each nation pursued its own priorities for delivery within their devolved agreements, there were also overarching institutional arrangements that supported the exchange of ideas in a more informal way (Clifford and Morphet 2015).

All UK nations operate within the EU, UN and WTO frameworks, which also means some common issues are apparent, not least in the timing of implementation (Dühr et al. 2010; Morphet 2013; Mayer-Sahling and Goetz 2009). In the case of planning, this was through both the British–Irish Council, which subsequently established a working group on spatial planning and the five administrations group, which comprised the chief planners in the four UK nations and Ireland (Morphet and Clifford 2018). Nevertheless, there was a keen sense that, within these broader parameters, policies in all areas should be distinctive and not seen to converge after devolution (Keating 2010, Allmendinger 2001).

The 2004 NPF was followed by the second National Planning Framework, NPF2, in 2009. The difference between the two NPFs is that NPF2 was intended to be far more specific about development priorities and implementation. NPF2 was a means through which the spatial consequences of policies for 'economic development, climate change, transport, energy, housing and regeneration, waste management, water and drainage, catchment management and the protection of the environment' could be considered (Scottish Executive 2009, Foreword from the Cabinet Secretary). The foreword to NPF2 also heralded its role in shaping the future approach to territorial planning in Scotland with the role of aligning strategic investment priorities. Although this can be viewed as a spatial planning approach, this term was never used in Scotland in the same way as defining a new approach in England and Wales (Adams 2008). Like NPF1, it maintained a strong economic focus and set out to be the spatial expression of all government policies. NPF2 also recognised that it worked within the EU framework expressed though the European Spatial Development Perspective (ESDP) (CEC 1999) and national spatial policies in other parts of the UK. Further, NPF2 focussed on specific operational relationships with spatial plans from bordering areas such as the North East region in England (McGuiness et al. 2015). It also created the context for the city regions – Edinburgh, Glasgow, Aberdeen and Dundee – which required the creation of strategic development plans (SDPs) for their areas, which went wider than the central Scotland economic belt (Bailey and Turok 2001). There was also a commitment to devolution of central functions within Scotland, as well as devolution to Scotland (Keating et al. 2009).

NPF2 (Scottish Executive 2009) created the spatial framework for the future of Scotland. It identified a range of key challenges, including the economy and its relationship with place. Secondly, it highlighted the challenges of sustainable development, including the issues of climate change, transport, energy, waste and new technologies. The third key challenge was seen in the changing size of Scotland's people and households, with recent downturns in population being reversed through in-migration and higher fertility rates, with a projected increase in households of 19 per cent by 2031. This had implications for homes, infrastructure and public services. The last challenge set out in the NPF2 was Scotland in the world. NPF 2 then went to identify how these challenges were to be met through a variety of targets, policies and proposals. It also concentrated on the need to deliver what was proposed in NPF2 through a variety of delivery agencies and private investments.

NPF2 also contained key proposals for Strategic Transport Corridors, electricity transmission, water and drainage. It also established spatial perspectives for a series of regional areas within Scotland, as well as their sub-regional components. These provided a framework for both the SDPs and local development plans (LDPs) that would follow, and although promised in the planning white paper, the NPF did not contain any detail of the way in which it would be delivered, other than through the development planning system, as set out in the *Development Planning Circular 1* (Scottish Executive 2009). However, this approach was more spatially defined than the system introduced in England in 2008 for NSIPs, where sector-specific but primarily spatially generic national policy statements were introduced (Morphet and Clifford 2017).

When NPF3 was adopted in 2014, the Scottish government set out its role as creating a context for local planning for the period 2014–2044 and described it as sitting at the top of the hierarchy of Scottish development plans. NPF3 was used to identify projects as 'national developments' that were regarded as essential to Scotland's strategic spatial development and included major strategic transport, water and drainage and waste management infrastructure. Many of these projects were already the subject of consultation as part of the development of other strategies and programmes. For new projects, identification in the NPF3 was the mechanism for establishing the need for such developments and facilitating their delivery through the consenting process. All LDPs had to be in conformity with NPF3.

The role of city regions in Scotland was also foregrounded in NPF3, based on their economic potential. In this approach there was a focus on the wider city region, with NPF3 defining broad areas that were primarily defined as travel-to-work areas for Glasgow and Edinburgh, including Stirling, Perth, Dundee and Tayside and Aberdeen and the North East and Inverness. Each area was to produce a strategic plan based on a relationship between the government and the local authorities with the defined areas. It also identified strategic towns that were important in the rural economy and centres for activity and services and also key coastal town and ports. NPF3 also contained a focus on major infrastructure, including energy and transport, through a priority to establish resilience.

City Regions

City regions are defined as being important as part of the economic future of Scotland. The development of SDPs for four city regions in Scotland – Aberdeen, Dundee, Edinburgh and Glasgow – was regarded as providing national leadership. In the *Review of Scotland's Cities* (Scottish Executive 2002), it was stated that 'devolution has provided an opportunity to put Scotland at the forefront of modern integrated approaches to territorial management within the UK' (p5). This approach to spatial planning at the sub-regional level is a potential forerunner for sub-regional planning within other parts of the UK. The boundaries of the four regions, Edinburgh, Aberdeen Dundee and Glasgow, were reviewed in 2002 (Halden, 2002) based on transport, housing and retail catchments areas. This was also published at the same time as an analysis of Scotland's city regions (Scottish Executive 2002). As Glasson and Marshall (2007) demonstrate, these two reports were set amidst amongst an extensive line of studies of the economic role of the city regions.

The proposal that city regions should have their own strategic planning arrangements, which span across the local authorities in the city region, was included within the Planning, etc. (Scotland) Act (2006) as a formal planning scale and created SDPs as the means of planning for them. These brought together development planning and action programmes, which must prepared once the plan has been published. In the areas that are included within the SDP, local authorities also had to prepare an LDP. Where there is not an SDP, then local authorities must only prepare an LDP. Glasson and Marshall (2007) also point out the links between this approach and that of Scottish Enterprise, which also promotes the role of Scotland's cities in building future economic success (Scottish Enterprise 2006).

The introduction of SDPs in effect identified and created the city regions and introduced sub-regional planning in Scotland. It also marked the second significant spatial planning initiative. Although not mentioned in the 2005 planning white paper, this sub-regional focus combined both economic and spatial planning in an integrated way, including the greater interrelationship with economic delivery agencies; these plans can provide a means of planning and delivering economic investment and infrastructure at this sub-regional scale. On the other hand, they are reliant on a traditional planning approach for their process of development plan adoption and there is a slight difference between the approaches for SDPs and LDPs as set out in *Planning Circular 1* (Scottish Government 2009). There were also proposals for additional city region plans, which would also contain infrastructure requirements for short (five years), medium (ten years) and long terms (20 years) (para 60).

> To work together to prepare a city region plan. Councils on whose a statutory requirement is placed to draw up a city region plan shall establish a joint committee with a mandatory membership. Other councils, key agencies or infrastructure providers should be invited to work with a joint committee where they have a role in delivering the strategy.
>
> (Scottish Government 2009 para 63)

SDPs have developed in practice. The Edinburgh and South East Scotland SDP covers six local authority areas – the Borders, Fife and the four Lothian authorities – and a committee has been set up. In Aberdeen, two of the four local authorities in the city region had been working on a structure plan in the previous system and decided to publish this before beginning work on the SDP (Aberdeen and Shire Strategic Development Planning Authority 2009). In Glasgow, there are eight local authorities that make up the city region. The SDP has been taken forward through the work of an existing joint committee for Glasgow and the Clyde Valley that was previously set up for the structure plan. In Dundee, there are four local authorities, including Fife, which is also part of the Edinburgh city region, and they have set up TAYplan (Tayplan Strategic Development Plan Authority) to undertake the SDP work. All the local authorities within the four city regions were also required to develop an LDP for their areas. These related to each local authority's community plan. In England, there is no equivalent of a local authority community plan that works across each city region in this way.

Both SDPS and LDPs are required to include action plans that set out their delivery mechanisms and approaches, including a programme. However, the SDPs cover more than one local authority area and a framework for democratic governance must be established to agree the strategic approach and programme whilst also supporting implementation. All the four city regions' SDPs are managed by a Strategic Planning Authority established through designation by the Scottish government and operate as joint committees between all the local authorities comprising the city region area. The main purposes of strategic planning are set out in the Planning (etc.) Scotland Act 2006.

The framework for the preparation of SDPs and their method of adoption, which is through a process of examination, are both under the auspices of the Scottish government as set out in the 2006 Planning, etc. (Scotland) Act. Advice on the process and form of the SDP was expanded through the Guidance Circular 1 (Scottish Executive 2009) and is summarised in Table 8.1. Each SDP must be in conformity with the Scottish NPF. In each area covered by an SDP, each local authority comprising the SDP also must prepare a local plan, which is required to be in conformity with the SDP. Outside those areas with no SDP, LDPs for each local authority are prepared. The LDPs must also include an action programme that indicates how the plan proposals are to be implemented.

The SDP guidance promotes a strategic planning framework that both allows for a vision of the area based on evidence and consultation and also requires a focus on its delivery.

The most advanced SDP in Scotland is that for Dundee and its FEA, known as TAYplan, which was adopted in 2012, following which a review was commenced in 2013. Compared with most local planning documents, the TAYplan strategic planning document is short and innovative in its form. It has 26 pages and it is more diagrammatic in its form than has been usual for this kind of document. The plan is structured more like a business plan, starting with the current position for people, place, employment, infrastructure, energy and environment and then, moving on, the outline of where the city region would like to be in 2032. It is more like an EU Integrated Territorial Investment (ITI) strategy (CEC 2015). The plan is focussed on addressing the route to achieving its objectives through setting out locational priorities for both more settlement growth and locations for improvement.

Table 8.1 SDPs: Required Contents

Section 7(1) of the 2006 Planning, etc. (Scotland) Act requires SDPs to contain:

1. A **vision statement**. This is a broad statement of how the development of the area could and should occur and the matters that might be expected to affect that development, including:

- the principal physical, economic, social and environmental characteristics of the area;
- the principal land uses in the area;
- the size, composition and distribution of population in the area;
- the infrastructure of the area (including communications, transport and drainage systems and systems for the supply of water and energy);
- how that infrastructure is used; and
- any anticipated change in these matters.

2. A **spatial strategy**. This is a broadly based statement of proposals as to the development and use of land in the area.

3. An analysis of the relationship with development and land use proposals in **neighbouring areas** that are likely to affect the SDP area.

4. Any other matter the SDPA consider appropriate.

Like any company, TAYplan identifies its assets and then continues to examine how these assets can be used to contribute towards achieving its longer-term objectives. This includes the identification of twelve key locations, which the SDP states are key to achieving the sub-region's success, whether for housing or employment growth. Further, the SDP states that LDPs should align with and implement these priorities. Housing is expected to be within existing settlements to fulfil sustainable objectives and there is an emphasis on reinforcing existing town centres. The SDP is also focussed on waste and energy infrastructure to fulfil wider-than-FEA needs.

The TAYplan action programme was adopted in June 2012 and is owned by a range of agencies responsible for the delivery of the specific projects, including Scottish Water, the Scottish Environmental Protection Agency, the NHS and Scottish Enterprise. The action programme includes programmed projects within diagrammatic maps and then lists the projects on schedules grouped by lead level of delivery, starting with those infrastructure projects being led by the Scottish government. Next, the projects included within the SDP are listed, including the timing and phasing, lead delivery agency and funding. Each individual project has a monitoring statement and supporting evidence and, in some cases, such as employment land and housing, the delivery is shown as being through the LDP. Where appropriate, such as in transport, projects are cross-referenced to the delivery agency's programme. Finally, the action programme includes a table identifying housing needs, land allocation and likely differences between need and supply of housing land.

A revised TAYplan was submitted to the Scottish government in 2016 and approved in 2017 as part of a four-year review programme. This plan identifies 11 transformational projects as the key priorities and then describes the policies that will support their delivery. For other settlements in the areas, there is an emphasis on placemaking above any specific land use provision, such as housing. This form of SDP continues to differ from other similar plans for FEAs in the rest of the UK in the way that it combines economic investment priorities and proposals with land use planning. The proposals contained within the SDP are based on evidence and also assessed both through environmental impact assessment and formal planning processes. This provides greater certainly for potential investors than that offered in the strategic economic plans in England, where the processes are separated and frequently in contention with each other.

Like TAYplan, the SDP for Glasgow and the Clyde Valley was adopted in 2012. It is also constructed more as a business plan than as a traditional development plan with clear ways in which decisions about strategic locations have been determined. It also has a robust economic base and focus for the plan, although within a sustainable context. It has also identified the strategic drivers of change and has linked these through cross linkages between the spatial vision and the spatial development strategy. It has identified key strategic growth areas and 20 economic investment locations together with a green infrastructure context and the associated environmental action required. These locations are set within a spatial vision and a development strategy that are accompanied with diagrammatic maps and schedules. The key objectives, which act as cross programmatic themes, are competitiveness, environmental actions, sustainable communities, infrastructure planning and strategic development priorities. These come together in a spatial model that identifies six key areas and an approach for the community growth areas. In the longer term, the relationship between the city region and its rural hinterland has been identified as requiring further development. Unlike the TAYplan, there is a greater emphasis on housing requirements and locations and these are associated with the economic proposals for the SDP.

The accompanying action plan, published in July 2012, is set out in relation to proposals but the contents are less specific about funding and responsibilities than the other SDP action programmes. Like TAYplan, it identifies those projects that are to be delivered through national programmes and includes each of the community growth areas that link employment development with new housing. It also includes a list of key strategic centres for the FEA. The action plan is specific about the proposals that are led by individual local authorities but less clear about the delivery though LDPs.

Both TAYplan and the Clydeplan FEAs are river valleys and the relationship between the city and its hinterland is long established. The second two SDPs differ from this. Aberdeen is coastal and, as an FEA, has an area that stretches out into its marine area. The oil and gas business has generated its own economy, which is in and around Aberdeen with its own growth pressures but it is also an FEA with a wider international hinterland that has an interest and stake in the city region. Edinburgh and Aberdden's FEAs also share a more international dimension with Aberdeen. Edinburgh has always been key in its location for government, which has expanded since devolution in 1999. It also has become the location of the headquarters of the Secretariat of the British–Irish Council and has a strong commercial base particularly associated with the banking industry. The Glasgow and Clyde Valley Plan, now known as Clydeplan, has also been updated and the latest version was approved in 2017 (Clydeplan 2017).

The SDP for the Edinburgh city region, SESplan, developed more slowly than that for TAYside and was adopted in 2013. The strategy compromises three key elements: the vision, the strategy and the action programme. The plan uses diagrammatic plans to outline its strategy, whilst the projects are identified by the individual local authorities that make up the city region. It has identified 13 locations for strategic development and has developed five sub-areas within the city region, where further policy is set out. The plan identifies policies for the selection of employment and housing sites in a more traditional way than TAYplan, leaving it to the local authorities to identify specific locations within the urban areas. The action programme is set out in the five sub-regions identified for the main policy discussion in the plan. The SESplan appears to be a more traditional planning document than that published by TAYplan and is less strategic in its content, leaving much for the local authorities to determine within its overarching framework, unlike TAYplan, which was more definite about key strategic locations.

The final SDP, for the Aberdeen city region, is like that for Edinburgh in that it was approved in 2014. Like SESplan, it also takes a more traditional approach to setting out its strategy, focussing on housing numbers as a key element of its spatial strategy. There is less use of an evidence-based approach than in Glasgow and TAYplan. The plan sets out a strategic vision and strategy but is structured through its approach to four key growth areas, which are seen to be more important than the key objectives of economic growth, sustainable development, population growth, the quality of the environment, sustainable mixed communities and accessibility. The implementation of the plan moved directly into housing delivery.

The more traditional structure planning approach of the Edinburgh and Aberdeen plans may be based on their secure economic bases, with the attendant pressures on housing provision, unlike Tayside and Glasgow and the Clyde Valley. The SDP for Edinburgh has been through a four-year review. In this iteration (SES 2016), the SDP is more diagrammatic than its previous format and it has now been aligned to support the emergent City Deal for the region. The City Deal is focussed on infrastructure and economic investment although there are no specific proposals included in the revised SDP. While there is an initial focus on place making, the remaining elements of the plan are more similar to a traditional planning format with a focus on issues such as the Green Belt and housing. Further, the examination of the SDP through the formal process did not appear to specifically identify City Deal issues although these may have been incorporated in specific topic areas such as infrastructure.

The Scottish government commissioned a review of the SDPs (Murray 2014) that found that, while the SDPs were performing well, they were not working as effectively as they might be for their areas. The review recommended that the process of preparing the SDPs would benefit from more community engagement and scrutiny. Further, it was recommended that there should be a shift from a hearing to an examination, like the approach in England. In terms of their content, the review recommended that there should be much more focus and guidance on providing housing at a strategic planning level. In considering the way that SDPs had dealt with infrastructure, there was a real concern that there had not been an adequately strategic approach to issues such as waste, energy, water and flooding, nor any alignment to programmes, resources and delivery. Finally, the review recommended that there should be a greater link with the NPF.

Scotland adopted an Agenda for Cities in 2011 and this was later updated (Scottish Government 2016). It was supported by the Scottish Cities Alliance and explicitly anticipated the EU's Urban Agenda (UA). As part of this policy delivery, the Scottish government also entered into a series of city region deals that are vertical contracts between the UK government, the Scottish government and local authorities. The first deals to be agreed were those for Edinburgh, Glasgow and Inverness and the islands. Further deals have been agreed for Stirling and the Tay cities area. The city region deals are focussed on an economic narrative but when they are considered in detail, they incorporate many of the approaches found in the City Deals in England, particularly in the provision of housing in the deal for Edinburgh. The Edinburgh city region deal has been included in the approach to revising the SDP although this relationship appears to be very general. All city region deals are with multiple local authorities that broadly represent FEAs. The topics in each deal are set as general objectives without some of the specific outcomes defined, as in the English City Deals. However, unlike the English City Deals, they are explicit about relating to city regions.

One key issue in the development of these Scottish city regional deals is their relationship to devolution. All the matters included within the deals are contained within the powers devolved to the Scottish government and there appears to be no policy explanation provided as to why the UK government is a senior and guiding partner in these arrangements. They can be viewed as EU territorial pacts, anchored in *Europe 2020*, and this would suggest a more contractual approach across the tiers of government. It could also be the UK government made funding available to these areas conditional on its involvement.

Local Development Planning

Since the review of national approaches to planning in Scotland, as set out in 2004, the Scottish Government has had as one of its objectives to make the planning system 'fit for purpose' although the purpose was not then clearly defined. (Scottish Government 2018 np). The 2006 Act required that the new development planning system consider the plans and policies of other public agencies and that it also be consistent with policies in neighbouring local authorities. In 2009, *Development Planning: Planning Circular 1* was published (Scottish Government 2009a) and it stated that the planning system should be plan-led, LDPs were to be kept up to date and there should be a focus on outcomes (para 5). In addition to setting out requirements for SDPs for the four cities, it identified development plans that covered the rest of Scotland. Although defined as a development plan, the approach outlined by Circular 1 is very like that set out in the first version of PPS 12 (ODPM 2005), in its focus on:

- An evidence base;
- A spatial strategy;
- A vision statement;
- Proposals map;
- Resources available for implementing the plan;
- Alignments with neighbouring local authorities.

There are some key differences between English local plans and the LDP approach being implemented in Scotland. English local plans are less focussed on the delivery of other public bodies, apart from the approach taken to draw together infrastructure development in infrastructure delivery plans that accompany local plans. In Scotland there is a duty placed upon public bodies to cooperate and this extends beyond their immediate project programmes. LDPs in Scotland have not been required to adopt a spatial planning approach and are not so delivery-focussed. In 2018, the Edinburgh City Region Deal was signed by the Prime Minster, which serves to emphasize the roles of the UK and the Scottish governments in this initiative.

Community Planning

Community planning is much stronger in Scotland than in England and at the local level, there are Single Outcome Agreements (SOAs) that bind together the delivery of public sector organisations. SOAs have been operational since 2008 and were reviewed in 2012. The SOAs are focussed on reducing inequalities and achieving this through focussed actions. The socio- economic conditions in each local authority area are mapped and measured on a regular basis and include targeted outcomes for older people, health and employment. The Scottish government produces a menu of SOA indicators, which are then the target of local action. While all the public bodies are involved, there is also engagement for local Community Planning Partnerships (CPPs), comprising local people, and they are supported in their work through national provision of resources.

The approach to community planning in Scotland is part of the commitment to devolution to the lowest levels although as Sinclair (2008) argues, this may incorporate some inherent tensions between local determination and centralised control of objectives (Fenwick et al. 2012). Similar local strategic partnerships were established in England from 2000 onwards, although without any legal basis. They were abandoned after 2010, when there was greater focus on the economic dimension of partnership at the local level through local enterprise partnerships.

In Scotland the role of community planning has been reinforced through the Community Empowerment (Scotland) Act 2015. In this, there is an increased role of community participation in the process, which is extended in its statutory basis. Through these participatory processes, the CPP is required to focus on smaller localities that need greater focus on improvement. While Pemberton (2017) argues that there has been a filling-in of community level plans across the UK, the approach in Scotland differs markedly from that in England. In Scotland, the process is imposed by the government and each local authority area has a CPP. Further, from 2015, each CPP must focus on smaller areas that require improvement. This is in comparison with England, where the process of neighbourhood planning is dependant on local choice and is frequently supported by higher socio-economic groups in an effort to maintain their wealth (Bradley et al. 2017) and control development (Sturzaker and Shaw 2015).

Planning Reform in Scotland: A Move to Convergence with England?

In 2015, the Scottish government commissioned an independent review of the planning system (Beveridge et al. 2016), with the purpose of simplifying the system while also making Scotland more attractive to domestic and international investment. It was also focussed on innovation and inclusive growth. To achieve these objectives, the review recommended an approach to the planning system that retained the primacy of the LDP but removed the sub-national strategic planning tier that had been introduced in 2008 for the larger urban sub-regions. This strategic approach was proposed to be replaced by a greater role for national policy making, where planning policy was to be more integrated with other policies, including transport and marine investment. One recommendation in the review was to introduce an approach to LDP examination similar to that introduced in England in 2004 – that is, to review the plan against a series of 'gate checks' not dissimilar to the English tests of soundness.

Another area where the Scottish system was recommended to reform to be similar with the English system was through the way in which housing should be foregrounded as a particular objective of plan making. However, unlike in the English system, where there is no National Planning Policy Framework (NPPF) or top-down system for housing allocation, the review proposed that regional housing targets should be set out through the Scottish government's NPF. A national approach was recommended for the delivery of infrastructure, through the establishment of a national agency, again, that was similar to the National Infrastructure Commission for England. Allied to this, it was recommended that there should be a fund established and that infrastructure providers should be required to work together. This is a main difference with the approach in England, where infrastructure providers must work within the terms set for them by their regulators. These reforms in Scotland were recommended to be delivered through a more streamlined approach to development management and improved and stronger leadership of planning services in local authorities. The review also proposed that local authorities should share services although it did not mandate that they do so, and that a planning graduate intern programme system should be established.

The Scottish government responded to the report and then committed to introducing planning reform through a government white paper. This was followed by a Planning (Scotland) Bill in December 2017. This incorporated the proposals in the independent review and started to merge systems together, including that for community planning and local planning, which had been separate. Another area of reform is the creation of regional partnerships to promote strategic planning, so, while the formal sub-regional partnerships established in 2008 are theoretically concluded, in effect a similar approach is being substituted. Further, these regional partnerships will be combined with a greater national role, across the whole of Scotland, to include rural as well as urban areas. These new arrangements are proposed to be the principle way of directing the transport infrastructure programmes. The NPF is to be redirected to focus on city regions as part of Scotland's urban policy. This will also align with the commitments made to achieve the UN's NUA, as agreed by the UK government in October 2016. It will also maintain a linkage with the EU's UA policies (CEC 2016).

For local plans, the reform includes a more streamlined approach and integration with community plans. This dual approach at the local level was in force in England until 2008, when the role of the SCS was included within the

LDP. The new LDPs in Scotland will have a renewed focus on delivery through the creation of implementation programmes. This is very much in alignment with government approaches in England (Quartermain 2018) although these specific changes have not been introduced.

What is interesting to note is that, after the creation of a separate approach to LDPs in Scotland, with a focus in national infrastructure delivery, the proposals for change set up in the 2017 bill will have the effect of making Scotland's system more similar to that in England. This is demonstrated through the increasing role of housing and the focus on sites. The LDP adoption process will also be similar to that in England although the processes will operate under different names. While the English local plans have infrastructure delivery plans as part of their delivery focus, the plans in Scotland appear to be going a stage further and incorporating these plans as delivery programmes.

If there is an alignment between the Scottish and English planning systems after a period of distinct practice, what might be the pressures for such changes? They are unlikely to be coming from the Westminster government, as planning is a devolved matter. It seems more likely that those pressures are appearing from outside the UK, through international bodies. The focus on housing in the UK is a constant pressure made by the EU and OECD, while the need to focus on cities and their role in the national economy is present in UN, EU and OECD initiatives. The OECD is also focussing on the benefits of vertical and horizontal integration between places in order to be able to maximise the benefits of investment and reduce the disbenefits of policy and delivery contestations (Charbit and Romano 2017).

Cook and Clifton (2005 p445) argue that Scotland has been more visionary in its economic policy and with the focus on knowledge being exported and coming into Scotland as main considerations.

References

Adams, D. (2015). Urban land reform briefing paper no 7: Response to Scottish Government report to its Land Reform Review Sounding Board on its recent housing and regeneration consultation. https://policyscotland.gla.ac.uk/wp-content/uploads/2015/11/ulrbp7-response-to-sounding-board-report1.pdf (accessed 9 July 2018).

Adams, N. (2008). Convergence and policy transfer: An examination of the extent to which approaches to spatial planning have converged within the context of an enlarged EU. *International Planning Studies*, 13(1), 31–49.

Allmendinger, P. (2001). The head and the heart: National identity and urban planning in a devolved Scotland. *International Planning Studies*, 6(1), 33–54.

Allmendinger, P. M. (2006). Escaping policy gravity: the scope for distinctiveness in Scottish spatial planning. In M. Tewdwr-Jones & P. M. Allmendinger (Eds.), *Territory, Identity and Spatial Planning: Spatial Governance in a Fragmented Nation* (pp. 153–166). Abingdon: Routledge.

Bailey, N., & Turok, I. (2001). Central Scotland as a polycentric urban region: Useful planning concept or chimera? *Urban Studies*, 38(4), 697–715.

Beveridge, C., Biberbach, P., & Hamilton, J. (2016) *Empowering Planning to Deliver Great Places: An Independent Review of the Scottish Planning System*. Edinburgh: Scottish Government.

Bradley, Q., Burnett, A., & Sparling, W. (2017). Neighbourhood planning and the spatial practices of localism. In S. Brownill & Q. Bradley (Eds.), *Localism and Neighbourhood Planning: Power to the People?* (pp. 57–74). Bristol: Policy Press.

CEC (1999). *European Spatial Development Perspective*. Brussels: CEC.

CEC (2015). *Scenarios for Integrated Territorial Investments*. Brussels: CEC.

CEC (2016). *Urban agenda for the EU*. Brussels: CEC. https://ec.europa.eu/futurium/en/urban-agenda-eu/what-urban-agenda-eu (accessed 10 July 2018).

Charbit, C., & Romano, O. (2017). Governing Together: An International Review of Contracts Across Levels of Government for Regional Development. OECD Regional Development Working Papers, 2017/04. Paris: OECD.

Clifford, B., & Morphet, J. (2015). A policy on the move? Spatial planning and state actors in the post-devolutionary UK and Ireland. *The Geographical Journal*, 181(1), 16–25.

Clydeplan (2017). Strategic development plan. www.clydeplan-sdpa.gov.uk/strategic-development-plan/current-plan/current-strategic-development-plan-july-2017 (accessed 19 August 2018).

Cooke, P., & Clifton, N. (2005). Visionary, precautionary and constrained 'varieties of devolution'in the economic governance of the devolved UK territories. *Regional Studies*, 39(4), 437–451.

Dühr, S., Colomb, C., & Nadin, V. (2010). *European Spatial Planning and Territorial Cooperation*. Abingdon: Routledge.

Fenwick, J., Miller, K. J., & McTavish, D. (2012). Co-governance or meta-bureaucracy? Perspectives of local governance 'partnership' in England and Scotland. *Policy & Politics*, 40(3), 405–422.

Glasson, J., & Marshall, T. (2007). *Regional Planning*. London: Routledge.

Halden, D. (2002). *City Regions Boundaries Study*. Edinburgh: Scottish Executive.

Keating, M. J. (2010). *The Government of Scotland: Public Policy Making after Devolution*. Edinburgh: Edinburgh University Press.

Keating, M., Cairney, P., & Hepburn, E. (2009). Territorial policy communities and devolution in the UK. *Cambridge Journal of Regions, Economy and Society*, 2(1), 51–66.

Lloyd, M. G. (1997). Structure and culture: regional planning and institutional innovation in Scotland. In R. MacDonald & H. Thomas (Eds.), *Nationality and Planning in Scotland and Wales* (pp. 113–132). Cardiff: University of Wales Press.

Lloyd, M.G., & Peel, D. (2009). New labour and the planning system in Scotland: An overview of a decade. *Planning, Practice & Research*, 24(1), 103–118.

Lloyd, M.G., & Purves, G. (2009). Identity and territory. The creation of a national planning framework for Scotland. In S. Davoudi and I. Strange (Eds.), *Conceptions of Space and Place in Strategic Spatial Planning* (pp. 71–94). Abingdon: Taylor and Francis.

McGuinness, D., Greenhalgh, P., & Pugalis, L. (2015). Is the grass always greener? Making sense of convergence and divergence in regeneration policies in England and Scotland. *The Geographical Journal*, 181(1), 26–37.

Meyer-Sahling, J. H., & Goetz, K. H. (2009). The EU timescape: from notion to research agenda. *Journal of European Public Policy*, 16(2), 325–336.

Morphet, J. (2013). *How Europe Shapes British Public Policy*. Bristol: Policy Press.

Morphet, J. & Clifford, B. (2017). *Infrastructure Delivery: The DCO Process in Context Main Report. June*. London: NIPA Insights. www.nipa-uk.org/uploads/news/(UCL)_Morphet_and_Clifford_-_NIPA_Main_Report_-_June_2017.pdf (accessed 9 July 2018).

Morphet, J., & Clifford, B. (2018). 'Who else would we speak to?' National Policy Networks in post-devolution Britain: The case of spatial planning. *Public Policy and Administration*, 33(1), 3–21.

Murray, K. (2014). *Review of the Strategic Development Plans in Scotland*. Edinburgh: Scottish Government. http://kevinmurrayassociates.com/wp-content/uploads/2014/04/ Slide1.jpg (accessed 10 July 2018).

ODPM (2005). *Planning Policy Statement 1: Delivering Sustainable Development*. London: Office of the Deputy Prime Minister.

Pemberton, S. (2017). Community-based planning and localism in the devolved UK. In S. Brownill and Q. Bradley (Eds.), *Localism and Neighbourhood Planning: Power to the People?* (pp. 183–198). Bristol: Policy Press.

Quartermain, S. (2018). The Government's Agenda for Planning. Speech to the National Planning Forum, March 20, Dentons, London.

Scottish Enterprise (2006). *Scottish Enterprise Operating Plan 2006–2009*. Glasgow: Scottish Enterprise.

Scottish Executive (2002). *Review of Scotland's Cities: The Analysis*. Edinburgh: Scottish Executive.

Scottish Executive (2009). *Edinburgh National Planning Framework 2*. Edinburgh: Scottish Government.

Scottish Government (2009). *Scottish Planning Series: Planning Circular 1 2009: Development Planning*. Edinburgh: Scottish Government. www.gov.scot/Publications/2009/ 02/13153723/0 (accessed 19 July 2018).

Scottish Government (2016). *Scotland's Agenda for Cities*. Edinburgh: Scottish Government.

SES (2016). *Proposed Strategic Development Plan*. www.sesplan.gov.uk/proposed-sdp -2016.php (accessed 10 July 2018).

Scottish Government (2018). Planning and architecture. https://beta.gov.scot/policies/pla nning-architecture/overseeing-planning-system/ (accessed 19 July 2018).

Sinclair, S. (2008). Dilemmas of community planning: Lessons from Scotland. *Public Policy and Administration*, 23(4), 373–390.

Sturzaker, J., & Shaw, D. (2015). Localism in practice: Lessons from a pioneer neighbourhood plan in England. *Town Planning Review*, 86(5), 587–609.

Wannop, U. A. (2014). *The Regional Imperative: Regional Planning and Governance in Britain, Europe and the United States*. London: Routledge.

Wilson, D., & Game, C. (2011). *Local Government in the United Kingdom*. Basingstoke: Palgrave Macmillan.

Further Reading

Aberdeen and Shire Strategic Development Planning Authority (2009). Aberdeen City and Shire Structure Plan, Aberdeen. www.aberdeencityandshire-sdpa.gov.uk/ (accessed 18 August 2018).

Allmendinger, P. (2003). Re-scaling, integration and competition: Future challenges for development planning. *International Planning Studies*, 8(4), 323–328.

Allmendinger, P., & Haughton, G. (2010). Spatial planning, devolution, and new planning spaces. *Environment and Planning C: Government and Policy*, 28(5), 803–818.

Allmendinger, P., Morphet, J., & Tewdwr-Jones, M. (2005). Devolution and the modernization of local government: Prospects for spatial planning. *European Planning Studies*, 13(3), 349–370.

Danson, M., & Lloyd, G. (2012). Devolution, institutions, and organisations: Changing models of regional development agencies. *Environment and Planning C: Government and Policy*, 30(1), 78–94.

Harkins, C., & Escobar, O. (2015). *Participatory Budgeting in Scotland: An Overview of Strategic Design Choices and Principles for Effective Delivery*. Glasgow: GCPH, WWS.

Lloyd, M. G., & Peel, D. (2005). Tracing a spatial turn in planning practice in Scotland. *Planning Practice & Research*, 20(3), 313–325.

Lloyd, M.G., & Peel, D. (2008). Reconstructing regional development and planning in Scotland and Wales. In J. Bradbury (Ed.), *Devolution, Regionalism and Regional Development: The UK Experience* (pp. 166–182). London: Routledge.

Lloyd, M. G., & Peel, D. (2012). Soft contractualism? Facilitating institutional change in planning and development relations in Scotland. *Urban Research & Practice*, 5(2), 239–255.

MacKinnon, D. (2015). Devolution, state restructuring and policy divergence in the UK. *The Geographical Journal*, 181(1), 47–56.

Morphet, J. (2010). Reflections on alterity in Irish and Scottish spatial planning: Fragmentation or fugue. *Journal of Irish and Scottish Studies*, 4(2), 173–204.

Morphet, J. (2011a). *Effective Practice in Spatial Planning*. Abingdon: Routledge.

Morphet, J. (2011b). Delivering infrastructure through spatial planning: The multi-scalar approach in the UK. *Local Economy*, 26(4), 285–293.

Peel, D., & Lloyd, G. (2007). Community planning and land use planning in Scotland: a constructive interface? *Public Policy and Administration*, 22(3), 353–366.

Pemberton, S., Peel, D., & Lloyd, G. (2015). The 'filling in'of community-based planning in the devolved UK? *The Geographical Journal*, 181(1), 6–15.

Purves, G. (2006). Quality and connectivity: The continuing tradition of strategic spatial planning in Scotland. In N. Adams, J. Alden, J. David, & N. R. Harris (Eds.), *Regional Development and Spatial Planning in an Enlarged European Union* (pp. 107–127). Aldershot: Ashgate.

Purves, G., & Lloyd, M. G. (2008). Identity and territory: The creation of a national planning framework for Scotland. In S. Davoudi and I. Strange (Eds.), *Conceptions of Space and Place in Strategic Spatial Planning* (pp. 86–109). Abingdon: Taylor and Francis.

9 Planning in Wales

Introduction

When devolution was first introduced in 1999, the Welsh Assembly had softer powers than those devolved to the Scottish Parliament. However, since the Government of Wales Act 2006, the Welsh Assembly Government (WAG) has had the power to promote sustainable development. The Welsh Assembly did not have law making powers until after the Silk Commission (Welsh Assembly Government 2012a), so, up to that point, planning powers in Wales were included alongside, although distinct from, planning powers for England in the same legislation. The Planning and Compulsory Purchase Act 2004 set out the powers for Wales and the approaches differed.

There had been considerable discussion in Wales, before devolution was implemented, about whether Wales would create a distinctively different system from that operating in England (Tewdwr Jones 2001). In practice the new planning system in Wales prioritised sustainability far more than either England, which remained focussed on housing, or Scotland, which had a strong preference for infrastructure. While in England spatial planning was introduced at the local level, in Wales it was introduced through the Wales Spatial Plan (WSP). At the same time, the LDP system remained very similar to that in England prior to the 2004 Planning and Compulsory Purchase Act. Wales was also included in the Planning Act 2008, which introduced NSIPs and CIL into the English planning system.

The Planning (Wales) Act was introduced in 2015 and provided separate legislation for planning. It created the legal basis for a new NPF and SDPs similar to the system in Scotland between 2003 and 2017. This legislation introduced a plan-led system that is described as being 'front loaded' in the same way as the one in England. The new planning system for Wales has similarities to that in Scotland, as LDPs in Wales are to be linked to wider public-sector providers and local priorities through the provisions of the Well Being of Future Generations (Wales) Act 2015. In this chapter the planning system in Wales is reviewed, first in the context of difference and then as the system has evolved to one of potential convergence.

National Planning in Wales

At the point of devolution, there were concerns about the fragmentation of spatial policy in the UK and the economic effects this might have. While there has never been a single spatial plan for the United Kingdom, the first planning priority in Wales, as in Scotland, was to prepare a plan for the whole of the nation. As Alden (1999) commented, the major concern was about the interlinkages between parts of the UK through the mechanisms of multi-level government. In practice, each UK nation developed a different set of scalar priorities in their approach to planning from 2000 onwards. Northern Ireland was the first to publish a significant regional plan (Morphet 2010). Wales focussed on sustainability in the WSP and Scotland on infrastructure, also at the national level. In England, after 2004, there was a focus on developing the local planning system. While the systems were divergent within an overall framework, Powell (2001) set out the ways in which officials between the four nations were working together to support common policy making.

Prior to devolution, the Welsh Office previously had limited numbers of staff and, consequently, there was a significant dependence on the Department of Environment, Transport and the Regions (DETR) in England for policy development lead (Powell 2001). Nevertheless, there were some distinctive elements to planning in Wales, such as a single consolidated document for land-use planning (Planning Guidance [Wales] Planning Policy 1996; updated 1999) (Welsh Assembly Government 1999). However, following devolution in 1999, the WAG decided that spatial planning was an important tool for its own work. In this respect, there was a commitment to more inclusive and speedier preparation of national planning guidance. Furthermore, it was announced in 'Better Wales' (National Assembly for Wales 1999) that a new spatial framework for planning in Wales was to be produced and framed by the ESDP. A further key driver was concern over the coordination of the spatial impacts of a range of sectoral policies (Harris and Hooper 2004).

While the WSP had a strong sustainable focus, the relationship between spatial planning and EU policy has always been present, particularly with the support provided for the Welsh economy. The interconnection between planning and economic policy and the role of planning as part of the redistributive mechanisms for investment were both underlying features and potential tensions in the system (Tewdwr Jones and Phelps 2000). The development of the WSP was consciously undertaken within the context of a newly devolved governance system that took the opportunity to align its national planning process with the approach for spatial planning emerging through the EU (Harris et al. 2002). The introduction of the ESDP (CEC 1999; Faludi 2004) was increasingly seen as underpinning EU policy, which had a spatial or territorial dimension. As a significant recipient of EU funding, Wales was concerned with ensuring that opportunities were maximised through the adoption of the spatial approaches that were epitomised in the ESDP. Following the introduction of the WAG in 1999, this became an early objective. Before devolution, the EU programmes directly associated with the

ESDP had been delivered through EU structural funding programmes, but following 2000, the evolution of a more widely integrated approach between EU spending programmes and spatial policy emerged, not least through a new policy of territorial cohesion. The development of the WSP was an opportunity to create a plan that had Wales as its focus and could identify its key vision for the future for Wales, identify where investment was required to deliver this investment and establish a new relationship with its stakeholders and partners in the process.

The development of the WSP was undertaken by the WAG through a stakeholder group. The Assembly was able to build on some existing institutional capacity within Wales but also to develop this further (Harris et al. 2002). At the same time, there was pressure to develop a distinctive 'Welsh way' of doing things. However, seen from the perspective of central government officials who remained in post over the transition to the Welsh government, even after devolution, Wales was seen to be heavily reliant on policy development and research commissioned by English departments of state (Powell 2001). This may not have been a popular view at the time and led to a more distinctive approach for a new plan for the nation.

So, if Wales wanted to introduce spatial planning at a national level, it would need to forge its own approach. In part, it looked to the other nations in the UK for examples (Morphet 2010). In Northern Ireland, there was seen to be a more spatial approach to planning, integrating economic development with infrastructure planning based on emerging EU models in the Baltic. There were also links with Scotland. Other models included Regional Planning Guidance in England, although this was undergoing a parallel process of reform. The Assembly commissioned research to identify the common components of spatial planning methodologies (Harris et al. 2002) to advise the process. Reviewing this with hindsight, the research does not contain any of the key features that would now distinguish a spatial planning approach – for example, integration, delivery and investment. However, although not operationalised into a methodology, the key identifying features were emerging, particularly through the recognition of the spatial consequences of policy making.

The objectives for Wales that were set by WAG after devolution were sustainable development, tackling social disadvantage and ensuring equal opportunity (Welsh Assembly Government 2000) and these were the focuses and drivers of the WSP. Harris et al. (2002 p563–564) described the functions of the first WSP as providing a spatial context for all policies in Wales and providing a means of assessing all policies in their process of consideration by the WAG. They went to describe the WSP as offering a strategic framework for investment and a means of expressing the differences and characteristics of the geographical areas within Wales. These purposes differed from any found in any English spatial plan at any scale.

The WSP was also seen as the 'spatial expression of the policies and programmes of the National Assembly of Wales and others' (Welsh Assembly Government 2001 p2). The WSP thus had a policy coordination role across other sectors, including transport, economy, environment, culture, etc. (Harris and Hooper 2004 p154). The development of the WSP drew on the policy documents and plans that had been prepared for Wales and developed a sub-national approach to policy development and delivery.

This approach is interesting in that it did not require that the WSP have a separate vision and agenda, but rather that it perform the role as a tool for spatial delivery. It also did not have its own evidence base but used that established for the Welsh Assembly. Thirdly, it introduced the concept of 'functional areas' – now more usually described as functional economic areas (FEAs), subsequently used as an institutional construct across other parts of the UK – to recognise the difference between administrative areas and those that work together through economic or environmental geography.

These functions and features of the WSP represented significantly different approaches that had not been used before in practice. As an innovative approach, the Assembly could argue that it had created a spatial plan that had a common use of evidence and represented existing places rather than creating a separate vision. As an innovative approach, the Assembly could argue that it had created a spatial plan that had a common use of evidence and represented existing places rather than creating a separate vision. These components represented essential components of spatial planning as a delivery mechanism. Further, the assessment of the spatial implications for policy and delivery was based on sustainable principles. The development for the WSP as a coordinating document initially relied upon the identification of explicit spatial elements of the other key plans and strategies. However, some of the key strategies had no spatial references and required an assessment of implicit spatial policies (Harris and Hooper 2004). This work extended to all the published plans and strategies, which helped to identify specific locational requirements for facilities, such as waste facilities and areas of spatial interest, such as rural areas and locations where specific investment was identified or proposed, particularly in the Plan for Wales (2001) (Harris and Hooper 2004).

In the 2015 Planning (Wales) Act, a National Development Framework (NDF) for Wales was introduced. This was a different concept from that of the WSP and has become a formal part of the development planning system. It also designated Developments of National Significance, which are like NSIPs in England and were formerly included in the 2008 Planning Act. The focus of the 2015 Act is on modernising the planning system and making it more effective and efficient through strengthening the role of the local plans within the context of the NDF and SDPs. Like the changes in the planning systems in Scotland, and before that, in England, it switches the planning focus to the provision of housing, together with jobs and infrastructure, as primary objectives for the planning system.

Planning for investment in infrastructure in Wales was undertaken through a process that was separate from the WSP (Welsh Assembly Government 2012). Unlike infrastructure planning in Scotland and England, the Welsh approach included social and community infrastructure in addition to transport and environmental projects. In this investment plan, subsequently updated in 2015, there was an assessment of specific projects as well as commentary on different sectors. There was also a commitment to engagement from the community and an identification of the mechanisms for project delivery. In 2017, the Welsh government introduced a new Mutual Investment Model (MIM) for projects, which shares the costs between the government and the private sector, and the first projects have been for schools, health and transport. The scheme appears to be similar to those used by the UK government through the private finance initiative (PFI) and are set within EU rules for public–private partnerships (PPPs) (Ashurst 2017), where risks are shared between the government and the contractor (Bing et al. 2005). Experience in the use of the PFI and PPPs has been variable within the UK and the National Audit Office in England has found that projects can only be successful and provide value for money where there is a strong client (NAO 2011), so this may be a significant issue in future delivery in Wales.

The Planning (Wales) Act 2015 did not lose the link with the former focus on sustainability and the WAG published a diagram that demonstrates how the spatial planning system will deliver sustainability through complementary legislation of the Well Being of Future Generations (Wales) Act 2015 and the Environment (Wales) Act 2016. Planning policy and practice in Wales are supported by a national research programme, which is commissioned to investigate approaches to policies before they are implemented. At the national scale, research was undertaken to identify what the thresholds for Developments of National Significance should be, with a focus on the development of infrastructure that is typical in Wales, such as open cast mining (Welsh Assembly Government 2017).

Sub-National Planning

The WSP (2004) provided for sub-regional planning that included Assembly members as well as local authorities and other interests in the areas that were identified in the plan. As a 20-year vision, the WSP emphasised inter-sectoral delivery and interrelationships between all policies that have spatial implications. It also created a new sub-national geography and focussed on six sub-regions of Wales, recognising the role of multi-level government and the vertical integration of policies and proposals between the national, sub-regional and local levels. The sub-regional scale was identified in the WSP with emphasis on its governance, through the presence of Welsh Assembly members and civil servants of each sub-national board. This enshrined a 'top–down' direction within the sub-regional areas set out through the strategic visions included in the WSP.

In practice, although the six areas identified set out a strategic vision, their boards met rarely and, in some cases, do not appear to have met at all. While Allmendinger et al. (2010) define this as useful uncertainty to change the spatial conceptualisation of Wales, these defined areas appear to be top–down, institutional constructions on which to create FEA governance, as in England and Scotland, or local government reorganisation to a smaller number of local authorities. They have been an attempt to promote change but, in effect, they have been paper exercises that have not delivered a strategic approach but rather a nudged compliance through the framework of the WSP (Heley 2013).

In 2011, the Welsh government instituted a review of city regions in Wales (Haywood 2012). The report found that the three major city regions in Wales were underperforming economically in comparison with other city regions in the UK and needed a specific policy focus if they were to address these issues. The report recommended that having an integrated approach to planning would help to improve connectivity and create a more secure platform for investment. The report further recommended that housing should be considered within the city region rather than at the local level. The report also drew attention to governance models in other cities, including Vancouver and Edinburgh. There was also a recommendation to establish an integrated passenger transport authority that would support the economic growth objectives and there had already been earlier proposals for this approach to improve economic and transport links (Barry 2011).

In response to the Haywood Report, the Welsh government announced in 2013 that it intended to adopt the same model of strategic planning as Scotland, with specific planning frameworks and a legal backing. The Planning (Wales) Act 2015 replaced the existing six sub-regional areas that had been defined with the legal frameworks provided through the Strategic Planning Areas (SPAs). Before implementing these areas, the Welsh government commissioned research into the methods that should be used to identify these strategic areas (Healy et al. 2015). Minsters were enabled to define the SPAs and then appoint a planning board to prepare a plan in these areas, which are required to comprise at least one local authority and at least part of a second local authority. However, there is an expectation that while minsters will designate the areas, the request to do so will come from the locality – that is, from the bottom up – in a way like that used in England to progress the nudged establishment of combined authorities (Townsend 2017). As part of the process, the local authorities must identify why an SPA is required and what its benefits will be – similar again to the cases that had to be made for CAs in England.

In this research study, four thresholds were identified that could be used to assist in identifying the SPAs:

1   What are the areal units that you will use to designate the eventual boundaries?
2   What thresholds are to be used to determine whether an area should be included in a strategic planning area or omitted?
3   What weight is to be given to the choice between balance and concentration?
4   A choice may also need to be made regarding the extent to which the boundaries reflect desired outcomes, rather than simply respond to existing patterns of activity (Healy et al. 2015 p5).

The final major determining point identified by Healy et al. is the political decision that will be made and it appears that the threshold questions set out in the report will act as a technical mechanism. However, it is unclear whether these will be sufficient to overcome the political networks and existing local spatial relationships expressed through transport and other cultural connections. In establishing a technical approach to the definition of these area, there are key issues about whether they should be economic or environmental in their character. If the journey to work area is a primary defining concept, then a city region may be the outcome. On the other hand, taking a balanced and polycentric approach may be more suitable for rural areas. The report does not suggest one approach over another and, in allowing for the possibility of differing styles of SPAs, has offered its own flexibilities that will suit government decision making.

This research was taken into consideration during the preparation of the Planning (Wales) Act 2015, which then introduced a power that allowed the government to designate SPAs with strategic planning panels comprised of local authority members for the local authorities included in these locations. These seem very similar, though, to those areas established under the WSP. If a strategic planning panel is established in an area, then an SDP will be prepared that will cover cross-border areas within the SPA, including transport and housing, and will be part of the formal development plan. The Welsh government has indicated that there might only be two or three of those SPAs in Wales and not all areas will be included. However, at the same time, the Welsh government has announced its intention to reduce the number of local authorities in Wales from 22 to eight or nine, and, as Winter (2016) states, if this proposal is implemented, then there may be less need for SPAs, although this may depend on their ultimate role and purpose. SPAs may also be used to combine groups of these new local authorities together into three sub-regions in Wales.

However, a major issue that needs to be considered, given the slow progress to develop integrated spatial planning approaches in the six areas identified in the WSP, is what will encourage or incentivise local authorities to take this approach. As Heley et al. (2013) demonstrate, differing definitions can be used for the same place – so, for example, in Swansea, there could be a city region focussing on the economy or there could be a Swansea Bay area focussing on its environmental unity. There are also considerations about who defines the issues facing sub-national economies and has the capacity to act in these settings that will make some difference. As Bristow and Healy (2015) demonstrate, there are also issues of dependency on the national government to provide more funding to address economic decline, rather than the resilience of agency to attempt to make self-directed change within the sub-region. While the institutional actors within sub-regions, including the public and private sectors, can learn to work together, it is unclear whether this is within the commitment to a local framework and action plan or whether it is a nudged compliance to demonstrate commitment that will in turn produce national financial support.

At the same time as the development of SPAs, City Deals were introduced into Wales. These are supported by the UK government despite dealing with policy issues that have been devolved. Like the changes in the Planning (Wales) Act 2015, City Deals are also anchored in the Haywood Report (Welsh Assembly Government 2012c). In addition to strategic planning reforms, the report made several recommendations around the development of skills, infrastructure and innovation. The Haywood Report also argued that establishing city regions would mean working together and that individual local authorities would have to cede some of their powers if they were to make any gains from joint working. The city region in the Valleys area of South East Wales was primarily based on the transport system, which could improve connectivity and access to jobs (Barry 2011). However, there was no specific reference to either city – Newport and Cardiff – in that area. Further recommendations were made for the Dee Merseyside partnership to be strengthened. Other institutional recommendations were addressed to reducing the skills gap, involving universities and establishing public transport executives to integrate transport planning and delivery. There was also a nod towards promoting sustainability. Finally, the report was open on the governance arrangements, which it considered could be determined locally.

While the context for this review lies within the wider urban agenda that was being developed though the OECD and the UN for Habitat III in Quito in 2016, the main driver was encouraging public bodies in Wales to organise in order to maximise the beneficial outcomes they could generate from the next round of EU cohesion programmes, which commenced in 2014. To achieve this, there needed to be more devolution to local authorities (CEC 2013) although up to this point there had been reluctance to further devolve more powers and funding from the Welsh government. There was a prevailing view that devolution from Whitehall to Cardiff meant that no further devolution was required but through the EU cohesion regulation (CEC 2013) and the subsequent partnership agreement that UK made changed this. So, in creating larger units of government, there were opportunities for both more strategic approaches to cohesion delivery and the maintenance of government influence over the programmes and projects selected.

The nudged, bottom-up compliance was reinforced through city and growth deals provided by the UK government. In November 2017, the National Assembly for Wales's Economy, Infrastructure and Skills Committee produced a scrutiny report on the economic regions in Wales. These have now been operationalised as four regions. Around Cardiff, ten local authorities were awarded a City Deal in 2016 (the Cardiff Capital Region [CCR] City Deal) and the four authorities around Swansea had a similar deal in 2017 (the Swansea Bay City Deal). These two regions set up informal governance arrangements to bid for these deals. These are now being translated into formal regional boards, although there have been concerns expressed about their membership and transparency (NAW 2017). A deal for North Wales was agreed in December 2017 (HMG 2017) and an expression of interest in a fourth deal for Mid Wales has been registered. In the 2017 Budget, the Chancellor of the Exchequer announced that the whole of Wales could be covered with deals (HMT 2018). It is uncertain whether such an approach has been proposed to support the final delivery of the EU 2014–2020 cohesion programme prior to Brexit or whether this is a post-Brexit measure to support local economies. It may be both. There has also been silence on the link between these deals, local government reorganisation and SPAs.

The CCR City Deal is a quasi-contract between the local authorities, UK central government and the Welsh government. It provides funding to improve local transport infrastructure and interoperability by establishing a non-statutory regional transport authority. It also includes commitments to improve skills, enterprise, growth and housing. However, the ten local authorities will be expected to fund the investment programme through their own borrowing although the local authorities have also requested some additional borrowing flexibilities, including the retention of business rates. While the CCR is run by the elected councillors from the local authorities, it is appointing a Regional Economic Partnership Growth Board to advise it. The Swansea Bay City Deal covers four local authority areas and is described as creating an internet coast. It is managed by the local authorities in conjunction with the Welsh and UK governments as a joint committee of local authorities.

Thus, at sub-regional level within Wales, there are a number of overlapping and potentially integrated initiatives. The role of the SPAs with their boards may be responsible for City Deals or they both may be led by new groupings of larger local authorities, once reorganised. With so much potential uncertainty at the local and sub-regional tiers of governance, progress may be slow. However, it also appears that structures that are potentially similar to CAs in England could be emerging in Wales and Scotland in a form of nudged local government reorganisation. While planning has been recognised as an important component in achieving these spatially integrated approaches to sub-regions, the City Deals take the more English view that planning has to be managed rather than harnessed to achieve the changes required.

Local Development Planning

Since the 2004 Planning and Compulsory Purchase Act, local authorities in Wales were required to prepare LDPs. These plans are examined and assessed against tests of soundness in a similar way to those in England. However, the WAG has powers, in relation to the local plans, which include the abilities to call in the plan and direct two or more local authorities to work together on a plan.

Planning Policy Wales (Welsh Assembly Government 2016) sets the context of the LDP as being part of the local wellbeing plan that must be prepared for each local authority as set out in the Well Being of Future Generations Act 2015. The LDP therefore does not sit within policy isolation but performs the same kind of role as the WSP in acting as a spatial representation of public policy. The Well Being of Future Generations Act provides a means for organisations to work together for the benefit of local people in local authority areas. This approach is more meaningful than the duty to cooperate in England and is similar to the approach that was in practice in Scotland through community planning. Its English equivalent is the wellbeing strategy, but this does not include requirements for the local organisations to work together, nor for the local plan to work within it. In reviewing the relationship between wellbeing and spatial planning in Wales, Jones and Spence (2017) have identified it as a significant component of place planning, which includes commitments from local authorities. This approach includes commitments to prevention of harmful change and long-term outcomes as well as collaboration, integration and involvement.

In 2015, the Welsh government published a manual to support the process of preparing LDPs although it was not government guidance. This manual follows the changes that were introduced into the Welsh planning system in the Planning (Wales) Act 2015. While the manual includes a delivery agreement, this is taken to be the delivery of the production of the plan, not the delivery of the content of the plan, which is the case elsewhere in the UK. However, the manual states that the plan has to be capable of implementation. Much of this implementation approach is related to managing the negative effects of development and mitigation. It also approaches the delivery of the plan as being primarily the responsibility of others, rather than that of the local authority adopting the plan.

Community Planning

Community planning in Wales has been associated, as in Scotland, with modernisation and improvement in the public sector (Pemberton 2017) and was closer to the model of English system of community strategies introduced in 2000. However, in the Planning (Wales) Act 2015, there is a new provision for place plans as supplementary planning guidance to be prepared by town and community councils in conjunction with local authorities. Place plans are similar to community plans in Scotland, in that they are required to focus on locations that are in need of specific attention rather than more affluent places, as is the case in England (Bradley et al. 2017). Place plans are intended to be a bridge between the LDP and the wellbeing plan in specific locations, so that the aspirations of the place can be located in evidence and delivered through the LDP. As with neighbourhood plans in England, there is a strong local authority involvement but there are also opportunities for town and community councils to take a lead. In Wales, the parallel preparation with the LDF means that the place plan can be used for consultation and engagement but also to inform the local authorities of the priorities for a specific settlement.

While there is strong central support from the Welsh government for place plans, Bishop (2017) proposes that there should be guidance or a manual to assist those preparing these plans. Bishop also bases his views on experience from England, preparing parish and neighbourhood plans over many years.

Design Council Wales has prepared a 'Shape My Town' toolkit that is available to groups that suggest design guidance. This toolkit seeks to bring together and integrate wellbeing and active travel issues with the place plan and ensure that they are considered in a common way. This means that, unlike neighbourhood plans, the health objectives can be incorporated in the place plan form the outset in a more integrated way (Jones and Spence 2017).

The role of place plans and neighbourhood plans in Wales and England differ. In Wales, place plans are designated as supplementary planning guidance, as 'a means of setting out more detailed thematic or site specific guidance on the way in which the policies of an LDP are to be interpreted and applied in particular circumstances or areas' (Welsh Assembly Government 2015 p21). In England, neighbourhood plans must be aligned with the local plan and form part of it for determining planning decisions.

References

Adams, N. (2008). Convergence and policy transfer: An examination of the extent to which approaches to spatial planning have converged within the context of an enlarged EU. *International Planning Studies*, 13(1), 31–49.

Alden, J. (1999). Scenarios for the future of the British planning system: The need for a national spatial planning framework. *Town Planning Review*, 70(3), 385–407.

Allmendinger, P., Haughton, G., Counsell, D., & Vigar, G. (2010). *The New Spatial Planning*. Abingdon: Routledge.

Ashurst (2017). A new model for Welsh infrastructure: 'MIM's the word!' *Infraread*, 3 October. www.ashurst.com/en/news-and-insights/insights/mutual-investment-model/ (accessed 1 January 2018).

Barry, M. (2011). *Metro for Wales' Capital City Region, A-Connecting Cardiff, Newport and the Valleys*. Cardiff: Institute of Welsh Affairs. www.iwa.wales/news/2011/02/a-metro-for-wales-capital-city-region-3/ (accessed 9 July 2018).

Bing, L., Akintoye, A., Edwards, P. J., & Hardcastle, C. (2005). The allocation of risk in PPP/PFI construction projects in the UK. *International Journal of Project Management*, 23(1), 25–35.

Bishop, J. (2017). Place plans in Wales. Presentation to Planning Aid Wales Conference, 7 February. www.planningaidwales.org.uk/place-plans-rolling-out-the-concept-2/?lang=en (accessed 10 July 2018).

Bradley, Q. (2017). Neighbourhood planning and the impact of place identity on housing development in England. *Planning Theory & Practice*, 18(2), 233–248.

Bristow, G., & Healy, A. (2015). Crisis response, choice and resilience: Insights from complexity thinking. *Cambridge Journal of Regions, Economy and Society*, 8(2), 241–256.

CEC (1999). *European Spatial Development Perspective*. Brussels.

CEC (2013). Regulation (EU) No 1301/2013 of the European Parliament and of the Council of 17 December 2013 on the European Regional Development Fund and on specific provisions concerning the investment for growth and jobs goal and repealing Regulation (EC) No 1080/2006. www.jobsandgrowthni.gov.uk/regulations/regulation-title-2 (accessed 5 July 2018).

Cole, A. (2013). *Beyond Devolution and Decentralisation: Building Regional Capacity in Wales and Brittany*. Manchester: Manchester University Press.

Faludi, A. (2004). Territorial cohesion: Old (French) wine in new bottles? *Urban Studies*, 41(7), 1349–1365.

Harris, N. (2006). Increasing and spreading prosperity: Regional development, spatial planning and the enduring 'prosperity gap' in Wales. In N. Adams & J. Alden (Eds.), *Regional Development and Spatial Planning in an Enlarged European Union* (pp. 87–106). London: Routledge.

Harris, N., & Hooper, A. (2004). Rediscovering the 'spatial' in public policy and planning: an examination of the spatial content of sectoral policy documents. *Planning Theory & Practice*, 5(2), 147–169.

Harris, N., & Thomas, H. (2009). Making Wales: spatial strategy making in a devolved context. In S. Davoudi and I. Strange (Eds.), *Conceptions of Space and Place in Strategic Spatial Planning* (pp. 43–70). Abingdon: Taylor and Francis.

Harris, N., Hooper, A., & Bishop, K. (2002). Constructing the practice of 'spatial planning': A national spatial planning framework for Wales. *Environment and Planning C: Government and Policy*, 20(4), 555–572.

Haywood, E. (2012). *City Regions Advisory Group*. Cardiff: Welsh Government.

Healy, A., Burgess, S., Webb, B., & Kazmierczak, A. (2015). Exploring methods for the identification of Strategic Planning Areas. Research report for the Welsh Government. Cardiff: University of Cardiff.

Heley, J. (2013). Soft spaces, fuzzy boundaries and spatial governance in post-devolution Wales. *International Journal of Urban and Regional Research*, 37(4), 1325–1348.

HMG (2017). Fuelling the momentum for a North Wales growth deal, 27 June. www.gov.uk/government/news/fuelling-the-momentum-for-a-north-wales-growth-deal (accessed 23 July 2018).

HMT (2018). Fuelling the momentum for a Mid Wales growth deal. Press notice, 16 March. www.gov.uk/government/news/fuelling-the-momentum-for-a-mid-wales-growth-deal (accessed 23 July 2018).

Jones, M., & Spence, A. (2017). Empowering local people through the planning process: The emerging practice of 'Place Planning' and its contribution to community well-being in Wales. In L. Brotas, S. Roaf, & F. Nicol (Eds.), *Design to Thrive* (pp. 4493–4500). Edinburgh: Network Comfort and Energy Use in Buildings. http://eprints.uwe.ac.uk/32988 (accessed 9 July 2018).

Jones, R., Goodwin, M., Jones, M., & Pett, K. (2005). Filling in 'the state: Economic governance and the evolution of devolution in Wales. *Environment and Planning C: Government and Policy*, 23(3), 337–360.

Lloyd, G., & Peel, D. (2008). Reconstructing regional development and planning in Scotland and Wales. In J. Bradbury (Ed.), *Devolution, Regionalism and Regional Development: The UK Experience* (pp. 166–182). London: Routledge.

Morphet, J. (2010). *Effective Practice in Spatial Planning*. Abingdon: Routledge.

NAO (2011). *Lessons from PFI and Other Projects*. London: NAO.

National Assembly for Wales (1999). *Better Wales*. Cardiff: NAW.

National Assembly for Wales (2017). *City Deals and the Regional Economies of Wales Economy, Infrastructure and Skills Committee Report November*. Cardiff: NAW.

Pemberton, S. (2017). Community-based planning and localism in the devolved UK. In S. Brownill and Q. Bradley (Eds.), *Localism and Neighbourhood Planning: Power to the People?* (pp. 183–198). Bristol: Policy Press.

Powell, K. (2001). Devolution, planning guidance and the role of the planning system in Wales. *International Planning Studies*, 6(2), 215–222.

Rees, T., & Chaney, P. (2011). Multilevel governance, equality and human rights: Evaluating the first decade of devolution in Wales. *Social Policy and Society*, 10(2), 219–228.

Tewdwr Jones, M. (2001). Planning and the National Assembly for Wales: Generating distinctiveness and inclusiveness in a new political context. *European Planning Studies*, 9(4), 553–562.

Tewdwr Jones, M., & McNeill, D. (2000). The politics of city-region planning and governance: Reconciling the national, regional and urban in the competing voices of institutional restructuring. *European Urban and Regional Studies*, 7(2), 119–134.

Tewdwr Jones, M., & Phelps, N. A. (2000). Levelling the uneven playing field: Inward investment, interregional rivalry and the planning system. *Regional Studies*, 34(5), 429–440.

Townsend, A. (2017). Combined authorities – where next? *Town and Country Planning*, September, 343–353.

Welsh Assembly Government (1999). *Planning guidance (Wales) planning policy 1996. Updated 1999*. Cardiff: Welsh Assembly Government.

Welsh Assembly Government (2000). *Wellbeing in Wales Consultation Document*. Cardiff: Welsh Assembly Government.

Welsh Assembly Government (2001). *Wales Spatial Plan*. Cardiff: Welsh Assembly Government.

Welsh Assembly Government (2012a). *Report of the Silk Commission on Devolution in Wales*. Cardiff: Welsh Government.

Welsh Assembly Government (2012b). *Wales Infrastructure Investment Plan for Growth and Jobs*. Cardiff: Welsh Government.

Welsh Assembly Government (2012c). *City regions review report*. Cardiff: Welsh Government. https://gov.wales/docs/det/publications/120710-city-regions-final-report-en.pdf (accessed 10 July 2018).

Welsh Assembly Government (2016). *Place Plans Pilot Projects Proposal*. Cardiff: Welsh Government. https://gov.wales/about/cabinet/decisions/previous-administration/2016/jan-mar/planing1/cs0840/?lang=en (accessed 10 July 2018).

Welsh Assembly Government (2017). *Research into the Thresholds and Criteria for Development of National Significance in Wales Final Report*. Cardiff: Welsh Government.

Winter, G. (2016). Comparison of the planning systems in the four UK countries. Research paper.Cardiff: National Assembly for Wales.

10 Planning in Northern Ireland

Introduction

In Northern Ireland, until 2015, planning was primarily undertaken by central government, with responsibility for planning policy, local plans and development management. This chapter will discuss the continuing role of central government in strategic planning and policy and local planning in the new local authorities that have been established following the Review of Public Administration (RPA) (Knox and Carmichael 2006). It will also consider the relationship to wider strategic planning approaches emerging between Northern Ireland (Murray 2004) and the island of Ireland's spatial planning initiative (Peel and Lloyd 2015).

The development of planning in Northern Ireland has been contextualised by the peace agenda since the Good Friday Agreement (GFA) (often known as the Belfast Agreement) in 1998. The planning framework has been set by this wider political agenda, which has influenced planning at all spatial scales. The GFA and the associated EU PEACE programmes, which started in 1989 and have continued since, have had a considerable influence on the way in which planning is conducted and the key locations identified for growth. The GFA has also led to operational agreements for spatial planning across the island of Ireland, where there are key issues for the planning and provision of inter-connecting infrastructure and utility services as well as links between key functional economic areas (FEAs,) including the growth of the FEAs across the border (Blair et al. 2007).

The GFA led to the establishment of institutional arrangements for working across the United Kingdom and Ireland, which continue to play an important part in the continuing discussions and negotiations between the UK, the EU and Ireland (Taillon 2017). As part of the GFA, the British–Irish Council was established and this has subsequently introduced a series of working groups between members. The group on spatial planning was established at the suggestion of the Minister for Planning in Northern Ireland in 2009 and has developed a regular pattern of meetings where information is exchanged between the planning chiefs of each of the BIC member governments (Clifford and Morphet 2015a). Following the GFA, the introduction of Northern Ireland into the devolved settlement for the UK, through the St Andrews Agreement in 2006, has led eventually to a return to local authority local plan making and determination of planning applications in 2015.

Strategic Planning in Northern Ireland

It can be argued that Northern Ireland was the first part of the UK to develop a systematic approach to strategic planning. In the mid-1990s, a strategic plan was commenced that was proposed to cover the FEA of the Belfast City Region. However, the increasing development of regional planning within the EU together with the application of EU structural funds programmes in Northern Ireland from 1989–1999 (known as the PEACE I programme), led to a decision to broaden the scope of this strategic plan to cover the whole of the territory in a 'regional' plan and to expand its policy coverage to include regeneration and strategic infrastructure.

The development of a spatial planning approach in Northern Ireland was included in the GFA (1998). As Neill and Ellis (2008) state, 'the Agreement was novel in that for the first time, spatial planning was acknowledged as having a crucial and constitutionally recognised role in preparing the region for what was hoped to be an enduring peace' (2006, p. 133). It also represented a significant break with the planning processes, which up to that time had 'a long history of almost slavishly following policy practices in Britain' (McEldowney and Sterrett, 2001; 47), but as Morrissey and Gaffikin (2006) argue, in order to reshape the structural weaknesses in the economy and social distribution of services, a spatially led approach was appropriate.

However, some of the thinking in advancing a spatial planning approach to developing a programme for Northern Ireland had begun before this (Morphet 1996). Consideration of the emerging integrated approach to territorial cohesion and the wider changes in approaches to EU structural funding, of which the whole of Ireland had been a significant beneficiary, was a key stimulus. Changes in EU programmes were being implemented for urban and rural areas (Morphet 1998 p147), both of which would have significant implications for existing funding streams. The format of the plan was influenced by the developing pattern of plan making in other EU areas, influenced by the EU's policy publications, *Europe 2000* (1991) and *Europe 2000+* (1994). A more outward and networked approach to spatial planning was suggested, where the boundaries depended more on the economic and physical characteristics of Northern Ireland rather than the administrative boundaries. This approach had been applied at an early stage by the Baltic Sea meta-region (Baltic Sea Secretariat 1994; Nadin and Shaw 1998; Zaucha 1998), which had considered the whole of their area in terms of key components and challenges, commonly summarised as 'pearls' (successful economic and environmental locations), 'strings' (communications) and 'patches' (locations that were more challenged, such as those with high unemployment or specific issues, such as islands). These three challenges were aligned to EU and domestic spending programmes and with the delivery character of spatial planning.

Although the resulting Regional Development Strategy (RDS) in Northern Ireland, *Shaping our future* (2001), did not use the same nomenclature as the Baltic Sea plan, it was a key influence on its approach. By the time of its publication, a further element of commitment to commence some initiatives for cross-border planning liaisons were also made. The process of plan development and publication was led by the Department of Regional Development (DRD) and was focussed on locations for development, infrastructure and key nodes of economic activity, including the border area.

The development work on the RDS was also significantly and consciously informed by a spatial planning approach. It also represented an integrated approach in achieving a 'joined up governance' between three government departments (Berry et al., 2001, p.785). The development of the RDS was one of the first spatial planning documents to straddle the emerging relationship between the European Spatial Development Perspective (ESDP) and the EU's Structural Funds Programme (Neill and Gordon 2001), and there was always an intention to develop and establish a model for European 'good practice' in spatial planning.

The RDS was published in 2001 by the Department of Regional Development for Northern Ireland (DRDNI). The RDS was focussed on delivery at the regional and sub-regional levels, across a range of agencies and delivery vehicles. The sub-regional approach was devised to underpin the anticipated restoration of local government responsibilities for planning. This focus on delivery and shaping the funding that would be available in a cross sectoral way, integrating the range of a programmed investments for physical, social and economic change, fulfilled the spatial planning approach as identified in the GFA. The DRD leadership of the process emphasised, perhaps ten years before this occurred in England, the strong leading role of the economic component of the spatial plan.

The RDS was evidence-based and had a vision and a spatial strategy based on urban hubs, corridors, clusters and gateways. The process of developing the RDS was also highly participative, (Murray and Greer 2002; Murray 2009). It was also set within a sustainable, global-to-local context, the EU's institutional and within the a local social, economic and environmental context. The RDS related this spatial vision to the sub-regional level. Although geared towards implementation, the lack of a detailed implementation and delivery plan with identified funding, programmes and accountable delivery agencies might now be regarded as a weakness in the RDS, although the delivery element of the RDS was strong and well defined.

The examination of the RDS was through a public process that was themed and based on an inquisitorial approach rather than one that was adversarial. It also included a 'challenge' process by the panel examining the RDS (Murray and Greer 2002), which was put through the chair of the panel rather than through a cross examination of the participants in the process. As with RSSs in England, the RDS was subject to E iP as part of its process (Murray and Greer 2002), and so the influence of the RDS in the shaping of spatial planning processes at this scale continued.

The resources that were made available to implement the RDS were provided through the funding that was delivered through the EU in the Peace and Reconciliation Programme, including that funded by successive rounds of the

EU PEACE programme. This was initially established in 1987 but was boosted as part of the GFA. The approach within this EU funding package was through multiple steams of delivery. PEACE promoted cross-border working between Northern Ireland and Ireland and provided infrastructure investment, rural development and community-based projects at the local level. A cross-sectoral civic forum was established in Northern Ireland to manage and steer the processes of change and investment. This work continued with PEACE programmes that have continued within each subsequent EU cohesion programme. Much of the focus in each PEACE programme has been on community development and local decision making alongside major infrastructure investment and this has been considered to be one of its successes (Buchanan 2008).

Since its publication, the RDS has been the subject of a monitoring report each year with the first year's report entitled as the *First implementation and monitoring report September 2001–March 2003*. Subsequently, the implementation focus has been lost. where annual reporting have become outcome focussed assessments of progress against objectives and targets rather than of the delivery of components of the RDS. So, it is possible to assess the outcomes from the delivery of the RDS but not to view the extent to which it has been used as a means of sharing funding and investment decisions within Northern Ireland as a delivery programme.

In 2006, Northern Ireland became part of the devolved settlement of the UK through the St Andrews Agreement. This year also marked a shift in responsibilities for planning in central government. Up to this point, it had been led by the Department of the Environment (Northern Ireland) (DoENI), with the regional plan preparation led by the DRD. After 2007, the responsibility for planning was shared between three departments – DoENI, DRD and the Department of Sustainable Development (DSD) – and an independent planning appeals body was established.

There are various views of the success of the RDS, which Ellis and Neill (2006) believe has been greatly exaggerated. Their criticism relates to an initial 'optimism bias', which they see in the original document, and which, in their view, did not deal with the substantive issues for Northern Ireland in a fundamental way. As Berry et al. (2001) point out, there were tensions in central government. The three government departments that were brought together to create the RDS had, until just before this process, been part of the same department. There were potential issues of fragmentation and reforming, although the process was tied into to the wider delivery programmes of these new departments through their public service agreements. One of the key weaknesses, in hindsight, could be seen to be the lack of a more detailed delivery plan that identified which government department or agency had the responsibility for specific delivery (Berry et al. 2001). Murray (2009) has also argued that although a technically confident, positivist approach was taken, the RDS dealt less well with issues of 'identity, segregation, interconnections and potential' (p126).

An updated and revised version of the RDS was published, which carried forward the plan until 2035 (DRD 2012). This strategic plan for the whole of Northern Ireland identifies key urban metropolitan economic areas around Belfast and in the North West region. It also identifies a cross-border area with Ireland and includes key centres across the border as economic hubs as part of the network across the whole territory. Confusingly, the RDS identifies two tiers of policy guidance within it – that which covers the whole area and is called 'regional' and that which is tailored to the five elements of the spatial framework. The RDS continues to focus on nodes together with gateways and corridors, some of which have a specific economic role. The RDS identifies key locations for investment by both the private and public sectors and has a greater focus on infrastructure investment. It also has a key role as a planning policy document and contains strategic guidance for local development plans (LDPs). Local and other policy statements made by DOENI must be in conformity with it.

An investment strategy for Northern Ireland has also been published with an up-to-date pipeline report (Northern Ireland Executive 2011). This focusses on the key communications within Northern Ireland but also on some specific spatial regeneration projects, including the Titanic Quarter in Belfast and the UK City of Culture in Derry-Londonderry in 2013. While there are networks and communications projects, there is no cross reference, either to the RDS or to the national infrastructure programme, that has been developed by the UK government since 2010. However, there is mention of the funding for infrastructure provided through the UK government's block grant to Northern Ireland. There is no mention of European transport networks, policy or funding in the annual investment programme. The programme takes a wider approach than that in England and includes social and economic infrastructure for health, schools and skills (NI SIB 2011) in a way that is like the Wales Infrastructure Investment Plan (Welsh Government 2012). The infrastructure programme is managed by a strategic investment board that is a hybrid institution, described as a department of the Northern Ireland Executive and also as a company.

Cross-Border Planning

The GFA (1998) had three dimensions – one for internal governance, the second for relationships between the North and the South of the island of Ireland and the third between the Great Britain and Northern Ireland (Birrell 2012). The focus of the arrangements within the island of Ireland was on cross-border issues, particularly infrastructure that was subject to the oversight of the North–South Ministerial Council that was established. This is particularly an issue in the case of spatial planning and FEAs, as there are a number of city regions to be connected within the island of Ireland, including Belfast, Dublin and Cork together with a major FEA across the border, which has grown in importance and economic activity since 1999.

Since the GFA, there has been an increasing interest in planning for the whole of the island of Ireland, including where planning systems particularly come together in cross-border areas. Although the FEAs in the North – Belfast and Derry – and the South – Dublin, Cork and Limerick – are characterised by being city regions, the cross-border area is an active FEA but has no individual dominant settlement and movement patterns are through key transport crossings and corridors, particularly those by road. These have greatly expanded in number since the GFA and have important economic and social roles. Before, the number of road crossings of the border was restricted and had customs checks. The key border corridors are between Belfast and Dublin in the East and between Derry and Letterkenny in the North West. These two corridors are important in linking city regions. The FEA is structured by these corridors and the gateways that they pass through, which together make up the FEA. These gateways have also supported the development of changing housing markets in these border areas (Paris 2006).

The planning context for the border FEA is provided through two planning policy documents – the Border Regional Authority *Regional planning guidelines 2010–2022* (2010) in Ireland and the *Regional development strategy* (DRD 2001, 2012) in Northern Ireland. Both planning strategies from the North and South emphasise three key implementation priorities:

• Influencing capital investment within a spatial planning context;
• Supporting the gateways;
• Reforming the planning system to ensure horizontal and vertical consistency.

In these approaches, the Dublin–Belfast corridor has been identified as a mega-regional FEA (Cussen and Hetherington 2006; Walsh and Murray 2006). Murtagh and Shirlow (2012) argue that the potential for developing this corridor has been enhanced since devolution in Northern Ireland but that it has been delivered within a neo-liberal governance framework that would not have been possible before. The corridor has now become the area of fastest growth on the island of Ireland (Hughes 2015), with high levels of investment together with increased transport movements that have had wider spillover effects (Foley et al. 2017). However, it is not only in the Belfast–Dublin corridor that growth has been occurring, with other expansion noted in the North West between the cities of Derry and Donegal (Paris 2017).

These areas are also supported through a network of cross-border councils working through organisations such as the Ireland Central Border Area Network (ICBAN), one of three cross-border partnerships. The work of these partnerships is supported through EU INTERREG funding and through the work of the Centre for Cross Border Studies (CCBS). Spatial planning is recognised as one of the areas of cooperation in the ICBAN partnership, which is supported through the management board of the whole organisation together with a specific planners working group. The group is working on a spatial planning vision for the cross-border area and other issues being addressed include sustainability, telecoms and social inclusion (ICBAN nd). This spatial planning approach has also been supported by other cross-border work between communities. Cremer and O'Keefe (2016) illustrate the differences and distances that existed in cross-border interactions before the GFA and PEACE programmes and how this has been gradually changed through a range of approaches primarily supported by EU membership. However, the effects of the UK's EU Brexit referendum on cross-border working are considerable and are likely to frame much of the longstanding relationship that the EU has with the UK (Murphy 2016; CCBS 2017).

The FEA across the border in the island of Ireland is like the FEAs on mainland Europe, where collaborative approaches have also been supported by a specific EU initiative, the Transnational Operational Mission, which has been operating in six specific locations (Walsh and Knieling 2013) and which has been promoting transborder cooperation to support economic growth. The similarity between the new institutional arrangements within the island of Ireland since the Belfast Agreement in 1998, and particularly those for the North–South Ministerial Council (NSMC), have been likened to those of the EU by Tannam (2006), who argues that there are specific similarities in the arrangements.

These similarities in institutional arrangements are not identified as being *intentional* or replicating any specific EU institutions but rather based on lessons learned and policy transfer, for example, from other land borders within the EU, including France and Germany. Tannam goes on to state that the similarities between the operation of the NSMC and the EU are related to the cooperative working relationships between civil servants, which have been increased as a consequence of the implementation of EU cross-border programmes, which included six joint implementation bodies and six areas of cooperation, the latter of which included the environment. This work is also supplemented by cross-border units in each of the Irish government departments although not in the Northern Ireland government departments (Coakley, 2002). The NSMC secretariat has also acted as a means of communication on issues that may need to be resolved although there are no formal objectives to promote cooperation.

The British–Irish Council (BIC) was not developed in an equivalent form and has taken longer to develop an institutional character. Following the St Andrews Agreement on devolution (2006), the BIC took on a greater role. It had no permanent secretariat until 2012, although the BIC was hosted by the States of Jersey until then. After 2012, a new secretariat was formed, located in Edinburgh and staffed by secondees from the civil services of the BIC members. The BIC has also developed several specialist working groups, which have been established to explore common policy ground on a range of issues. One of these is specifically concerned with spatial planning.

In reviewing the work of the spatial planning task group of the BIC, Clifford and Morphet (2015a) found that there was a considerable exchange of ideas that, together with their conversations between bi-annual meetings, supported the development of a policy community between all the heads/deputy heads of planning in the four nations of the UK, Ireland, Jersey, Guernsey and the Isle of Man. In addition, a group of the heads of planning in the four UK nations and Ireland also meet regularly and there has been a considerable exchange of planners acting as advisers or in senior roles between the jurisdictions. These planners also share the political and practical issues in relation to the introduction of policy and the likely outcomes of such implementation. As a relatively small set of professionals in each of their respective administrations, the research found that the planners valued the opportunity to share issues and experience in this way; as one stated when asked about the value of the group to their work, 'who else would we speak to?' (Morphet and Clifford 2018).

Planning for the Island of Ireland

Any policy development and delivery for the island of Ireland includes both the governments of Ireland and the UK together with the Northern Ireland Assembly and any sub-state government that is involved in policy and delivery. Intertrade prepared an assessment of the mechanisms and benefits of collaborative action on spatial strategies for the island of Ireland (ICLRD 2006) although there was no immediate action taken. However, in 2011, these spatial planning frameworks and initiatives were set in the context of a consultation on a Framework of collaboration of spatial strategies for the island of Ireland (DRDNI and Department of the Environment Heritage and Local Government, Ireland 2011). This proposed framework was located within an EU territorial agenda (CEC 2011) and focussed on economic growth, which it expected to be promoted through collaboration in spatial planning. It also drew upon experience that had already been achieved through previous EU programmes. The proposed framework was concerned with strategies locations, corridors and energy networks. The proposed framework also built on the existing institutional governance networks between government departments and local and regional authorities that were already working together. ICLRD (Creamer, Keaveney and Blair 2011) also proposed a single monitoring framework for the island of Ireland to assess progress towards territorial cohesion, which fits within the wider monitoring framework of achieving the EU's objectives (Daly and González 2013).

Following consultation, the final version of the cooperation framework was published (DRD 2013). While the text focussed on the issues that were identified in the draft, a key focus was placed on continuing work of the border regions. There was also a consideration of the economic growth areas and of the environmental and sustainability issues in a way that suggested that all contributing government departments had their interests included. The framework also identified the objectives of working together on major infrastructure projects and establishing common monitoring arrangements. However, in the appendix, there is a list of all the EU legislation that is relevant to both jurisdictions and how this provides a platform for common working although this is not specifically addressed in the framework text.

A major consideration of this spatial planning approach for the island of Ireland is whether it is a soft or a transitional space. Walsh and Knieling (2013) argue that it is a soft space although there are several ways in which planning initiatives have been taken forward across the border, while Peel and Lloyd (2015) argue that this has been part of a process of spatial diplomacy. Another assessment of this approach is that it is a part of a process of transitional territorialism (Pemberton and Morphet 2014), which is a staging post to some firmer destination. One option for a stronger relationship between Northern Ireland and Ireland could be through the establishment of a European Grouping of Territorial Cooperation (EGTC) (CEC 2017; Clifford and Morphet 2015).

The New Local Planning Agenda

At the local level, the role of area, local and subject plans, which were introduced in 1972, continued, with the plans being prepared by DOENI, rather than by local authorities. Pressure for reform of the development planning system came following a report of the House of Commons Northern Ireland Affairs Committee, *The Planning System in Northern Ireland*, in 1996 (Cullingworth and Nadin 2006), but changes in response to this have been overtaken by the RPA. This was launched in 2002 with the objective of rescaling responsibilities within the state, including planning, and returning many functions to a newly established local government tier.

In Northern Ireland before 1973, planning powers were exercised by local authorities but after this date, they were brought into central government with an obligation to consult local authorities. Since then the exercise of all planning functions has been through central government with policy and local development management divisions of DoENI and this has operated as a single planning authority (McCandless, 2011).

At the local level, development planning in Northern Ireland had been largely unreconstructed from the model that was established in 1972, although recommendations were made for changes over time. However, following the publication of the RDS there was a growing recognition of the need for a relationship between the RDS and the use of the LDP as a delivery mechanism. The discontinuity between the RDS and the development plan system, particularly when making decisions on specific applications, came to a head in 2005, when a joint ministerial statement was issued between the DRD and DOENI. In this, the slow progress in reviewing the development plans was recognised as a threat to 'the successful implementation of the RDS' (para 16). As a result, the statement confirmed that decisions on planning applications would be made within the context of the RDS and that all development plans had to be in conformity with the RDS.

Much of the delay in the changes to the system has been dependent on the RPA, which commenced in 2002 and which focussed on the rescaling of responsibilities within Northern Ireland. A central feature of this has been the development of a new model of local government, delivered through 11 newly formed local authorities. Planning has always been a key component of these reforms, with the expectation that a new system would be delivered through the local authorities. In 2007, the Northern Ireland Assembly Government invited Greg Lloyd to provide advice to them on the reform of the land use planning system within Northern Ireland (Lloyd 2008).

The terms of reference for Lloyd's report and its subsequent recommendations did not suggest the wider introduction of spatial planning at the local level. Instead, it reaffirmed a separate land use planning system not connected with the wider planning and delivery responsibilities of the new local authorities when they are set up. Further, it proposed the insertion of a new regional tier of planning without any reference to the relationship with the RDS and it did not make these relationships clear. The consistent references to land use planning in Lloyd's report serves to identify its separation from a spatial planning approach that would be more integrated. Although development control is proposed to be changed into development management, it is not clear how its delivery role would be implemented. In Northern Ireland, for the time being at least, infrastructure planning is being conducted at a regional, i.e. national, scale and at the local level there is a reaffirmation of a separate traditional development planning system.

The ministerial response to Lloyd's paper moved planning closer to the spatial planning agenda at the local level. In the report Planning reform: emerging proposals (2008), one of the key purposes of the new local plan-led system is the co-ordination of public and private investment within the overall framework of supporting economic and social needs of communities within Northern Ireland. Like in Scotland, Wales and England, local authorities will have to produce and present a management scheme for LDP preparation and there will also be a statement of community involvement. The objectives of the new planning system are like those in Scotland, Wales and England, that is, to promote economic growth. The development planning and development management are now undertaken by the 11 new local authorities. Significant planning applications will be determined centrally in the same way as they are in Scotland and England and regional policy will also be retained, to be developed centrally.

The new approach to local development planning is focussed on speed and stakeholder engagement. A plan strategy will be developed in association with site -specific policies and proposals and these will be the two separate components of the LDP. Additionally, the development plan will be closely allied to the community plan developed by the district councils, like the approaches in Scotland and England. The role of the LDP in identifying and supporting delivery is contained in the functional objectives. The examination of the plan documents will move from an adversarial to an inquisitorial process and the plan will be examined against tests of soundness, with English and Welsh models being provided as examples (DOENI 2015 Annexes 4 and 5). The LDP will need to be in general conformity with regional policy although this is to be interpreted at the local level. It will also have a focus on delivery and be required to include measures for implementing the plan which can also include delivery agreements and master plans.

The Planning (Northern Ireland) Act 2011 set out the general requirements of the new local development system, which was followed by the Planning (Local Development Plan) Regulations (Northern Ireland) 2015. The structure of the LDP is in two parts, with the planning strategy being prepared and adopted first and then followed by the local policies plan. In these regulations, the ways in which the system is to be implemented were set out, including approaches to consultation and preparation of evidence and its use, in preparing the preferred options paper, which in turn forms the basis for the plan strategy. This has to contain the strategic vison and the strategic policies for meeting the objectives identified. The government later published guidance on the preparation and use of evidence in these processes (DOENI 2015).

In 2015, 11 new local authorities were formed, each with planning powers, while DOENI still described planning as a shared responsibility between local and central governments. The local development plans sit within the RDS (2012). Like in Scotland and Wales, and formerly in England, the LDP must take into account the local community plan, which is designed to promote the economic, social and environmental wellbeing of the area. The government is responsible for legislation, guidance and the strategic framework and while this is the case in the other nations of the UK, it is not elsewhere described as a shared responsibility. As Turley (2017) points out, for these new LDPs, this will be the first revision for a generation. The process of preparing LDPs in Northern Ireland is in its early stages. In Belfast, a preferred options paper for consultation was published in January 2017 and following a report on this consultation, the draft plan strategy will emerge.

References

Baltic Sea Secretariat (1994). *Vision 2010: The Baltic Sea Plan Towards a Framework for the Spatial Development of the Baltic Sea Region*. Karlskrona: Baltic Sea Secretariat.

Berry, J., Brown, L., & McGreal, S. (2001). The planning system in Northern Ireland post-devolution. *European Planning Studies*, 9(6), 781–791.

Birrell, D. (2012). *Comparing Devolved Governance*. London: Palgrave Macmillan.

Blair, N., Adair, A., & Bartley, B. (2007). Delivering cross border spatial planning: Proposal for the island of Ireland. *Town Planning Review*, 78(4), 485–509.

Border Regional Authority (2010). Regional planning guidelines 2010–2022. www.nwra.ie/wp-content/uploads/Planning-Guidelines-for-the-Border-Region.pdf (accessed 10 July 2018).

Buchanan, S. (2008). Transforming conflict in Northern Ireland and the border counties: Some lessons from the peace programmes on valuing participative democracy. *Irish Political Studies*, 23(3), 387–409.

CCBS (2017). Briefing paper 1: A roadmap. Brexit and the UK-Ireland border: A new briefing paper series. Armagh: CCBS.

CEC (2011). *Territorial Agenda Territorial Agenda of the European Union 2020*. Brussels: CEC.

CEC (2017). European groupings of territorial cooperation. https://portal.cor.europa.eu/egtc/Pages/welcome.aspx (accessed 2 January 2018).

Clifford, B., & Morphet, J. (2015a). A policy on the move? Spatial planning and state actors in the post-devolutionary UK and Ireland. *The Geographical Journal*, 181(1), 16–25.

Clifford, B. & Morphet, J. (2015b). The British–Irish Council: Political expedient or institution in waiting? *The Journal of Cross Border Studies in Ireland*, 10, 91–106.

Coakley, J. (2002). Religion, national identity and political change in modern Ireland. *Irish Political Studies*, 17(1), 4–28.

Creamer, C., Keaveney, K., & Blair, N. (2011). *Planning and governance reform: Implications for inter-jurisdictional planning in the island of Ireland*. Maynooth: ICLRD. http://iclrd.org/2011/10/14/planning-and-governance-reform-journal/ (accessed 10 July 2018).

Cremer, C., & O'Keeffe, B. (2016). Raising the emerald curtain: communities and collaboration along the Irish border. In C. Crowley and D. Linehan (Eds.), *Spacing Ireland: Place, Society and Culture in a Post-Boom Era* (pp. 58–72). Manchester, Manchester University Press.

Cullingworth, J. B., & Nadin, V. (2006). *Town and Country Planning in the UK* (14th edition). Abingdon: Routledge.

Cussen, N., & Hetherington, J. (2006). Implementing the National Spatial Strategy and the Regional Development Strategy for Northern Ireland within the Dublin–Belfast corridor. In J. R. Yarwood (Ed.), *The Dublin–Belfast Development Corridor: Ireland's Mega-City Region?* (pp. 29–44). Farnham: Ashgate Publishing, Ltd.

Daly, G., & González, A. (2013). Key indicators for territorial cohesion and spatial planning: The reform of EU cohesion policy and the new role of spatial indicators. *Borderlands Journal of Spatial Planning in Ireland*, 3, 77–89. http://iclrd.org/wp-content/uploads/2011/08/Borderlands-TerritorialCohesionKITCASP-DalyGonzalez.pdf (accessed 9 July 2018).

DOENI (2015). *Local Development Plans DOE Environmental Evidence and Information Version 1.1.* September. Belfast: DOENI. www.planningni.gov.uk/index/advice/northern_ireland_environment_agency_guidance/doe_environmental_evidence_and_information_final_pdf.pdf (accessed 9 July 2018).

DRD (2001). *Regional development strategy for Northern Ireland 2025*. Belfast: DRD.

DRD (2012). *Regional Development Strategy RDS 2035 Building a Better Future*. Belfast: DRD.

DRD, & Department of Environment Community and Local Government (2013). *Framework for Co-Operation Spatial Strategies of Northern Ireland & the Republic of Ireland*. Belfast: DRD.

DRDNI, & Department of the Environment Heritage and Local Government, Ireland (2011). Spatial strategies on the island of Ireland: Framework for collaboration consultation document. www.housing.gov.ie/sites/default/files/migrated-files/en/Publications/DevelopmentandHousing/Planning/NationalSpatialStrategy/FileDownLoad,25407,en.pdf (accessed 19 August 2018).

Ellis, G., & Neill, W. J. (2006). Spatial governance in contested territory: The case of Northern/North of Ireland. In M. Tewdwr Jones and P. Allmendinger (Eds.), *Territory, Identity and Spatial Planning* (pp. 147–162). Abingdon: Routledge.

Foley, W., Shahumyan, H., & Williams, B. (2017). Quantitative assessments of the spatial distribution of business clusters in Ireland. *International Journal of Business Intelligence and Data Mining*, 12(3), 211–235.

Hughes, B. (2015). Effects of the 2002–2020 National Spatial Strategy (NSS) on Ireland's settlement growth, its cities and on other gateways and hubs. https://arrow.dit.ie/cgi/viewcontent.cgi?referer=https://scholar.google.co.uk/&httpsredir=1&article=1039&context=beschrecart (accessed 2 January 2018).

ICBAN (nd). Central border regional spatial planning initiative. www.icban.com/Spatia l-Planning (accessed 2 January 2018).

Knox, C., & Carmichael, P. (2006). Bureau shuffling? The review of public administration in Northern Ireland. *Public Administration*, 84(4), 941–965.

Lloyd, G., (2008). *Planning Reform in Northern Ireland Independent Report to the Minister of the Environment*. Belfast: DOENI.

McCandless, E. (2011). Peace dividends and beyond: Contributions of administrative and social services to peacebuilding. United Nations Thematic Review for the Peacebuilding Support Office, New York. http://s3.amazonaws.com/inee-assets/resources/p eace_dividends.pdf (accessed 9 July 2018).

McEldowney, M., & Sterrett, K. (2001). Shaping a regional vision: The case of Northern Ireland. *Local Economy*, 16(1), 38–49.

Morphet, J. (1996) *Scoping Paper on Regional Planning*. Belfast: DOENI.

Morphet, J. (1998). Local authorities. In P. Lowe & S. Ward (Eds.), *British Environmental Policy and Europe: Politics and Policy in Transition* (pp. 138–152). London: Routledge.

Morphet, J., & Clifford, B. (2018). 'Who else would we speak to?' National Policy Networks in post-devolution Britain: The case of spatial planning. *Public Policy and Administration*, 33(1), 3–21.

Morrissey, M., & Gaffikin, F. (2006). Planning for peace in contested space. *International Journal of Urban and Regional Research*, 30(4), 873–893.

Murray, M. (2004). Strategic spatial planning on the island of Ireland: Towards a new territorial logic? *Innovation: The European Journal of Social Science Research*, 17(3), 227–242.

Murray, M., (2009). Building consensus in contested spaces and places? The Regional Development Strategy for Northern Ireland. In S. Davoudi, & I. Strange (Eds.), *Conceptions of Space and Place in Strategic Spatial Planning* (pp. 125–146). Abingdon: Routledge.

Murray, M., & Greer, J. (2002). Participatory planning as dialogue: The Northern Ireland Regional Strategic Framework and its public examination process, *Policy Studies*, 23(3–4), 191–209.

Murphy, M. C. (2016). Northern Ireland and the EU Referendum: The outcome, options and opportunities. *Journal of Cross Border Studies in Ireland*, 11, 18–31. http://cross border.ie/site2015/wp-content/uploads/2015/11/CCBS-JOURNAL-2016.pdf (accessed 9 July 2018).

Murtagh, B., & Shirlow, P. (2012). Devolution and the politics of development in Northern Ireland. *Environment and Planning C: Government and Policy*, 30(1), 46–61.

Nadin, V., & Shaw, D. (1998). Transactional spatial planning in Europe: The role of interreg IIc in the UK. *Regional Studies*, 32(3), 281–289.

Neill, W., & Ellis, G. (2008). Spatial planning in a contested territory: The search for a place vision in post-troubles Northern Ireland. In C. Coulter, & M. Murray (Eds.), *Northern Ireland After the Troubles* (pp. 88–109). Manchester: Manchester University Press.

Neill, W. J. V., & Gordon, M. (2001). Shaping our future? The regional strategic framework for Northern Ireland, *Planning Theory and Practice*, 2(1), 31–52.

NI SIB (2011). NIB 2016 corporate plan 2016–9 and business plan 2016–7. Northern Ireland Strategic Investment Board. https://sibni.org/ (accessed 10 July 2018).

Northern Ireland Executive (2011). *Investment Strategy for Northern Ireland 2011–2021*. Belfast: NIE.

Paris, C. (2006). Housing markets and cross-border integration. In E. Yarwood (Ed.), *The Dublin–Belfast Development Corridor: Ireland's Mega-City Region* (pp. 205–230). Aldershot: Ashgate.

Paris, C. (2017). From barricades to back gardens: Cross-border urban expansion from the City of Derry into Co. Donegal. In N. Moore and M. Scott (Eds.), *Renewing Urban Communities: Environment, Citizenship and Sustainability in Ireland* (pp. 114–131). Routledge: London.

Peel, D., & Lloyd, M. G. (2015). Towards a framework for cooperation: Spatial public diplomacy on the island of Ireland. *European Planning Studies*, 23(11), 2210–2226.

Pemberton, S., & Morphet, J. (2014). The rescaling of economic governance: Insights into the transitional territories of England. *Urban Studies*, 51(11), 2354–2370.

Taillon, R. (2017). The Belfast/Good Friday Agreement: Addressing 'the totality of relationships'. Speech given on 5 August 2017. Available at http://crossborder.ie/site2015/wp-content/uploads/2017/05/Speech-050817-1.pdf (accessed 2 January 2018).

Tannam, E. (2006). Cross-border co-operation between Northern Ireland and the Republic of Ireland: Neo-functionalism revisited. *The British Journal of Politics & International Relations*, 8(2), 256–276.

Turley (2017). Informing local development plans in Northern Ireland. www.turley.co.uk/intelligence/informing-local-development-plans-northern-ireland (accessed 14 December 2017).

Walsh, C., & Knieling, I. (2013). Creating a space for cooperation: Soft spaces, spatial planning and territorial cooperation on the island of Ireland. Paper presented at AESOP-ACSP Joint Congress, Dublin, 15–19 July 2012. www.researchgate.net/profile/Cormac_Walsh/publication/256461730_CREATING_A_SPACE_FOR_COOPERATION_SOFT_SPACES_SPATIAL_PLANNING_AND_TERRITORIAL_COOPERATION_ON_THE_ISLAND_OF_IRELAND/links/0c960522dc4c426c18000000.pdf (accessed 14 December 2017).

Walsh, J. A., & Murray, M. (2006). Critical reflections on the National Spatial Strategy and the Regional Development Strategy for Northern Ireland within the Dublin–Belfast corridor. In J. Yarwood (Ed.), *The Dublin–Belfast Corridor: Ireland's Megacity Region* (pp. 45–58). London: Routledge.

Welsh Government (2012). *Wales Infrastructure Investment Plan for Growth and Jobs*. Cardiff: Welsh Government.

Zaucha, J. (1998). VASAB 2010 Transnational Cooperation in the Spatial Development of the Baltic Sea Region. In U. Graute (Ed.), *Sustainable Development for Central and Eastern Europe* (pp. 163–179). Berlin, Heidelberg: Springer.

11 Delivery Through Planning

Introduction

How does planning deliver? Is a plan enough or should a local authority and other public agencies be responsible for its delivery once it is agreed? The role of planning in delivering places, investment and development is provided through a range of mechanisms. Firstly, there are plans that are formally adopted and have a legal basis for determining development and, on occasion, the compulsory purchase of land from owners. In addition, there are other forms of plans, including supplementary planning documents (SPDs) and neighbourhood plans, that are part of the development plan. There are also master plans and design-based proposals that are prepared, frequently by land owners and developers, to frame development.

In local plans in England, there is an infrastructure delivery plan (IDP) (Morphet 2011) and in Scotland, a proposed programme that will work to deliver the local development plan. These IDPs comprise projects that have a formal commitment to be delivered by their sponsors. The range of agencies and institutions that implement plans goes across all organisations, including the public, private and voluntary sectors and hybrid bodies, such as universities, that are in all three sectors. Some plans and policies are made by the government, including those for Nationally Significant Infrastructure Projects (NSIPs) and major development areas around infrastructure investment. The UK government had a programme to deliver new towns in the past and are reviving their role in development through proposals for the Oxford, Milton Keynes and Cambridge arc as a growth area (NIC 2016). The government also incentivises other locations to promote delivery through the Homes England agency and specific growth and City Deals (DCLG and DBEIS 2017).

Planning may also be delivered through programmes and projects. Here, there may be specific locations for the implementation of plan proposals, such as new community facilities or infrastructure improvements. The plan can be a core component on the pathway to deliver these projects, as it will signify an intent and an agreement about the purpose of the project, its location and when it is expected to be delivered. This timing may be a factor in relation to other projects, where there can be dependencies between projects, such as the provision of facilities in relation to new housing development being completed. The project's timing may also be significant in achieving specific events, such as major sporting or cultural events.

Another way that planning is involved in delivery is through the submission and determination of planning applications (Greed 2014). These can be made whether or not there is an extant, up-to-date and adopted local plan. They will be determined within the framework of the existing plan and any emerging plans together with national policy and EU regulations that are appropriate to the specific proposals in the planning application, its site and context. All planning applications need to be considered on their merits within these policy frameworks and are frequently modified though negotiation that can take place before the planning application is submitted or between the time of submission and determination. Sometimes there is a continuous process of negotiation that may start long before an application is submitted and continue following its approval through the closure of any associated legal agreements that are required to secure specific contributions or other development matters before construction can commence (Morrison and Burgess 2014; Fox-Rogers and Murphy 2014). In some cases, these relationships become familiar and there can be less distinction between the formal process, the respective roles that are played and the outcomes (Fox-Rogers and Murphy 2015).

Achieving Delivery Through Planning

Delivery through planning requires a range of methods and approaches that need to be considered as part of the plan making process. One test of the deliverability of local plans in England is that of commercial viability (DCLG 2018). However, plans can support delivery in a variety of ways. This can be through the designation of sites for specific purposes, the intention to implement objectives through site assembly, which may involve acquisition by compulsory purchase, and policies that apply to specific types of sites and locations.

As Barrett (2004) reflects, the interest in implementation has varied over the years. Sometimes, there is more focus on theory and ideologically based policy making, with a statement of the objectives being more important than the achieved outcome. There are also some expressed cultural views that delivery-based policy is of a lesser order than more conceptually anchored approaches. Here, there may be an assumption that a policy is good, but if it fails, is it those who are implementing it who are at fault?

As Alexander and Faludi (1989) remind us, there is an assumption that changes that are made because of a plan or planning activity are better than those made without one. All planning is an attempt to guide, if not control, what occurs in the future, to achieve some specific ends or to prevent other consequences. This might be to reinforce the role of one specific town centre over another, to support the preservation and enhancement of heritage assets or reduce development pressure on specific locations. However, as Alexander (1981) asks, is a failure to implement a plan a failure overall? Wildavksy (1989) would take this view, whereas Faludi (2013) considers that the detachment between a plan and its subsequent delivery encompasses flexibility.

This flexibility can be taken further into fuzzy plan making (de Roo and Porter 2016), which has less direct link with delivery. Fuzzy approaches to the analysis of planning have gained in analytical use (Allmendinger and Haughton 2010; Allmendinger 2017) and they need to be located within the political theories of scalecraft and statecraft (Morphet 2017a). Fuzziness is as much a mechanism for delivering change as more specifically defined approaches (Arnott 2015). Fuzzy planning is a tool of depoliticisation, that is, intentional to achieve defined outcomes, such as rescaling spatial policies (Fraser 2010) and implementing international agreements (Olesen and Richardson 2011). The act of preparing a plan or undertaking planning regulation, no matter whether from a firm or fuzzy perspective, has some influence on who makes decisions and on delivery outcomes. Where governments are using fuzzy planning to achieve state rescaling, the decisions may be shifted between scales of governance without any transparent policy reset.

What does delivery mean? In the case of planning, it is concerned with the fulfilment of the policies and objectives of the plan as they apply to locations and land uses. The plan may identify locations for specific types of development or areas that are protected for environmental reasons, which may prevent development or allow it only to occur in specific ways. Plans may also include codes for design, engagement, construction and delivery. Much of any plan's delivery will be achieved by the private sector, through housing, employment or leisure projects. However, public sector organizations and utilities will also be involved in the delivery of these outcomes. It is also the case that, in the planning system introduced in England and Wales in 2004, spatial planning has meant a greater emphasis on delivery of the plan than before (Nadin 2007; Morphet 2009). Initially this has been achieved through the test of deliverability in the tests of soundness for any plan that is supplemented by the IDP (Morphet 2011). As Shaw and Lord (2007) pointed out, this shift from policy making to a focus on delivery was challenging for practicing planners. As it challenged existing culture, planners needed a new understanding of the way this new system would operate on the front line, which was not provided (Clifford 2013).

Policy that leads to delivery is complex and requires the engagement of a range of actors, even where the organisation considers the outcome as a priority. Erickson et al. (2017) identify a range of 'mandates' or requirements that form part of the process of implementation. There are other implementation challenges that may relate to the organisational capacity and the skills required. Further, there may be individuals or organizations that take a different view from those promoting the plan. These interests may be competing for attention, time and resources within the organisation and specific outcomes can be the sites of intra organisational conflict (Tsaturyan and Müller 2015; Morphet 2015). There are also issues about who will be the senior responsible owner (SRO) for the project's completion and delivery and whether this will be direct or through an arm's length organisation or outsourced agency (Patanakul et al. 2016).

The production of planning is an issue related to the culture of the profession (Booth 2011) and professionalism itself (McClymont 2006; Hendler 1991). This inevitably brings into consideration the way that judgements are made (Vigar 2012) and the extent to which practitioners can be objective arbiters of the issues they are required to advise on. Frequently, these concerns arise because professionals are seen to be objective. However, planners employed by clients in to promote development may not be regarded as being professionally objective. There is a concern about the quality of professionals and sometimes there is suspicion from academics about the ways in which these decisions are made outside some objective position (Breheny 1989; Bartunek and McKenzie (2017).

Much of the discussion about delivery has been concerned with addressing culture change – that is, how planners, particularly in the public sector, can change the way they operate their practice (Shaw and Lord 2006). This is regarded as a challenge of change without necessarily being clear about the problems of the current practices or the expected outcomes (Sartorio et al. 2017). Some of these issues may be about the methods of working and increasing efficiency (Inch 2012) while others may be a concern to address the resistance that planners may be offering when they consider that there are issues about quality of plan and decision making in comparison with pressures for speed in these processes.

While much of the pressure for culture change is focussed on planners, there has been less consideration of contextual factors for these practices. These may be outside the organisation and related to the speed of change in government regulations and operating frameworks. There may also be changes in the market, as occurred in 2008 at the time of the economic downturn (Taylor 2013). These contextual pressures may occur inside the organisation, given fewer available resources, reductions in staff, timing of local elections and objectives of local politicians. Much may also relate to the relative power relations between departments inside the organisation (Nadin and Stead 2008). In some cases, these external and internal pressures may lead to planners' voices and views being silenced (Grange 2016).

There are also varying views about the effectiveness of these models. For example, some argue that the detachment or split between the organisation and the delivery agency can reduce the commitment to the outcome and in some situations, the outcome can be diluted. There can also be mixed priorities for delivery – the agency will be focussed on the client's requirements for delivery, but this will be set in the context of the delivery organisation's own priorities and financial targets. On the other hand, it is argued that using an arm-length organisation as a contractor for delivery can create easier conditions for control. The contractor can be instructed in a direct way and does not have to cope with the intra-organisational differences that might affect the delivery of a project if undertaken internally. The introduction of new public management (NPM), which was more focussed on performance inside and outside the organisation, also has some resonance here (Pollitt and Bouckaert 2011). NPM was an attempt to bring the activity of public administration into the process of government and not to regard it as a separate activity (Bryson et al. 2014). NPM brought a focus on the consumer and the quality of the outcomes, which was intended to focus the role of public expenditure and resource management. Hood and Dixon (2015) argue that the result has been more complaints and not much improvement but this charge is not altogether convincing. While public administration and government remain separate in central government, local authorities have become more attuned to their users and needs and increased public satisfaction. This focus has had a key influence on delivery priorities and modes (Van Dooren et al. 2015).

Plan Led Delivery

The preparation of a plan for an area, particularly where it has a legal status, is an important and fundamental part of achieving delivery of both specific developments and wider locational change (Erickson et al. 2017). The process of plan making includes a range of dimensions that are brought together in one place and these processes are undertaken over time. The focus of a plan and its content will depend in part on its scale. A strategic plan will vary from a neighbourhood or site master plan. However, they each share some key characteristics and components that shape and make the plan. These all contribute to the delivery of the plan's objectives. Plans are not documents that only have policy application; they are delivery intentions that are put into programmes and will be delivered through projects.

Policies and proposals within plans are posited on the assumption that whatever is proposed for implementation will have the outcome expected. These approaches are based on theories and models that assume the same outcome will follow as might have occurred elsewhere. They provide generalised models of cause and effect although they are frequently not examined to consider whether the same outcomes will derive from similar policies in distinct locations and at various times. That is, they are not examined against any positivist tests or tests of falsifiability (Popper 1957), nor is there any assumption that there may be unintended consequences arising in one location in comparison with another (Boudon 1982). In some cases, theories have not been tested and while the parameters of the theory might seem to be similar, the location or prevailing economic trends may mean that the implementation has a different outcome.

While the intention, structure and form of the plan are set to lead to delivery, what factors will have an influence on the transition from plan production and project delivery? As Berke et al. (2006) discuss, this is a continuing challenge and one that has been confronted in New Zealand. As they point out, in England, the US and New Zealand, development continues whether or not there is an adopted and up-to-date plan and the plan base together with case decisions will form the basis of delivery. This means that the decisions may not recognise more recent objectives or, indeed, protections and requirements that have not yet been enshrined in legislation.

However, Berke et al. (2006) indicate that plans can be assessed on their deliverability by monitoring subsequent performance and conformance, which are useful concepts to consider. Using a range of monitoring methods, it is possible to examine how the plan was implemented and whether proposals that come forward from developers enabled the plan's policies and proposals to be implemented. Subsequently, did this implementation lead to the outcomes anticipated? The second approach of conformance assesses the extent to which the wider policies within the plan, which come into effect for development applications, were used or whether they were challenged. Another aspect of conformance is where proposals in the plan are directly challenged by developers when they promote development that diverges from that set out in the plan. In these cases, these proposals may be initially refused by the local authority but subsequently upheld on appeal to the Secretary of State. An issue here is whether the challenge would be effective if staff were better skilled. Alternatively, the new proposals outside planning policy may be more acceptable than the original, given the passage of time since the plan was made.

Plans can enhance their deliverability through different mechanisms within them. These include the objectives that are set out to deliver them, the direct inclusion of specific land allocations and projects and the regulatory controls that support the proposals made by third parties that have not been engaged in promoting the plan. While the policies will have a significant role in framing the plan, the specific proposals, delivered by the local authority promoting the plan in conjunction with others, such as other agencies in the public sector or the private sector, may have the leading role in making the changes in the delivery of the plan's expected outcomes. When considering these different approaches, Dalton et al. (1989) found that the direct investment approach was more successful than relying on regulation.

There are other factors to consider when assessing successful implementation. Laurian et al. (2004) suggest that the primary issue is the organisation's commitment to the implementation of the plan and whether the plan is set out in a form that can be delivered. This may need some specific tests in the consideration of the plan's form so that the implementation commitments are clearly defined, as is the process for their delivery. Laurian et al. describe this as implementation depth and breadth and these are useful concepts for considering the plan as it is drafted. Where policies across the plan are not implemented, this may be because they are developed in a way that is too general. For example, having a plan policy that gives priority to housing for older people may be a broad commitment, which is not owned by any constituency and has no delivery means or resources associated with it.

An alternative approach might identify which locations would best suit older people, what kinds of development and tenure would reflect their needs and whether there is a range of extra care housing being developed as part of local wellbeing strategy. Once specific locations and types of development have been indicated, the plan may then continue to identify which would be the best organisations to implement these developments, whether the needs of one group will have priority over others and how these developments might be funded. Some proposals may also be to improve the surrounding public realm or increase capacity at local facilities for those who have time to enjoy cultural and leisure activities. This approach may also consider alternative forms of delivery and the methods required to monitor whether the overall outcome, such as better use of under-occupied housing or reductions of extended stay in hospital beyond discharge, has been addressed.

On policy-led delivery, an important consideration will be to understand which issues have been prioritized. Kingdon and Thurber's (1984) approach to agenda setting, how it is possible to determine when a policy's time has come, is a crucial issue here (Morphet 2017a). In some locations, policies may be brought forward very quickly but in others, they will be left and perhaps never implemented. There is also a key role for monitoring to see whether plan-based policies are being delivered in practice or whether other forces are at work either to attempt to undermine or break the policy or leave it alone altogether.

Development Led Delivery

The development industry in the UK forms a major part of the economy and is a barometer of the economy's health (IPF 2013). Development-led delivery is also subject to pressure from promoters and applicants who want to implement their proposals regardless of the plan-led policies. These forces may attempt to exert informal power through influence with politicians or other local figures. In attempting to achieve their development, they may use the most experienced and successful planning consultants and legal counsel (Ericksen et al. 2004). In times of economic stress or where there are political priorities, there may also be pressure to reduce requirements for contributions or development mitigation from those promoting development in order to achieve these wider objectives (Fox-Rogers and Murphy 2014).

Here, delivery may also be met by organised opposition, such as that from community groups. This is a longstanding approach to opposing change in the UK, and particularly in England (Grindrod 2017), and may be focussed on development in general or on specific types of development, such as energy plants (Devine-Wright 2014). The role of Nimbyism towards development is regarded as a means to reduce the level of housing provided nationally, with a particular concern about the provision of social and affordable housing (Scally and Tighe 2015; Matthews et al. 2015). Some communities will be against new social and affordable housing on the basis that it will drive down existing property prices. In some cases, politicians collude with communities to seek social and community infrastructure as part of planning contributions rather than affordable housing, as they appreciate that this will make a planning application more politically acceptable.

While plans set the context for land use regulation, every development requires a proposer and a funder to enable it to be delivered. The proposers for the development may be motivated by a range of reasons. Firstly, they may want to develop for their own purpose, including a house, shop or office. More frequently, those promoting development are intermediaries in the market, who have invested in acquiring land in a location they consider that the market will favour and where planning permission for their proposed development will be granted. Their business, as land agents, is to make a profit by acting as this intermediary, by operating a land market. Developers engage in this market as a means of finding land to implement their projects. An agreement to purchase the land for development may start early in the acquisition or planning process or the development may be completed without an occupier, as can occur when the market changes. In some cases, the risk is shared between owners through a joint venture company (McAllister et al. 2015; Hawkins et al. 2016).

The process of making a planning application for a development in England is expected to be determined within a fixed period for smaller and larger developments. In practice, a high proportion of planning applications are now determined through local authorities by officers who have the delegated powers to issue a planning consent using the powers that reside in the council as whole. For larger developments, or in some cases where developments receive objections, these may be considered by planning committees made up of several councillors who are expected to hear reports on the proposals and may also hear from public objectors before making decisions. The reports on the analysis of the impact of the development will be based on normative assumptions of the impact of the development, whether this is on traffic movements, numbers of employees or contribution to the local economy.

As part of the process of negotiation with the local authority, there will be a requirement that developers agree a contribution, which will be frequently referred to as 'planning gain' (Crook et al. 2015). Through this process, the local authority has a right to request a contribution from the proposer of a planning application to mitigate the impact of the development on the locality. This contribution may be either in cash or in kind – that is, affordable or social housing, community facilities or open space, for example. The developer will factor in the cost of this contribution in their development appraisal and the negotiation will frequently reflect how much of this allocation will be agreed, given that this financial allocation and how it will be used are not known to the local authority. The role of developers' contributions has also been a principle mechanism for the delivery of housing in England (Crook and Whitehead 2002).

The use of some development contributions can add to the value and likely saleability of housing in comparison with other houses on the market. These negotiations sit within the viability assessments considered previously.

In England, there is also a second and supplementary approach to collecting developer contributions through community infrastructure levy (CIL). The level and area covered by CIL will be designated in each local authority area, following a formal exanimation by the independent planning inspector. When introduced, the government expected CIL to be a primary form of charging for development contributions but this has not yet been applied in all locations. It also can be applied differently from the mitigation contributions, in that the

CIL may be spent in any part of the local authority although it may only be used for predetermined types of infrastructure. There are also regulations about the way in which development contributions and CIL may be used together. Some local authorities have decided not to use CIL, as they regard it as a development disincentive

The scale of development is based both on the designation of sites for specific uses, such as housing or employment, in local plans but the planning system also allows a developer to seek planning consent on non-designated sites where the profits may be higher if the development proposals are accepted through an independent appeal process (Nadin and Cullingworth 2007; Pacione 2016; Bradley and Sparling 2017). Where the owner of the land seeks to obtain a planning consent on non-designated land, this provides considerable potential for higher profits, not least if the land is currently within a lower land value use.

Government Led Delivery

Unlike other members of the EU, the UK does not have a spatial plan for investment and infrastructure delivery. While such national plans exist in Scotland (Scottish Government 2014), Wales (Welsh Government 2013) and Northern Ireland (DRD 2010), there is no specific plan for England. The government sets planning policy in general and has more recently started to engage in strategic delivery though its own agencies, including Homes England and the Highways Agency, and using specific growth and City Deals to incentivise the type of development the government wishes to see delivered.

Nationally Significant Infrastructure Projects

One of the key ways in which government is supporting the delivery of NSIPs in England is the system established through the 2008 Planning Act. This provides a means by which specific categories of national infrastructure can apply for a development consent order and there is a guarantee of the time that the process of examination and decision making will take once the application has been accepted. Since the system was implemented, over 70 applications have been submitted and only three have been refused. The NSIP regime is primarily a legal rather than a planning process, with no requirement on scheme promoters to establish the principle of development, which is already included within an EU regulation (Morphet 2017a) and subsequent national planning statements (NPS) approved by Parliament. When the system was first introduced, it was run by the independent Infrastructure Planning Commission but in 2011, it was incorporated within the Planning Inspectorate National Service (PINS). This means that the policy is set and the decision on each proposal is made by the same government department, albeit on a recommendation from PINS after an independent examination.

While the system has been working well, there have been fewer proposals for NSIPs than were initially envisaged although the new system has meant that more applications have been able to be considered at the same time than under the previous system, which relied on planning inquiries. However, even for those NSIPs submitted, far fewer have been implemented. In some cases, this has been due to the type of infrastructure being implemented, with energy proposals subject to national energy auctions. There have been some concerns that the reason for this lower take-up was related to the increasingly detailed nature of the discussions on the proposals, which appeared to be going against the more general nature of the conceptualisation of the entire system. In research undertaken to investigate this issue, it was found that most of the efforts of scheme promoters and their professional teams had been on the achievement of the development consent order (DCO) rather than on the completion of the project (Clifford and Morphet 2017; Morphet and Clifford 2017a). Further, the need for detail was driven by both the issue of public consultation and the need to achieve a DCO that is deliverable for the scheme's constructors (Morphet and Clifford 2017b).

The National Infrastructure Commission

Within England, the delivery of infrastructure, including broadband, is being led by the National Infrastructure Commission (NIC), established in 2015. While the NIC describes its position as independent, it is an agency of the government. The initial terms of reference the NIC was given were not to focus on an infrastructure plan for the whole of England, as exists in Scotland (Scottish Government 2015), Wales (Welsh Government 2017) and Northern Ireland (ISNI 2011) but rather to focus on specific locations, such as the North of England, and at the same time establish an evidence base on which to make future recommendations. Since then the NIC has published proposals for future work on a national infrastructure assessment, the Oxford, Milton Keynes and Cambridge Growth Corridor, freight, roads and new technologies.

While the work of the NIC has some spatial dimensions, it has not been linked with England's industrial strategy (DBEIS 2017), which takes a sectoral approach to economic investment and growth. Nor does it relate to the strategic plans likely to emerge from the combined authorities (CAs) that have been established in England. The approaches in other UK nations are far more integrated and there is a basic assumption that these strategies need to be integrated and mutually reinforcing. In England they remain separate.

Utilities

While utilities are primarily provided by private sector bodies in England, they are defined as services of public interest within the EU and much of their operations are subject to government regulation. These regulatory offices can intervene on charging policy, level of service and the amount of the market taken by any supplier. The government can influence the quality of national infrastructure by requiring the regulators to change standards of supply, as in broadband and in codes of connection, which both have geographical dimensions. Some services, such as those for rail, are more hybrid and although they have a regulator, also have been in and out of public ownership. While they are not utilities, the government runs the roads through Highways England. This is an intermediate body, with its role as an agency used to determine interdependent decision making on highway projects.

Local Authority Direct Delivery

Local authorities can lead development through several means:

Placemaking

Placemaking is generally understood to be the art and practice of building communities through places (Pierce et al. 2011) and local authorities can intervene to achieve this in many ways. They may undertake this master planning on major sites or on their own land, which they have acquired, hold or have assembled through purchase (Collinge and Gibney 2010; Cilliers and Timmermans 2014). The local authority may be undertaking place making on their own or with partners. Local authorities generally promote place making as a means of regenerating economic activity, for example, in locations with heritage assets, town centres or specific locations, such as parks or riversides (Pendlebury and Porfyriou 2017). Place making approaches may also be used to support investment or other objectives, such as place calming or improvements in creating safe places. This might be achieved through selective development or improvement to the urban realm. Much of place making is concerned with design and appearance or development, as well as the activity that is contained within it.

Regeneration

Local authority-led development may also focus on regeneration, which is primarily, but not exclusively, concerned with major changes within existing places to improve their appearance and performance. Regeneration may be of town centres that are underperforming and is frequently associated with projects in which the local authority has some legal or financial interest (Roberts et al. 2016). Another form of regeneration is on housing estates that are owned by the local authority. Here, regeneration may include the redevelopment of existing housing or other associated land, such as garage sites (Morphet and Clifford 2017c). It may include new landscaping and intensification for development through the addition of floors or wings at the ends of existing buildings. In some cases, local authorities seek to achieve a mix of tenures on their existing housing land by generating mixed development to create income that will then be reused for other improvements on the site or simply on estates elsewhere.

The government provides some funding for estate regeneration and while some investment borrowing is still available, many local authorities have hit their set debt cap and are unable to progress with further development until they pay down existing debt. The debt cap is set by the government and, unlike in the private sector, it does not relate to the current asset value of the properties against which investment loans are raised.

Developing Housing

While local authorities in the UK, including England, were major providers of housing in the immediate post-war period to the late 1980s, when they were no longer in receipt of government grant and were required to offer right to buy of their stock as subsidised rates. The government also imposed restrictions on the use of capital receipts and reinvestment in the existing stock. Many local authorities sold their stock to housing association in large-scale voluntary transfer, while others passed the stock to an arm's length management company.

While some local authorities have continued building housing over the period since the late 1890s, most had stopped until after the 2011 Localism Act. In this legislation, local authorities were enabled to act as individuals and establish companies that could develop housing. The pressures to develop housing were motivated by a range of factors, including the increasing rise of housing need not being met by the private sector, the increase in homelessness of all types of households (caused by unfettered landlord behaviour) and the removal of a main source of income to local authorities (the revenue support grant) by the government (Morphet and Clifford 2017c). Other local authorities have been motivated by the failure of the private sector to implement planning consents for housing, or to abandon housing sites altogether and not progress development. Another concern has been that local authorities have been required to negotiate development contributions with developers, only to see developers return for a renegotiation to reduce their contributions after planning permission has been granted. Further, even where planning permission is granted and development has commenced, the developer may only build out 30–50 dwellings a year on a major site, leaving the site and contribution traffic a local issue and problem. The government recognised these issues in the housing white paper *Fixing Our Broken Market* (DCLG 2017).

Faced with these problems and challenges, local authorities have slowly started to act directly. In most cases, this has been through a problem-solving approach – that is, to deal with one issue, such as homelessness, and from there go on to tackle another issue, such as unimplemented consents. In other local authorities, councils have taken a more strategic approach by identifying a target number of dwellings they want to provide in their area through variety for means. These include direct council building, the use of joint venture companies and using their planning powers to assemble land for others to develop (Morphet and Clifford 2017c). The local authority housing developments are built out in their entirety and are frequently tenure-blind. The local authority may sell some of the properties and offer others in shared ownership schemes and others are offered on a rental basis, both at affordable and social rent levels, using cross-subsidies within the scheme to offer lower rental properties. In some cases, local authorities have negotiated affordable properties through development contribution agreements and although in the past these have been passed to housing associations, a hybrid between public and private organisations, housing associations are not primarily focussed on new builds and are not taking on these properties. Hence, local authorities are taking them on directly and putting them into their own stock, if they have it, or creating a wholly owned housing company to manage the houses.

While local authorities are unlikely to become house builders to the same degree as they were in the period 1945–1988, when, for example, they contributed to 400, 000 housing completions in 1971, their interest in providing housing is growing. They are increasing their role in delivery. In some cases, their housing companies are acquiring stock from the open market. Elsewhere, they have acquired hostels and bed and breakfast accommodations that house homeless people or they have built hostels specifically for homeless people. Nearly half of those engaging in development are building for specific groups and special needs, such as older people or people with mental or physical disability.

References

Allmendinger, P. (2017). *Planning Theory* (3rd edition). London: Palgrave Macmillan.

Allmendinger, P., & Haughton, G. (2010). Spatial planning, devolution, and new planning spaces. *Environment and Planning C: Government and Policy*, 28(5), 803–818.

Allmendinger, P., & Haughton, G. (2012). Post-political spatial planning in England: A crisis of consensus? *Transactions of the Institute of British Geographers*, 37(1), 89–103.

Alexander, E. R. (1981). If planning isn't everything, maybe it's something. *Town Planning Review*, 52(2), 131–142.

Alexander, E. R., & Faludi, A. (1989). Planning and plan implementation: Notes on evaluation criteria. *Environment and Planning B: Planning and Design*, 16(2), 127–140.

Arnott, R. J. (2015). Reflections on Calgary's spatial structure: An urban economist's critique of municipal planning in Calgary. https://papers.ssrn.com/sol3/papers.cfm?abstract_id=2693740 (accessed 9 July 2018).

Barrett, S. M. (2004). Implementation studies: Time for a revival? Personal reflections on 20 years of implementation studies. *Public Administration*, 82(2), 249–262.

Bartunek, J. M., & McKenzie, J. (2017). Reviewing the state of academic practitioner relationships. In J. M. Bartunek & J. McKenzie (Eds.), *Academic–Practitioner Relationships: Developments, Complexities and Opportunities* (pp. 1–10). London: Routledge.

Berke, P., Backhurst, M., Day, M., Ericksen, N., Laurian, L., Crawford, J., & Dixon, J. (2006). What makes plan implementation successful? An evaluation of local plans and implementation practices in New Zealand. *Environment and Planning B: Planning and Design*, 33(4), 581–600.

Booth, P. (2011). Culture, planning and path dependence: some reflections on the problems of comparison. *Town Planning Review*, 82(1), 13–28.

Boudon, R. (1982). *The Unintended Consequences of Social Action*. London: Macmillan.

Bradley, Q., & Sparling, W. (2017). The impact of neighbourhood planning and localism on house-building in England. *Housing, Theory and Society*, 34(1), 106–118.

Breheny, M. J. (1989). Chalkface to coalface: A review of the academic–practice interface. *Environment and Planning B: Planning and Design*, 16(4), 451–468.

Bryson, J. M., Crosby, B. C., & Bloomberg, L. (2014). Public value governance: Moving beyond traditional public administration and the new public management. *Public Administration Review*, 74(4), 445–456.

Cilliers, E. J., & Timmermans, W. (2014). The importance of creative participatory planning in the public place-making process. *Environment and Planning B: Planning and Design*, 41(3), 413–429.

Clifford, B., & Morphet, J. (2017). Infrastructure delivery: The DCO process in context. www.nipa-uk.org/uploads/news/(UCL)_Clifford_and_Morphet_-_NIPA_Technical_Report_-_June_2017.pdf (accessed 9 January 2018).

Clifford, B. P. (2013). Reform on the frontline: Reflections on implementing spatial planning in England, 2004–2008. *Planning Practice & Research*, 28(4), 361–383.

Collinge, C., & Gibney, J. (2010). Connecting place, policy and leadership. *Policy Studies*, 31(4), 379–391.

Crook, A. T. D., & Whitehead, C. M. (2002). Social housing and planning gain: is this an appropriate way of providing affordable housing? *Environment and Planning A*, 34 (7), 1259–1279.

Crook, T., Henneberry, J., & Whitehead, C. (2015). *Planning Gain: Providing Infrastructure and Affordable Housing*. Chichester: John Wiley & Sons.

Dalton, L. C., Conover, M., Rudholm, G., Tsuda, R., & Baer, W. C. (1989). The limits of regulation evidence from local plan implementation in California. *Journal of the American Planning Association*, 55(2), 151–168.

DBEIS (2017). Industrial strategy. www.gov.uk/government/policies/industrial-strategy (accessed 4 July 2018).

DCLG (2014). *Viability: A General Overview*. London: DCLG.

DCLG (2017). Fixing our broken housing market. Housing white paper. London: DCLG.

DCLG, & DBEIS (2017). City deals and growth deals. www.gov.uk/government/policies/city-deals-and-growth-deals (accessed 9 January 2018).

De Roo, G., & Porter, G. (2016). *Fuzzy Planning: The Role of Actors in a Fuzzy Governance Environment*. London: Routledge.

Devine-Wright, P. (Ed.) (2014). *Renewable Energy and the Public: From NIMBY to Participation*. London: Routledge.

DRD (2010). *Regional Development Strategy RDS 2035*. Belfast: DRD.

Ericksen, N. J., Berke, P. R., & Dixon, J. E. (2004). *Plan-Making for Sustainability: The New Zealand Experience*. London: Taylor & Francis.

Faludi, A. (1987). *A Decision-Centred View of Environmental Planning* (Vol. 38). Oxford: Pergamon.

Fox-Rogers, L., & Murphy, E. (2014). Informal strategies of power in the local planning system. *Planning Theory*, 13(3), 244–268.

Fox-Rogers, L., & Murphy, E. (2015). From brown envelopes to community benefits: The co-option of planning gain agreements under deepening neoliberalism. *Geoforum*, 67, 41–50.

Fraser, A. (2010). The craft of scalar practices. *Environment and Planning A*, 42(2), 332–346.

Grange, K. (2016). Planners: A silenced profession? The politicisation of planning and the need for fearless speech. *Planning Theory*, 16(3), 275–295.

Greed, C. (2014). *Investigating Town Planning: Changing Perspectives and Agendas.* London: Routledge.

Grindrod, J. (2017). *Outskirts: Living Life on the Edge of the Green Belt.* London: Sceptre.

Hawkins, C. V., Hu, Q., & Feiock, R. C. (2016). Self-organizing governance of local economic development: Informal policy networks and regional institutions. *Journal of Urban Affairs*, 38(5), 643–660.

Hendler, S. (1991). Ethics in planning: The views of students and practitioners. *Journal of Planning Education and Research*, 10(2), 99–106.

Hood, C., & Dixon, R. (2015). What we have to show for 30 years of new public management: Higher costs, more complaints. *Governance*, 28(3), 265–267.

Inch, A. (2012). *Changing the Culture of Scottish Planning: Interpreting New Regulations, Shaping New Practices, Relationships and Identities.* Sheffield: Sheffield University.

IPF (2013). The role of commercial property in the UK economy. http://www.ipf.org.uk/resourceLibrary/the-role-of-commercial-property-in-the-uk-economy–march-2013-.html (accessed 9 July 2018).

ISNI (2011). *Investment Strategy for Northern Ireland 2011–2021.* Belfast: ISNI. http://isni.gov.uk/home/ (accessed 9 July 2018).

Kingdon, J. W., & Thurber, J. A. (1984). *Agendas, Alternatives, and Public Policies.* Boston: Little, Brown.

Laurian, L., Day, M., Berke, P., Ericksen, N., Backhurst, M., Crawford, J., & Dixon, J. (2004). Evaluating plan implementation: A conformance-based methodology. *Journal of the American Planning Association*, 70(4), 471–480.

Matthews, P., Bramley, G., & Hastings, A. (2015). Homo economicus in a big society: Understanding middle-class activism and NIMBYism towards new housing developments. *Housing, Theory and Society*, 32(1), 54–72.

McAllister, R. R., Taylor, B. M., & Harman, B. P. (2015). Partnership networks for urban development: how structure is shaped by risk. *Policy Studies Journal*, 43(3), 379–398.

McClymont, K. E. (2006). *Ideology, Legitimacy and Values in Practice: Reconceptualising Professionalism in Town Planning.* Doctoral dissertation, University of Sheffield.

Morphet, J. (2009). Local integrated spatial planning: The changing role in England. *Town Planning Review*, 80(4–5), 393–414.

Morphet, J. (2011). *Effective Practice in Spatial Planning.* Abingdon: Routledge.

Morphet, J. (2015). *Applying Leadership and Management in Planning: Theory and Practice.* Bristol: Policy Press.

Morphet, J. (2017a). Sub-regional strategic spatial planning: The use of statecraft and scalecraft in delivering the English model. *Town Planning Review*, 88(6), 665–682.

Morphet, J. (2017b). *Beyond Brexit.* Bristol: Policy Press.

Morphet, J., & Clifford, B. (2017a). Infrastructure delivery: The DCO process in context. www.nipa-uk.org/uploads/news/(UCL)_Morphet_and_Clifford_-_NIPA_Main_Report_-_June_2017.pdf (accessed 9 January 2018).

Morphet, J., & Clifford, B. (2017b). The national infrastructure planning regime: The role of local authorities and communities. *Town and Country Planning*, August, 296–302.

Morphet, J., & Clifford, B. (2017c). *Local Authority Provision of Housing.* London: NPF and RTPI.

Morrison, N., & Burgess, G. (2014). Inclusionary housing policy in England: The impact of the downturn on the delivery of affordable housing through Section 106. *Journal of Housing and the Built Environment*, 29(3), 423–438.

Nadin, V. (2007). The emergence of the spatial planning approach in England. *Planning, Practice & Research*, 22(1), 43–62.

Nadin, V., & Cullingworth, B. (2007). *Town and country planning in the UK*. Abingdon: Routledge.

Nadin, V., & Stead, D. (2008). European spatial planning systems, social models and learning. *disP–The Planning Review*, 44(172), 35–47.

NIC (2016). *Cambridge, Milton Keynes and Oxford Corridor: Interim Report*. London: National Infrastructure Commission.

Olesen, K., & Richardson, T. (2011). The spatial politics of spatial representation: relationality as a medium for depoliticization? *International Planning Studies*, 16(4), 355–375.

Pacione, M. P. (2016). Residential development in the urban fringe: A conflict interpretation. *Geography Research Forum*, 13, 12–31.

Patanakul, P., Kwak, Y. H., Zwikael, O., & Liu, M. (2016). What impacts the performance of large-scale government projects? *International Journal of Project Management*, 34(3), 452–466.

Pendlebury, J., & Porfyriou, H. (2017). Heritage, urban regeneration and place-making. *Journal of Urban Design*, 22(4), 429–432.

Pierce, J., Martin, D. G., & Murphy, J. T. (2011). Relational place-making: The networked politics of place. *Transactions of the Institute of British Geographers*, 36(1), 54–70.

Pollitt, C., & Bouckaert, G. (2011). *Public Management Reform: A Comparative Analysis – New Public Management, Governance, and the Neo-Weberian State*. Oxford: Oxford University Press.

Popper, K. (1957). Philosophy of science. In J. H. Muirhead (Ed.), *British Philosophy in the Mid-Century* (pp. 182–183). London: George Allen and Unwin.

Roberts, P., Sykes, H., & Granger, R. (Eds.). (2016). *Urban Regeneration* (2nd edition). London: SAGE.

Sartorio, F. C., Thomas, H., & Harris, N. (2017). Interpreting planners' talk about change: An exploratory study. *Planning Theory*. http://journals.sagepub.com/doi/abs/10.1177/1473095217742183 (accessed 15 December 2017).

Scally, C. P., & Tighe, J. R. (2015). Democracy in action? NIMBY as impediment to equitable affordable housing siting. *Housing Studies*, 30(5), 749–769.

Scottish Government (2014). *National Planning Policy Framework 3*. Edinburgh: Scottish Government.

Scottish Government (2015). *Scottish Infrastructure Plan*. Edinburgh: Scottish Government.

Shaw, D., & Lord, A. (2007). The cultural turn? Culture change and what it means for spatial planning in England. *Planning, Practice & Research*, 22(1), 63–78.

Taylor, Z. (2013). Rethinking planning culture: A new institutionalist approach. *Town Planning Review*, 84(6), 683–702.

Tsaturyan, T., & Müller, R. (2015). Integration and governance of multiple project management offices (PMOs) at large organizations. *International Journal of Project Management*, 33(5), 1098–1110.

Van Dooren, W., Bouckaert, G., & Halligan, J. (2015). *Performance Management in the Public Sector* (2nd edition). London: Routledge.

Vigar, G. (2012). Planning and professionalism: Knowledge, judgement and expertise in English planning. *Planning Theory*, 11(4), 361–378.

Welsh Government (2013). *Wales Spatial Plan*. Cardiff: Welsh Government.

Welsh Government (2017). *Wales Infrastructure Investment Plan for Growth and Jobs*. Cardiff: Welsh Government.

Wildavksy, A. B. (1989). *Speaking Truth to Power* (2nd edition). Abingdon: Routledge.

Part III

Planning's Persistent and Emerging Challenges

12 Planning and Health

Introduction

The role of spatial planning in providing wider and deeper approaches to delivery has extended beyond the physical manifestation of place to the way that places deliver social and economic outcomes (Morphet 2009). The development of integrated approaches to public policy and delivery (Stoker 2011; Morphet 2008) have not only been manifest in joint services such as the merger of the local authority and health services but also in support systems such as the common use of shared evidence in local authorities, such as the Joint Strategic Needs Assessment (JSNA) (NHS 2017) and the local Well-Being Strategy (NHS 2011). There are also shared duties to involve and cooperate with communities and each other, local responsibility to align budgets and joint scrutiny with a greater focus on the technology of governmentality (Imrie and Raco 2000; Huxley 2007).

Services have to demonstrate how they work together not only within and between agencies but also over administrative boundaries. A new role for directly elected mayors in health policy and delivery in Manchester and London (Sandford 2017) may achieve a new kind of service integration, with positive support from the National Health Service (NHS). However, the government department that is responsible for the NHS may be less culturally aligned with integrative working.

Another approach to drawing together public service policy and delivery is through the advisory work of Public Health England (PHE). Since 2010, local authorities have been directly responsible for public health, although PHE has continued to provide research and advice on local authority policies for health and other areas, including planning. Here, there has been advice on major design approaches, such as the healthy towns initiatives (PHE 2017c), to more detailed approaches to creating non-obesogenic environments (PHE and LGA 2013). Local authorities have also attempted to manage the number of hot food takeaways near school gates to reduce children's access to fast food (PHE and LGA 2014; PHE 2017b; MoL 2017b). Some local authorities have also tried to control opportunities for other dependencies, such as gambling, through the management of betting shops and over-the-counter credit shops (RSPH 2015). The opportunities for smoking have also been addressed in some locations, as has providing safe locations for those with drug dependency.

The relationship between planning and health through access to and location of facilities is also a key consideration. Since the early 2000s, there has been a gradual erosion of access standards for public facilities, including hospitals, clinics and general practitioner (GP) surgeries. While there is the opportunity for local authorities to set local standards (DCLG 2012 para 174), this has been used rarely. Instead the delivery of health facilities has been more concerned with provider concerns to assist the NHS estate managers to generate income to support service delivery. This has led, in many cases, to city centre hospitals being redeveloped or reused while out-of-town sites, reliant on car access and with less public transport, have been preferred for main health locations. This has resulted in public concerns about parking charges generated by hospitals in England, although these charges have been removed in Scotland and Wales. At the local level, primary health access is again dependent on GP preference, supported through local decision making.

Context for Planning and Health Policy

The relationship between planning and public health is now being explored more extensively. Until 2010, some strategic interrelationships were noted at the regional level (Kidd 2007; Harris and Hooper 2004; Pilkington 2009; Haughton et al. 2010). However, since then, these have switched to a more local relationship, with the transfer of public health functions to local authorities in the 2006 NHS Act and the 2012 Health and Social Care Act. Here the focus is on managing public health, primary care budgets and mental health provision for the local authority area. Local clinical commissioning groups (CCGs) were also established through the 2012 Health and Social Care Act and replaced primary care trusts on 1 April 2013. CCGs are also responsible for considering the distribution of pharmacies. Some services, such as ambulance provision, still operate locally but are controlled centrally and not through the CCG. At this local level, the relationship between planning and health has related to public and mental health issues and the location and provision of health facilities (Forsyth et al. 2010; Barton et al. 2010; 2015; Barton 2005).

The development of active citizens and the notion of responsibilisation in policy delivery (6 et al. 2010) particularly have also heightened the awareness of provision and capacity for more active engagement in health by individuals (Halpern et al. 2004; Mulgan 2009). Public health approaches include encouragement to take exercise and the provision of safe and secure environments. The relationship between planning and health is increasingly recognised, whether this is through issues such as air quality, obesogenic environments or the relationship between green spaces and mental health (Barton and Pretty 2010; Nutsford et al. 2013). This chapter will consider current approaches suggested by research and exemplify the ways that they have been used in practice. The chapter will also consider the barriers to increasing working relationships between planning and health and how they have been addressed in some locations.

Finally, there has been an increasing set of issues around the costs of running the NHS and access to care for specific groups. These include the elderly and, in some parts of the country, the rationing of types of surgery. The cost of supporting older people has increased as local authority funding for social care has been reduced. Many hospitals must keep older people in their beds as their discharge is delayed where no other suitable alternative care or housing is available. The number of care homes has reduced as the costs of running them have increased and there are differential costs and subsidies for care homes in different sectors. Some local authorities are now taking over or opening direct care provision as a means of providing better services and reducing payments to third party providers. While the provision of care home spaces has not been a main issue in local plans, it is increasingly seen as a crucial component of any housing strategy and of the wider concerns with housing provision in all local authority areas.

Planning for Health Outcomes

There are a range of sources of advice and guidance on the delivery of health outcomes through spatial planning, many of which also include examples and case studies. The government has produced planning practice guidance on the role of health and wellbeing in planning (DCLG 2017). This requires consideration of the determinants of health that have some specific relationships with planning, how to create healthy communities and the issues related to planning decision making on the location of health facilities. The NHS has also produced two introductory guides on the relationship between health and planning, one written for health professionals (2007a) and the other written for planning professionals (2007b). The guide written for health staff introduces them to spatial planning, includes some case studies and strongly encourages them to work with planners to support health delivery. The guide for planners on health concentrates more on public health than on the location of all health care facilities, so this might not provide a fully developed approach and will need to be extended in practice. The Royal Town Planning Institute (RTPI) has produced a good practice note on *Delivering healthy communities* (RTPI 2009), which provides some pointers to ways in which spatial planning can be used to deliver health outcomes.

A more detailed set of guidance on ways that health outcomes can be delivered through local plans has been prepared for health professionals through guides prepared by the NHS Healthy Urban Development Unit (HUDU) (HUDU 2013a and b, 2017a, 2017b, 2017c) and the Mayor of London (MoL 2017a). HUDU has a London focus but all its publications have a wider application and use in spatial planning elsewhere. The HUDU *Healthy Urban Planning Checklist* (2017a) encourages planners to be involved in developing a health infrastructure plan at the local level to secure the delivery of health outcomes. Another useful guide to identifying the evidence base required for spatial planning has been developed by PHE through an evidence review that supports planning practice in assessing planning proposals and in designing healthier places (PHE 2017c). A summary of the spatial determinants of health is shown in Table 12.1.

Table 12.1 The Spatial Determinants of Health

- Housing
- Transport
- Employment and skills
- Education and early life
- Access to services
- Liveability, open space and public realm
- Air, water and noise quality
- Access to fresh food
- Climate change

The development of a joint approach to identifying health needs alongside other concerns has been driven through the establishment of Joint Strategic Needs Assessments (JSNAs), which are now undertaken for every local authority area and are increasingly seen as the main source of evidence about local needs. Each JSNA has a data set that allows local and national comparisons of health outcomes to be made (DoH 2007; LGA 2011). These have now been evolved and sit within local health and wellbeing strategies (DoH 2011), which provide detailed assessments of the underlying health issues in every area, their location and prospects for their improvement. These strategies provide the guidance for local health expenditure priorities. While it may be assumed that health outcomes, such as life expectancy and morbidity, will be uniform in most local authority areas, these local health and wellbeing strategies, accompanied by local health data additionally provided by Office of National Statistics (ONS), indicate a different position. In some local authorities, there may be a variance of ten years or more in male life expectancy between two different parts of the same area (Congdon 2009).

This is a major challenge for local authorities to address, particularly where life expectancy rates are much below the national average. A main concern for planning is whether there are any policies or initiatives that can contribute to meeting this wider wellbeing outcome. The role that planning can play may depend on the determining issues but contributory causes that may be assisted by planning interventions include housing condition and quality, access to facilities, provision of shops for fresh foods (Griffiths et al. 2016), access to safe walking environments, air quality and fear of crime. There may also be a lack of community and social meeting places that can support people who have lower incomes or live alone. These issues are rarely included in local plans even where concerns are considerable and there are strong health priorities. Few local plans mention the health and wellbeing strategy as a source of evidence and a determinant of priorities.

Health Impact Assessments

Health impact assessments (HIAs) are 'a combination of procedures, methods and tools by which a policy, programme or project may be judged as to its potential effects on the health of a population, and the distribution of those effects within the population' (WHO 1999). A practical way of assessing whether any planning policy or proposal meets health objectives is by using HIAs (Glasson et al. 2013). The processes are like those used in sustainability appraisal and can be incorporated within it. The key reasons for undertaking an HIA are shown in Table 12.2.

There are different methods that can be used to make an HIA. The World Health Organization (WHO) suggests that there should be an initial scoping approach, which can then assess whether an HIA is required. It is also important to assess what role the HIA will have in decision making – will it be advisory or mandatory? Further, there will be issues about the role of medical or public health professionals in the HIA process, although Lock (2000) argues that it is a multi-disciplinary process that should include public engagement and span spatial scales. As with all impact assessments, several types of assessments may need to be undertaken at different stages in the process. There can be an HIA across the whole of a local plan, specific policies within it or in relation to individual development proposals.

The application of HIA, together with its tools and techniques, is at an early stage in its development and acceptance (Scott-Samuel 1998). However, there are some specific areas where HIA has been refined and developed, including, for example, for air quality (Thompson et al. 2014; Likhvar et al. 2015), in strategic environmental assessment for planning (Linzalone et al. 2014) and even for trade agreements (Ruckert et al. 2017). There are also assessment methods designed for urban (Carmichael et al. 2012) and rural areas (Swindlehurst 2005; Lee 2016).

In the development of specific use of HIA in planning, Forsyth et al. (2014) have suggested that this should be approached in a series of stages. This is based on the use of an initial review, then followed by the consideration of evidence and assessment against a checklist of questions. This can also include a structured workshop and the use of geographical information systems (GIS) in illustrating and assessing evidence. The methodology then follows that for environmental impact assessments (EIA) (Dunwoody and Johnson 2016; Cave et al. 2016) and business planning in considering status quo assessments and the appraisal of alternative scenarios, including the use of threshold analysis. As with other assessments, these will result in interpretation of the findings that are anchored to the initial objectives and the means of measuring the outcomes. There are also considerations of the relative weighting given to the whole HIA in comparison with other objectives, such as the need for jobs or housing, when considering a decision for development. Another barrier is the extent to which

Table 12.2 Why Do an HIA?

- To promote greater equity in health
- To promote evidence and knowledge-based planning and decision making
- To maximise health gain and minimise health loss by informing and influencing decision making in favour of health
- To reduce inequalities by addressing health impacts on vulnerable populations

public health professionals and planners understand the relative interests that can be considered and this can cause misunderstandings within and between organisations (Carmichael et al. 2012).

The HUDU rapid assessment tool checklist for assessing the health impact of planning proposals (HUDU 2017b) identifies key topics to include with a HIA matrix, including access to services, housing and air quality, and then reviews the kind of evidence that is available to make local assessments about the relative importance of these issues. The checklist provides some questions to stimulate thinking on issues within the matrix and provides an opportunity for the responses to be included to build an assessment. There are also approaches that consider health impacts of specific aspects of planning such as transport (Mueller et al. 2015).

Developing Planning Policies for Health

One of the key considerations in planning for health is the inclusion of health outcomes as part of planning policy so that they can be considered as part of decision making on specific developments, including location, access and proximity to other local infrastructure, such as schools.

In a study undertaken in 2010, local plans were reviewed in response to a requirement to focus policies on local health priorities. This requirement was subsequently removed but while it was in effect, it resulted in a greater range of innovative policy design input, although no assessment was made of the outcomes in practice. These policies were focussed on public health issues, including obesity and specific chronic conditions including respiratory and circulatory diseases together with mental health and ageing. It also addressed road traffic accidents. The level of detail achieved for each of these policy interventions varies, with some acknowledging required action on alcohol and drug abuse, and is related to the extent to which planning policies can be constructed to intervene in these issues. Others were more proactive and detailed, e.g. the responses to road traffic accidents.

Although not necessarily seen as a central planning issue, some plans addressed mortality and life expectancy, including specific causes of death, such as cancer. Some considered detailed approaches about how to respond to the relationship between settlement policy and older people and the provision of local shops for vulnerable and older adults. Some tackled mental health issues through calm environments, safety and reducing fear of crime. In terms of access to services, many local plans linked these to transport policies but also to street cleanliness and attractiveness to encourage people to walk. Finally, some local plans addressed fuel poverty and saw this as a key issue to be tackled. In addition to the range of policy responses, there were also other health policies included, such as those specifically addressed to the health needs of Gypsy, Roma and Traveller communities.

The inclusion of an issue within a local plan needs to be based on evidence from the health and wellbeing strategy and the extent to which any health issue in the population varies from local and national averages. This will signal the need to consider a policy priority and include it in the local plan. While most local plans have not included evidence of this kind with associated policies, some local authority planners are being invited to sit on health and wellbeing boards (Morphet and Clifford 2017). Where this is not the case, there are opportunities to generate closer working and consider policy development and adoption in the local plan that may be expected to improve health outcomes of the population.

However, the intention to include a policy does not necessarily mean that the policy will be delivered or that the intended outcome will be achieved. Further, the recognition of the elevated level of smoking in the area or level of cancer deaths does not immediately lend itself to identifiable policies. In some cases, such as the reduction in teenage pregnancies, the response may come through more detailed development management policies, such as the provision of pharmacies. Similarly, on smoking, this may be an issue of planning control over smoking shelters. In some cases, local plans used town centre planning policy to reduce the number of drinking establishments through the Use Classes Order, promoting non-alcohol-based leisure and alternative land uses. Some local plans have also included access to fresh food, particularly for those living in deprived areas, and the provision of allotments as part of their health outcomes. In Table 12.3, the desired health outcome and the contributing local plans policies used by some local authorities are set out.

Planning for Health Care Facilities

Provision of funding for health services is provided through the CCG's purchasing services for their populations. The government provides funding and direct advice on premises for GPs and hospitals in England through the NHS Property Services, Ltd. NHS Property Services is 100 per cent owned by the Secretary of State and in turn owns the legal title to 4,000 assets. The organisation owns sites across England but retains a local focus, providing strategic and operational management of NHS estates, property and facilities. Additionally, many GPs own their own premises.

One of the key issues for planning is to consider the location and access to health care facilities of all types. Firstly, the local plan can adopt a standard for access for several types of facilities based in local evidence of use (DCLG 2017; MHCLG 2018). In applying these standards, the local plan can identify where there are gaps in provision. These standards and applications will also need to be developed and applied in conjunction with the CCG, as differential standards may be in practical operation between those localities where people have longer life expectancy than others. There may also be different standards applied in locations with more children or older people. A further consideration is the standard and quality of these facilities and whether they may need replacing in the immediate plan period. The preferences for the style of health care provision change regularly and it may be difficult to fix a specific model of

Table 12.3 Examples of Local Plans Policies to Deliver Health Outcomes

Health Outcome	Examples in Local Plans Policies
Overall satisfaction with the area	Using the survey of quality of life indicators as part of its evidence base; also linked to mental health
Adult participation in sport and active recreation	Enhancing access to facilities; accessing more active transport options; considering the pattern of development as one of the mechanisms for improving levels of activity; using health and wellbeing and sport and leisure strategies as part of the evidence base
Local council and police dealing with local concerns about anti-social behaviour and crime	Identifying fear of crime as key issue in issues and options paper; addressing anti-social behaviour as a key objective and addressing it through the night-time economy and the pattern of development in town centres; using the design of streets to promote feelings of safety
Rate of hospital admissions per 100,000 for alcohol-related diseases	Identifying alcohol abuse as a key issue and relating it to night-time economy policies for town centres
Number of drug users recorded as being in effective treatment	Identifying drug abuse as a key issue and assessing whether more community facilities for therapy centres or where meetings between individuals and their health professionals are required
Number of people, including children, killed or seriously injured in road traffic accidents	Developing a proactive policy on home zones to support safer travel and reduce child deaths from road traffic accidents (RTAs); reviewing the location of secondary school provision to reduce journeys to school across the town to minimise travel and accidents; requiring all planning applications for certain types of development to be accompanied by green travel plans
Emotional health of children	Identifying access to children's centres as critical; identifying fear of crime as a major issue; identifying the specific requirements for children and their families to live in safe environments
Effectiveness of child and adolescent mental health services (CAMHS)	Addressed schools and facilities for children with special needs through infrastructure delivery; specific policies on 'free play' environments
Services for disabled children	Addressing specific facilities requirements; prioritising the provision of facilities
Obesity in primary age children in reception	Identifying the links between childhood obesity and life expectancy and focusing on ways in which children can be more active from their early years and how planning can support delivery of mechanisms
Obesity in primary age children in Year 6	Identify child obesity as a specific issue to be tackled and addressing this through local transport actions, including improving access to facilities by walking, cycling and public transport, and improving personal safety through design improvements as well as green space improvements

Health Outcome	Examples in Local Plans Policies
Children and young people's participation in high-quality PE and sport	Promoting wellbeing; setting out how to achieve this through location, design and the pattern of development
Young people's participation in positive activities	Identifying the needs of young people; focussing on the locations where additional facilities are required, particularly in rural areas
Substance misuse by young people	Identifying issues of teenage drug dependency rates as key issue to be addressed though provision of community facilities and access to health
Proportion of children in poverty	Tackling child poverty in a holistic way; identifying most deprived areas; focussing growth and regeneration strategies to help to deal with this issue
16–18-year-olds who are not in education, employment or training (NEETS)	Identifying the needs of those who are deprived and meeting these through identified development opportunities to create more jobs; raising the aspirations of young people, their skills and education; retaining young people within the area through jobs
Self-reported measure of people's overall health and wellbeing	Encouraging local food production and processing to support both healthier living and wider sustainable objectives; promoting mental and physical health through green space, good environmental quality standards and access to safe forms of walking and cycling; undertaking HIA
All-age, all-cause mortality rate	Addressing health inequalities where health outcomes and life expectancy are lower; including mortality and life chances; addressing elevated levels of cancer deaths; designing streets to promote activity
Mortality rates for all circulatory diseases at ages under 75	Improving health outcomes, including mortality rates, as justification for the delivery of improvements in facilities, green space, opportunities for walking and cycling and linking improved facilities to programmes to improve activity levels by other agencies; identifying this as a specific target in annual monitoring
Stopping smoking	Controlling smoking shelters
Social care clients receiving self-directed support per 100,000 population	Identifying sites for more specialist open market housing for people needing onsite support or access to support for their existing and future populations, based on expectations that older people will want to live independently for longer; providing adequate dwellings for people who are in need; providing aid in a coordinated way
Delayed transfers of care	More support for carers to enable people to live at home, and more community and day care facilities to support older people living at home; potential of more jobs in the social care sector
People supported to live independently through social services (all adults)	Providing specific housing types for elderly people; a settlement policy to support independent living; reducing social exclusion for adults and older people

Health Outcome	Examples in Local Plans Policies
Health life expectancy from the age of 65	Promoting good health and wellbeing as part of commitment to social progress through providing community and physicals activities
Extent to which older people receive the support they need to live at home	Supporting maintenance of local shops for those who find it difficult to get out frequently; extra care housing, including discussing whether this should be in extra care communities or integrated into existing communities
Percentage of vulnerable people achieving independent living	Using Building for Life criteria as part of evidence base; providing local shops for those who find it difficult to get out
Adults with learning disabilities in settled accommodation	Lifetime homes for people who need support
Overall employment rate (working age)	Employment rates and unemployment as key issues in areas of high deprivation through employment, land and location policies; addressing unemployment
Working age people who are on out-of-work benefits	Identifying higher unemployment areas as locations for development, including new potential workplaces; reducing unemployment through supporting businesses to increase their turnover and monitoring it
Working-age people claiming out-of-work benefits in worst performing neighbourhoods	Identifying areas with higher unemployment and, in those areas, locations for development, including new potential workplaces
Amount of affordable housing delivered (gross)	Including amount of affordable housing provided
Percentage of non-decent council homes	Achieving decent homes through planning policy
Median earnings of employees in an area	Increasing income levels through regeneration and transport investment; associating income levels with access to affordable housing for the residents
Congestion and average journey time per mile during the morning peak	Congestion and air quality as key issues related to lack of investment in public transport in more socially deprived areas, giving poorer access to jobs; link between congestion and air quality
New business registration rate	Addressing new businesses and monitoring though VAT registration
Access to services	Re-siting GP surgeries into health clinics; improving access to local services by walking and public transport; addressing the needs of older people in rural areas, including access to services; co-location of services to improve accessibility
Per capita reduction in CO_2 emissions in la area	Addressing CO_2 reduction; location policies and decentralised energy generation

Health Outcome	Examples in Local Plans Policies
Tackling fuel poverty; percentage of people receiving income-based benefits and living in homes with low energy-efficiency rating	Identifying where there are the highest levels of fuel poverty and using policies to reduce through retrofitting
Improved street and environmental cleanliness	Enhancing streets in ways that will that encourage people to use them
Children travelling to school and mode of transport usually used	Redistribution of secondary school provision to reduce cross city journeys by school children; school travel plans for the whole area

delivery in the plan. It may be necessary to identify sites or locations for health care facilities without determining how they should be developed in the future.

As the provision of health care is purchased by the CCG, there is some competition between hospitals, and between hospitals and GPs, for the provision of services. This may have an effect in the longer term, if combined with other health funding for teaching hospitals and specialisms may favour one location over another. It is possible for some health facilities to be reduced on site but these may be replaced by others, such as social care housing for older people or for health care professionals. Planning can also plan for dual use facilities, including health care and libraries or sports centres, in a joint approach to social prescribing (Naylor 2016). The local plan also must consider provision for mental health facilities. These are frequently located in the community but may use premises above shops or in town centres that are not immediately visible in the street scene.

The provision of care of older people through specialist housing or homes is a key issue for the future of local plans and assessment of housing numbers. While these may not be considered as health facilities, they are as much part of the joint approach to health and social care and their availability can have a major effect on the way in which local hospitals can deal with delayed discharges. Similarly, having adequate housing available for health staff in hospitals can be a major consideration, as can access by public transport for all those working in and visiting the hospital.

Local authorities may be requested by health providers to contribute to the provision of facilities through developer contributions (HUDU 2013b). However, any assessment of the use of developer contributions needs to considered in the context that the NHS is a publicly funded service, free at the point of delivery and funded through taxation. Any request for funding of health facilities will need to be in the context of other development requirements in the area and may be in competition for use of funds for other health-related initiatives, such as design and delivery of non-obesogenic environments. Here, two parts of the NHS will be in competition with each other. Also, the provision of health care is now included within competition legislation (the NHS Act

2006) and any contribution will need to be considered carefully within state aid rules. Local authorities will need to take legal advice before making any contribution through development income, either through funding or premises. As an alternative, local authorities can take land from developers and hold in their ownership and then rent or lease the land to health providers. This would leave the land in a more flexible ownership for diverse kinds of health or community provision and provide an income stream for the local authority.

Social care is funded by the state and the user and this mixed pattern of funding is likely to continue in the future. Where there is a need for life-long homes for sheltered accommodation provided through a housing association of the local authority, this may be a provision that could be included in a developer's contributions in cash or kind or through Community Infrastructure Levy (CIL).

Healthy Communities Initiatives

As part of promoting a more comprehensive approach to delivering healthier places, the NHS has launched some initiatives as demonstrating exemplary approaches and trying to change existing practice. The NHS Healthy New Towns programme was launched in 2015. Through a competitive process, ten private sector housing sites were selected where specific themes were being progressed through design and delivery of places in conjunction with the developers. These themes included active travel and healthful food choices, new care models and the public realm (McCafferty 2016; Kleinert and Horton 2016). The housing sites vary in size and location, ranging from 800 units in schemes in Runcorn and Oxfordshire to 15,000 in Ebbsfleet in Kent, with other sites, including those for 8,000 homes in Cranford in Devon and 10,000 each in Northstowe in Cambridge and Barking Riverside in London.

These sites include some that were former government-owned land and most, if not all, appear to have direct sponsorships from Homes England, the government's housing agency. As yet there has been no evaluation of either whether houses on these sites will be attractive to purchasers or whether the approaches taken in design and other features included will lead to healthier outcomes for the residents. In December 2017, the NHS launched an initiative to attempt to share the early lessons from the Healthy New Towns programme with private sector developers, with a particular focus on affordable housing. This initiative calls for developers to sign up to work with health practitioners in the areas in which their sites are located.

The NHS is also undertaking other initiatives to support housing development, including making a commitment to build 26,000 homes on land in its ownership. The NHS Confederation, a membership body of health organisations, has called for the NHS to build housing for staff on its own land (Tapper 2017). The Secretary of State for Health gave a pledge at the Conservative Party conference that when NHS land is sold, NHS staff will be given first refusal on any affordable housing built, which is intended to benefit up to 3,000 families (Barnes 2017), but it was not clear how this would be implemented.

References

6, P., Fletcher-Morgan, X., & Leyland, K. (2010). Making people more responsible: The Blair Government's programme for changing citizens' behavior, *Political Studies*, 58(3), 427–449.

Barnes, S. (2017). NHS staff to get 'first refusal' on affordable homes. Inside Housing, 3 October. www.insidehousing.co.uk/news/news/nhs-staff-to-get-first-refusal-on-affordable-homes-52627 (accessed 4 January 2018).

Barton, H. (2005). A health map for urban planners: Towards a conceptual model for healthy sustainable settlements. *Built Environment*, 31(4), pp. 339–355.

Barton, H., Grant, M., & Guise, R. (2010). *Shaping Neighbourhoods for Health, Sustainability and Vitality* (2nd ed). London: E & F Spon.

Barton, H., Thompson, S., Burgess, S., & Grant, M. (Eds.) (2015). *The Routledge Handbook of Planning for Health and Well-Being: Shaping a Sustainable and Healthy Future*. Abingdon: Routledge.

Barton, J., & Pretty, J. (2010). What is the best dose of nature and green exercise for improving mental health? A multi-study analysis. *Environmental Science & Technology*, 44(10), 3947–3955.

Carmichael, L., Barton, H., Gray, S., Lease, H., & Pilkington, P. (2012). Integration of health into urban spatial planning through impact assessment: Identifying governance and policy barriers and facilitators. *Environmental Impact Assessment Review*, 32(1), 187–194.

Cave, B., Fothergill, J., Pyper, R., & Gibson, G. (2016). Amending the EIA Directive – an opportunity for health, environmental assessment and planning. *Town and Country Planning*, November, 495–498.

Congdon, P. (2009). Life expectancies for small areas: a Bayesian random effects methodology, *International Statistical Review*, 77, 222–240.

DCLG (2012). *National Planning Policy Framework*. London: DCLG.

DCLG (2017). The role of health and wellbeing in planning. Planning Policy Guidance. www.gov.uk/guidance/health-and-wellbeing#history (accessed 3 November 2017).

DoH (2013). Statutory guidance published on joint strategic needs assessments and joint health and wellbeing strategies. www.gov.uk/government/publications/jsnas-and-jhws-statutory-guidance (accessed 23 July 2018).

DoH (2011). JSNAs and joint health and wellbeing strategies explained. www.gov.uk/government/news/jsnas-and-joint-health-and-wellbeing-strategies-explained (accessed 3 January 2018).

Dunwoody, J., & Johnson, P. (2016). How to include health in EIA? *Town and Country Planning*, November, 492–494.

Forsyth, A., Slotterback, C., & Krizek, K. (2010). Health Impact Assessment (HIA) for planners: What tools are useful? *Journal of Planning Literature*, 24(3), 231–245.

Glasson, J., Therivel, R., & Chadwick, A. (2013). *Introduction to Environmental Impact Assessment*. Abingdon: Routledge.

Griffiths, C., Wilkins, E., & Morris, M. (2016). Associating food environments with obesity? *Town and Country Planning*, November, 465–469.

Halpern, D., Bates, C., Mulgan, G., Aldridge, S., Neales, G., & Heathfield, A. (2004). *Personal Responsibility and Changing Behaviour: The State of Knowledge and Implications for Public Policy*. London: Prime Minister's Strategy Unit, Cabinet Office.

Harris, N., & Hooper, A. (2004). Rediscovering the 'spatial' in public policy and planning: An examination of the spatial content of sectoral policy documents, *Planning Theory and Practice*, 5(2), 147–169.

Haughton, G., Allmendinger, P., Counsell, D., & Vigar, G. (2010). *The New Spatial Planning*. Abingdon: Routledge.

HUDU (2013a). *Hot Food Takeaways*. London: NHS London Healthy Urban Development Unit.

HUDU (2013b). *Planning Contributions for Health: Case Study Examples*. London: NHS London Healthy Urban Development Unit.

HUDU (2017a). *Healthy Urban Planning Checklist*. London: NHS London Healthy Urban Development Unit.

HUDU (2017b). *Rapid Health Impact Assessment Tool*. London: NHS London Healthy Urban Development Unit.

HUDU (2017c). *Rapid Health Impact Assessment Matrix Self Completion Form*. London: NHS London Healthy Urban Development Unit. www.healthyurbandevelopment.nhs.uk/wp-content/uploads/2017/05/HUDU-Rapid-HIA-Tool-3rd-edition-April-2017-self-completion-form.pdf (accessed 3 November 2017).

Huxley, M. (2007). Geographies of Governmentality. In *Space, Knowledge and Power: Foucault and Geography* (pp. 185–204). Farnham: Ashgate.

Imrie, R., & Raco, M. (2000). Governmentality and rights and responsibilities in urban policy. *Environment and Planning A*, 32, 2187–2204.

Kidd, S. (2007). Towards a framework of integration in spatial planning: An exploration from a health perspective, *Planning Theory and Practice*, 8(2), 161–181.

Kleinert, S., & Horton, R. (2016). Urban design: An important future force for health and wellbeing. *The Lancet*, 388(10062), 2848–2850.

Lee, R. (2016). Health inequalities in the urban fringe and rural localities. *Town and Country Planning*, November, 473–476.

LGA (2011). Joint strategic needs assessment: Data inventory. www.local.gov.uk/sites/default/files/documents/joint-strategic-needs-ass-41b.pdf (accessed 10 July 2018).

Likhvar, V. N., Pascal, M., Markakis, K., Colette, A., Hauglustaine, D., Valari, M., ... & Kinney, P. (2015). A multi-scale health impact assessment of air pollution over the 21st century. *Science of the Total Environment*, 514, 439–449.

Linzalone, N., Assennato, G., Ballarini, A., Cadum, E., Cirillo, M., Cori, L., ... & Soggiu, M. E. (2014). Health Impact Assessment practice and potential for integration within environmental impact and strategic environmental assessments in Italy. *International Journal of Environmental Research and Public Health*, 11(12), 12683–12699.

Lock, K. (2000). Health impact assessment. *BMJ: British Medical Journal*, 320, 1395–1398.

MHCLG (2018). *Revised National Planning Policy Framework 2018*. Cm 9680. London: MHCLG.

MoL (2017a). *A City for All Londoners*. London: Mayor of London.

MoL (2017b). Draft New London Plan Policy E9: Retail, markets and hot food takeaways. www.london.gov.uk/what-we-do/planning/london-plan/new-london-plan/draft-new-london-plan/chapter-6-economy/policy-e9-retail-markets-and-hot-food-takeaways (accessed 3 January 2018).

Morphet, J. (2008). *Modern Local Government*. London: SAGE.

Morphet, J. (2009). Local integrated spatial planning The changing role in England. *Town Planning Review*, 80(4), 383–415.

Morphet, J. & Clifford, B. (2017). *Local Authority Direct Provision of Housing*. London: NPF and RTPI.

Mueller, N., Rojas-Rueda, D., Cole-Hunter, T., de Nazelle, A., Dons, E., Gerike, R., ... & Nieuwenhuijsen, M. (2015). Health impact assessment of active transportation: A systematic review. *Preventive Medicine*, 76, 103–114.

Mulgan, G. (2009). *The Art of Public Strategy: Mobilising Power and Knowledge for Public Good*. Oxford: Oxford University Press.

Naylor, S. (2016). Thinking together, planning together, delivering together. *Town and Country Planning*, November, 483–485.

NHS (2007a). *A Guide to Town Planning for NHS Staff*. London: NHS.

NHS (2007b). *A Guide to the NHS for Local Planning Authorities*. London: NHS.

NHS (2011). Joint health and well being strategy explained. www.gov.uk/government/news/jsnas-and-joint-health-and-wellbeing-strategies-explained (accessed 9 July 2018).

NHS (2017). Joint strategic needs assessment. http://content.digital.nhs.uk/jsna (accessed 3 November 2017).

Nutsford, D., Pearson, A. L., & Kingham, S. (2013). An ecological study investigating the association between access to urban green space and mental health. *Public Health*, 127(11), 1005–1011.

PHE (2017a). Healthy new towns. www.england.nhs.uk/ourwork/innovation/healthy-new-towns/ (accessed 3 January 2018).

PHE (2017b). Health matters: Obesity and the food environment. www.gov.uk/government/publications/health-matters-obesity-and-the-food-environment/health-matters-obesity-and-the-food-environment–2 (accessed 3 January 2017).

PHE (2017c). *Spatial Planning for Health: An Evidence Resource for Planning and Designing Healthier Places*. London: PHE.

PHE, & LGA (2013). *Obesity and the Environment: Increasing Physical Activity and Active Travel*. London: PHE.

PHE, & LGA (2014). *Obesity and the Environment: Regulating the Growth of Fast Food Outlets*. London: PHE.

Pilkington, P. (2009). *Health Impact Assessment: Spreading Good Practice Among Public Health and Planning Professionals Baseline Briefing Exercise Activity in the South West*. Bristol: UWE.

RSPH (2015). *Health of the High Street*. London: RSPH.

RTPI (2009). Delivering healthy communities. RTPI Good Practice Note 5. www.rtpi.org.uk/media/6325/GPN5_final.pdf (accessed 10 July 2018).

Ruckert, A., Schram, A., Labonté, R., Friel, S., Gleeson, D., & Thow, A. M. (2017). Policy coherence, health and the sustainable development goals: A health impact assessment of the Trans-Pacific Partnership. *Critical Public Health*, 27(1), 86–96.

Sandford, M. (2017). Combined authorities. House of Commons Library Briefing Paper Number 06649, 4 July. London: House of Commons Library. https://researchbriefings.parliament.uk/ResearchBriefing/Summary/SN06649 (accessed 9 July 2018).

Scott-Samuel, A. (1998). Health impact assessment: Theory into practice. *Journal of Epidemiology and Community Health*, 52(11), 704–705.

Stoker, G. (2011). Was local governance such a good idea? A global comparative perspective. *Public Administration*, 89(1), 15–31.

Swindlehurst, H. (2005). *Rural Proofing for Health*. Newtown: Institute of Rural Health.

Tapper, J. (2017). 40,000 homes for medics and staff could be built on spare NHS land. *The Observer*, 10 June. www.theguardian.com/society/2017/jun/10/nurses-homes-nhs-staff-shortfall (accessed 4 January 2018).

Thompson, T. M., Saari, R. K., & Selin, N. E. (2014). Air quality resolution for health impact assessment: Influence of regional characteristics. *Atmospheric Chemistry and Physics*, 14(2), 969–978.

WHO (1999). Health impact assessment. Gothenburg consensus paper. Brussels: European Centre for Health Policy, WHO Regional Office for Europe. www.healthedpartners.org/ceu/hia/hia01/01_02_gothenburg_paper_on_hia_1999.pdf (accessed 9 July 2018).

13 Planning and Older People

Introduction

While the challenges of an ageing society are understood in broad terms, there has, as yet, been very little planning policy to address this issue or how a significantly older population may need to be considered in planning in the future. Policies have been focussed on housing that encourages downsizing and pathways into care, although the rate of development of purpose-built housing is slow. Future planning policies may require an increase in more localised day care facilities, such as those available for children, increased leisure and sports facilities for older people and different approaches to health care delivery that may have spatial consequences. It is also important to consider the role of older people in the labour force.

In the UK, as in many other countries, the proportion of the population that is over the state retirement age is increasing and people are living longer (OECD 2000). However, unlike other countries, the UK has a young population and the population is growing (ONS 2017). Further, the length of the period lived post-retirement age means that older people will probably pass through at least three or more transitions, out of a possible six, during the later periods of their life, as shown in Table 13.1. The first phase is pre-retirement, which may then move into the second phase of retirement and include a move from full-time to part-time working, volunteering, care for grandchildren or parents (Hill 2017) or engagement in hobby activities. A third transition occurs when people move into full retirement with good health and become active members of the community. An alternative to this phase occurs for those who decide to build a second career, which may be through consultancy based on former work experience or longstanding interests or hobbies. Some will take jobs in museums or retail at lower pay than their former employment, either to supplement their pension or remain in a social circle. A fifth transition may occur when a partner dies or when there is a health change for one partner that requires more close and supportive care. For many people, another transition comes in the last six months of their lives, when they might need considerably more care and support. These six stages may extend between ten and 40 years of life, with some being retired for as long as they have been at work (Stula 2012).

Table 13.1 Periods of Life in Older Age

Phase	Characteristics	Planning Issues
1. Pre-Retirement 50–60	May reduce hours, move home, take on more voluntary interests	Downsizing housing stock but may have children living at home
2. Partial Retirement 55–75	Active in work and voluntary activities, engagement in arts and culture	Labour market participation, journey to work and volunteering; may have children still living at home; divorce and demands on housing market; may be caring for grandchildren full or part time
3. Full Retirement – Good Health 65–80	Attendance and participation at cultural events, organised activities; less driving, more need for social contact for those living on their own	Main concerns are travel, personal safety, fear of crime; activities may depend on street lighting, public transport access, any downside to sheltered accommodation or purpose-designed housing for older people
4. Second Career 50–80	Change job; need for income because of low pension; work from choice	Labour market projections; journey to work considerations
5. Full Retirement – Caring 65–85	Less participation in social activities, more attendance at hospital and health facilities, manging household and other support	More dependency on community transport, use of car to attend hospital or health facilities, probably with a blue badge; may have concerns about income and fuel bills for those at home all day; adaptation of homes
6. Full Retirement – Cared for 70–100	At home, in a care home or in a hospice; less external activity, attendance at health facilities	Move out of house into supported accommodation; adaptation of home; more access to health facilities; possible access to hospice; cemetery and crematoria provision

All of this suggests that the needs of older people should be considered through these stages in the same ways as the different requirements of younger people, including families with children, rather than being regarded as homogenous. Older people, when first retired, may be very active and, if they have an adequate occupational pension and other financial resources, they may be supporting local arts and cultural activities, through providing audiences, volunteers and sources of research and knowledge. This may be extended for prolonged periods of activity during this phase. There may still be children living at home, needing some financial or domestic support, returning from university, on marriage breakdown or through inability to fund a separate home. At this stage, older people may also take some equity release from their pension or their home to support children or grandchildren in the purchase of their first home. There is also some evidence that older people are moving to larger homes to accommodate the needs of their adult children.

In the next phase, when they are full-time carers, older people may require more support themselves for travel to hospital or care in their own home. This may necessitate moving to a smaller home or a care facility with specific support. At these times, the location of the home may be important in terms of access to medical and other facilities and the level of support available through friends and family may be critical. This may also be a time when people must stay in hospital because they cannot be supported to live at home. This increases when they may need more intensive care, more hospital visits and end-of-life care options, including hospices.

What do these transitional phases mean for those considering a local plan or infrastructure provision for their area? Each area is likely to have its own ways of addressing these issues although advice and practices can be transferred from elsewhere. Some local authorities in England are setting out to be focussed on older people. In Leeds, the Older People's Forum is a partnership with older people working with the Centre for Ageing Better, which is proactively promoting the use of community and public transport, volunteering and housing. In Manchester, there is a discussion about creating an 'age friendly' city in recognition of the changing demographic profile (Buffel et al. 2016). Other localities are taking up the 'men in sheds' project, which is enabling older men to share their skills, offering some return to the community and improving social interaction (UKMSA 2017).

There is a universal view that older people need specialist support, without an understanding of their contribution to the labour market and their spending power (George et al. 2015). Older people may want to engage in these activities for their own wellbeing or because they now have more time to do so. They may also be keen to take on part-time work to provide some additional finance to supplement their pension. As there is a potential reduction in the migrant labour force from the EU following the Brexit Referendum, there may be much more demand for older people to enter the labour force to support services at all levels. Planning therefore needs to take into consideration housing needs (DCLG 2017a, 2017b), but also other contributions to the labour market, which need to be factored into assessments of working populations and which may be beyond traditional levels (Robertson 2016).

Finding Evidence About the Needs of Older People

Evidence of the needs and activities of older people for use in planning can be found in the the DOH's health and wellbeing strategy (DOH 2013) and extra care housing strategies at local levels. Levels of engagement in the labour market may be offered by local employers and employment agencies, while journey to work data may be extracted from regular journey information provided through free bus and travel passes. In London, older people have free travel on London transport services at all times, with free travel on rail after 9.30 on weekdays and all times at the weekend. Outside London, free travel may be confined to bus journeys and may be available after 9.30 in the morning.

This may shape the type of employment that older people obtain and they may be more flexible in their potential hours of work than those with child care responsibilities. There may also be local data on how many older people are caring for younger children to allow their parents to engage in the labour market. This may be a cheaper alternative than a day nursery and may only be for part of the week but this data provides some indication that supports the labour market levels of activity. Finally, many older people volunteer to support charities and cultural activities.

The Implications of an Ageing Society for Planning

When planners consider issues for older people in local plans, these are primarily focussed on the provision of specific housing needs, although even these inclusions tend to be general proposals. There may be some indication that housing for older people needs to be near town centres or accessible facilities, but no specific standards are set for these locations, nor for wider accessibility to other facilities, including leisure, transport and health facilities. In 2017, the government made a commitment that local plans in England should address housing for older people specially (DCLG/DWP 2017) and this might make some difference, not least in being the first time that these groups have been identified as needing specific allocations in housing policy and land supply. There is a general discussion and consideration of approaches to ageing in planning at the end of this chapter.

Working and Income

Older people may now spend much more time working after the state retirement age than previous generations. This may be because they are healthier and can contemplate a longer retirement period in comparison with their own parents. Older people may have state and occupational pensions but as more generations move into retirement, these pensions are likely to reduce and older people are more likely to work longer before they can receive a state pension. After leaving their main job, older people are entering the labour force in increasing numbers to supplement their pensions (ONS 2017). Transition from work can also lead to a loss of structure, identity and self-esteem in people's lives, which economic activity or regular volunteering can provide. Older people also receive free and concessionary travel, which means that they have fewer costs of working than before retirement (Green et al. 2014; Mackett 2017).

While the increase in labour market participation by those beyond retirement age may have changed following the removal of the legal age cap for those working, many may take jobs that are not the same as those they did for most of their careers (McNair 2006). The issue facing planners making plans and considering specific development proposals is what will be the proportion of the labour force comprised of older people and what jobs will they do. This may have an impact on considering the role of economic activity and growth in the area and may change perceptions of the attractiveness of specific locations for jobs. This might also have an impact on the assessment of job-related housing requirements, as those taking on these new working roles in older age may be already living within the area and not moving housing location for work. It may have some implications for travel to work assessments, as older people may travel to work using their free travel concessions and reduce demand for car parking. Older people may be willing to work later shifts or more flexibly, as they do not have childcare considerations.

Increasing the number of older people in the workforce will also be dependent on several factors. These include a willingness of employers to employ older people. Some retailers have a policy to employ older people and operational practices may be changing in other companies, particularly in the service sectors. There also may be a greater willingness of older people to work. Frequently, given their lower-paid jobs and interrupted working lives, women have lower pensions and may be more willing to work to supplement their income. Some are interested in maintaining a sense of purpose or a social circle. As there may be fewer workers available from the EU 27, as a result both of Brexit uncertainties and of the improvement of domestic economies, older people may be attracted into the labour force to meet these gaps.

It is also important to consider older people as doing unpaid work that contributes to the community and the economy (NCVO 2016; Arno et al. 1999). This is generally considered as volunteering and charity work, but also much unpaid caring for family members is undertaken by older people, which offsets the costs to the public sector. These roles are likely to continue, and not only for older people, as those in middle age may be caring for children and parents at the same time (Hill 2017). The extent to which older people are and could participate in the local labour market and the implications for housing and travel all need to be considered when preparing a plan or making employment projections. There will also need to be some adjustment in thinking as the state pension age in England increases to 68 in 2037–2039.

Housing

Much of the consideration about older people in planning is about housing. Housing for older people is a critical issue for older households and the focus is either on those households that wish to downsize after their families have left home or the needs of those older people who will require more direct care (Altman et al. 2013). There is generally a move towards encouraging older people to reduce the size of the property that they occupy to make it available for younger and larger households. This is the case in all tenures, whether in public housing, where some local authorities are building diverse kinds of stock to encourage downsizing, and in the private sector, where older people may no longer be able to fund the heating and maintenance costs required. For some older people, the value of their home will be used to offset care home costs by taking a charge on the property sale when it occurs. Wider public policy decisions about the caps and ceilings that may be applied to those using the value of their homes in this way were an issue in the 2017 UK general election, when there was a suggestion that £100,000 could be retained and beyond this, the funds available on the value of a house could be used for care costs although this was subsequently dropped.

Downsizing

Many of the issues related to downsizing relate to motivations, available housing options and experience (Pannell et al. 2012; Graham et al. 2015). While older people are in their active period of ageing, or whilst in the transition between working and needing more care – perhaps a period of 20 years after the state retirement age – there may be little incentive to move home, particularly if their social circle and family are still within the vicinity. However, the potential consideration to downsize or relocate to another part of the country may also depend on the availability of a reasonable pension or appropriate housing stock. While there are few providers of specialist housing stock for older people, with one company, McCarthy and Stone (2017), providing 70 per cent of the market, this may not be attractive to all. Further, some of the management costs and retentions on equity release may also discourage people from purchasing these dwellings. However, their locations, frequently on the edge of a town centre, are attractive to older people, as are the social activities and interactions that might be available.

Changing Household Patterns: Silver Splitters

The divorce rates are growing for older people and there is a new group of 'silver splitters' who are seeking rented accommodation rather than house purchase (Rudgard and Kirk 2017). Secondly, there are also older people who are helping their own families by providing them with accommodation (Morphet and Clifford 2017). This might be because children stay at home well into adulthood, as they cannot afford to purchase a home and, in some cases, older people are buying larger homes to accommodate their family – perhaps on divorce – who cannot afford to buy a separate home. For some older people, they are also still caring for their own parents as well as their children and this may provide pressures for bringing households together (Hill 2017).

Supported Living

In 2017, the government estimated that there were approximately 651,500 supported homes in Great Britain, the majority in England (85 per cent), and at any one time there are around 716,000 people living in supported housing. Social landlords are the main providers, with housing associations providing the majority (71 per cent) alongside local authorities and third-sector providers. A small proportion is provided by the private sector (Blood 2016; DCLG/DWP

2017). The provision of supported housing in its various forms enables the release of resources in health, where many older people have delayed discharge because there is nowhere else for them to go and this is popularly known as 'bed-blocking' (Fernández et al. 2018). While improved working relationships between health and social care are opening in some places, such as the Greater Manchester Combined Authority, the differences in funding, accountabilities and lack of integration between government departments responsible for housing and health mean that this continues to be a major issue at the local level (DCLG/DWP 2017).

Provision of those people needing more support and direct care, either in their own homes or in specialist facilities, is primarily by the private sector. While some local authorities provide care homes, the sector is dominated by private providers. These private facilities are inspected by the government's Care Quality Commission and there has been a growing public anxiety about both the costs of this provision and the quality of care that it provides to residents, with family members installing secure cameras to ensure that their family members are appropriately cared for. In some locations, local authorities, once the major providers of care, have decided to go back into direct provision.

The market for care is strongly influenced by the extent to which those using it, or their families, can pay for it. At present, many local authorities and care home owners will agree to take a charge on an older person's home to provide care, to be taken at point of house sale after death. There are political debates that remain unresolved about whether there should floors, ceilings and caps on the amount of funding being used in this way. A major challenge in providing supported housing for older people is in the supply of appropriate facilities. While there have been economic disincentives, there are also difficulties in finding appropriate locations and this is now a significant issue to be considered in local plans. Each area will have a supported housing commissioner as part of the health and social care team and it is important that local plan making engages with these commissioners to identify specific types of housing that are required or that might need to be adapted from other forms of housing use.

There is also a consideration of the design of new housing using lifetime homes standards, which mean that the internal layout of the dwelling and external access will provide for households into later life. These design standards include doorways, shower design and ramp access, amongst other issues. These design standards are shown on Table 13.2

The development of housing for older people with higher incomes is also emerging as a major business investment opportunity for some companies and investors. These might provide housing specifically designed for older people but can also include sports and social clubs with perhaps a nurse resident on site. The Association of Directors of Adult Social Services (ADASS) have identified the designs issues that planners might consider when assessing planning applications for housing for older people or housing that could be converted to their use in due course. These are shown on Table 13.3.

Table 13.2 Lifetime Homes Standard

- Parking standards and bay widths
- Approach to dwelling from parking (distance, gradients and widths)
- Approach to all entrances
- Entrances
- Communal stairs and lifts
- Internal doorways and hallways
- Circulation space
- Entrance-level living space
- Potential for entrance-level bed space
- Entrance-level WC and shower drainage
- WC and bathroom walls
- Stairs and potential through-floor lift in dwelling
- Potential for fitting of hoists in bedroom/bathroom
- Bathrooms
- Glazing and window handle heights
- Location of service controls

Source: Lifetime Homes 2010.

Table 13.3 Housing Standards for Older People

- Does the building promote or restrict independent living through its design?
- Are there identified factors that might limit the potentiality for change, internal pillars, asbestos, etc.
- Can the scheme support older people with a physical, sensory or mental frailty?
- Is the building wheelchair-accessible, and how accessible is the immediate area? Are there facilities for re-charging mobility vehicles?
- Is the building capable of making use of assistive technology, or to what degree is it doing so already?
- Are there good local facilities that are readily accessible?
- Is there sufficient storage space?

Source: ADASS 2011 p42.

There are also other issues to consider related to the design and longer term adaptability of new housing (housing for life) and in the Netherlands, 50 per cent of homes are requires to be built capable of adaptability and this is mainly being undertaken by housing associations (Stula 2012).

Care Homes

The provision of care homes can be by the public, private or voluntary sectors. The number of care homes in the UK has fallen as the economics of running such homes has become more difficult for providers. Some local authorities are closing care homes, e.g. in Devon, whilst other local authorities are opening them as businesses. The range of provision required for an increasing number of older people in UK society suggests that this needs to be considered in local planning policies, whether sites for care homes are allocated as part of overall housing land supply or designated through specific policies for town centres or urban extensions or garden villages. In some part of the country, hospital trusts with vacant land have been building supported housing and care facilities on their own estate and developing existing facilities for joint medical centres and care home facilities. However, at present these are local initiatives and there is no specific and considered policy assessment of the kind of provision that is required in any area or of how this may be delivered (BPF 2015).

There are examples of specific policies in the London Plan (GLA 2016), where boroughs are required to identify and address significant health and social care issues facing their area, for example, by utilising findings from Joint Strategic Needs Assessments (JSNAs). In translating this into local plan policies,

> Boroughs should ensure their public health team work with the local NHS, social care services and community organisations to:
> a regularly assess the need for health and social care facilities at the local and sub-regional levels; and
> b secure sites and buildings for, or to contribute to, future provision.
> (London Plan 2016 para 3.17).

Hospices

Hospices are primarily provided by the voluntary sector, but some places are funded through public sector budgets. Through fund raising, hospices may purchase existing buildings and convert them or provide purpose-built accommodation.

Experience of Housing for Older People in Other Countries

How do other countries cope with these issues and are there are examples that are useful to consider? Ball (2016) states that in the US, 17 per cent of the housing stock is for older people and in Australia and New Zealand, this is 13 per cent. In Canada, there has been some building for older people on university campuses, which allow for students to live with older people rent-free in return for providing some services – perhaps shopping, cleaning, washing and conversation. This also encourages a use of university facilities on campus all year round and can change the nature of the university as an institution. A similar approach is being trialled in Finland, where younger people are being provided with free accommodation in an older person's home in return for 3–5 hours' work per week for their neighbours (Macguire 2016). Another version of this, from the US, is, again, through universities' building retirement villages for their own faculty. These allow staff to move in and have a range of support and care to the end of life but also helps to maintain the intellectual and social life that academics had when they were working at the university. In Denmark, those over 75 and not in receipt of any social care are entitled to a home assessment to consider how their home might be modified. There has also been a policy to develop shared housing communities for those over 50 (Stula 2012).

Mental Health

IPSOS MORI (2015) found that concerns about mental health worried 22 per cent of people, compared with 50 per cent concerned about their physical health. Research also shows that older people's mental health benefits from access to or views over green spaces. This could have considerable implications for the design and location of specific facilities for older people identified in local plans, not least those worried about social isolation or not being able to meet family and friends. As Gale et al. (2011) discuss, there is little known about the relationship between older people's mental health and place, and in their study, they found that those older people who felt more positively about their neighbourhood had more positive mental health in later life. Mental health issues may range from anxiety or fear of crime, resulting in an unwillingness to leave the home (Foster et al. 2014; Lorenc et al. 2013). This could relate to media stories or direct experience of being attacked or robbed in the street. Other older people may have depression, which may have some connection with their neighbourhood, how it appears to them and the people who live there. However, Gale et al. (2011) found that where older people felt part of the community and where there was a greater sense of neighbourhood cohesion, their mental wellbeing was better.

Leisure

Older people are using their time in a variety of ways and may still distinguish their leisure time as being different from the daily round. Older people are now more engaged in international tourism and many take gap years when they retire (Patterson 2006). Advice on healthy living post-retirement is focussed on mental and physical activity. As older people maintain lifetime habits and practices of swimming and walking, others may join when they have more time available or are focussed on maintaining mobility. Environments may be able to absorb some of these activities, such as walking and cycling, relatively easily but other activities that need built facilities may come under increased demand pressure. Here it is possible to consider swimming pools, gyms and courts for games like badminton. As the population is more aware of the need to keep fit, these facilities may be under increased pressure for use. The demand assessments in their provision may need to take these issues for increased use into account. Also, leisure activities help to support social interaction and counteract isolation (Toepoel 2013).

Access and Transport

The design of environments for older people needs some consideration, particularly where there are or are expected to be higher numbers of older people (Metz 2003). As well as the design of public realm and considerate issues such as the length of time available on crossing points (Nathan et al. 2012), there were some other design approaches that make a difference in the likelihood that older people will walk in their neighbourhoods. What they found was that 'destinations that facilitate more social interaction, for example eating at a restaurant or church involvement, or provide opportunities for some incidental social contact, for example visiting the pharmacy or hairdresser, were the strongest predictors for walking among seniors' (p133). Public health benefits of access to public transport and walking and cycling are all part of the assessment of facilities in plan making for older people (Hupert and Galilee 2015).

Many older people drive although driving licences are reduced to a three-year term after the age of 70 in the UK, after which specific applications for renewal must be made. Older people may depend on their cars to get them to leisure and volunteering opportunities, including providing car services for others, such as taking them to hospital. Where there are caring responsibilities, the mobility of individuals may depend on cars being available. These issues are significant when considering parking standards for older people in purpose-designed development. In the UK, once people pass retirement age they are eligible for a concessionary bus pass although what this provides varies in each location; the requirements for car ownership may diminish over time and requirements for access to public transport may increase. Older people may use public transport more than they did previously, as they have time to plan their journeys, can travel off peak and maximise the free or low-cost travel available to them. In some locations, older people take the bus to the coast, country or market towns as a day out.

In considering plans and proposals for development for older people, there will be issues of location of development and car parking standards. Where facilities or housing are provided in town centres, there may be less need for car parking although this may not be the case for GP and other medical facilities where car-borne patients may be brought by their relatives. In these facilities, the practices of providing disabled or access bays for those needing more space to leave and enter a vehicle have been implemented and appear to work well. In town centres, the management of public services needs to ensure that there are no restrictions of footways from street furniture or advertising 'A' boards, which are matters of planning control. Where there are cycle paths, these need to be clearly demarcated to prevent pedestrian confusion and road-crossing points may need to offer longer periods where there are older people. There has been a recent innovation where an older person's smart phone can communicate with the crossing timer to allow a longer period for road crossing when used.

Wellbeing, Including Social Circles

Older people often need the opportunity to meet others and maintain a social circle. In the past, this has primarily been achieved though day care centres where there have been regular activities, frequently supported by a luncheon club. While older people may not be able to attend these facilities every day, they have provided some support. However, as austerity has reduced local authority budgets, the provision of day care and the associated facilities has been cut, with a focus in minimum care requirements. In some locations, day care and luncheon clubs are provided by charities and volunteers, but this is sporadic. Also, many of the community facilities used for day care are now occupied by nurseries for younger children as community building owners seek to maximise their income to reduce the effects of grant cuts and to maintain their other activities. Does this suggest a new model of day care that is akin to those services for younger children may need to be developed? Can day care be operated as a paid service in the same way as a nursery, where there are daily activities and lunch provided, but in a non-residential environment? Are au pairs for older people an option for the future?

Dementia

As the RTPI good practice note 'Living with dementia' (2017) points out, there are 850,000 people living with dementia in the UK, which is likely to increase to 2m by 2051. Because people with the initial stages of dementia are still living and working, the British Standards Institution (BSI) has launched a dementia-friendly communities code (BSI PAS1365: A code of practice for dementia-friendly communities) and the Alzheimer's Society has 215 registered dementia-friendly communities. The key issues to supporting dementia-friendly communities appear to relate to the quality of walkability and legibility in the local environment and the RTPI suggests that local authorities could undertake walkability audits in their areas. More detailed urban design advice is shown in Table 13.4.

Several countries are developing dementia care villages, particularly based on the Hogeweyk dementia village established in the Netherlands, which operates a range of care types within one care community. Canada is copying this model and in Australia, the first dementia village (Hosie 2017) includes accommodation for 90 people together with a cinema, supermarket, café and gardens. In Suffolk, a care centre has constructed a village high street to help dementia sufferers through stimulating memories of the past (BBC 2014). Some dementia housing providers go beyond this and in Ohio, US (Carter 2017) and in Switzerland (Hall 2012), replica villages are being created to remind people of the past and create town layouts that are easy to navigate and where staff wear uniforms that relate to the village rather than to a care environment.

Planning for Older People

Planning for older people will need to consider their requirements in all aspects of plan making. The Association of Directors of Social Services (ADASS) (2011) has calculated the forms of provision required per 1,000 of relevant populations 75+C, as shown in Table 13.5.

Table 13.4 Good Urban Design Is Essential for Improving the Ability of People Living with Dementia to Live Well

Good urban design is essential for improving the ability of people living with dementia to live well:

- Familiar environment – functions of places and buildings are obvious, any changes are small scale and incremental;
- Legible environment – a hierarchy of street types, which are short and narrow. Clear signs at decision points;
- Distinctive environment – a variety of landmarks, with architectural features in a variety of styles and materials. There is a variety of practical features, e.g. trees and street furniture;
- Accessible environment – land uses are mixed with shops and services within a 5–10-minute walk from housing. Entrances to places are obvious and easy to use and conform to disabled access regulations;
- Comfortable environment – open space is well defined with toilets, seating, shelter and good lighting. Background and traffic noise should be minimised through planting and fencing. Street clutter is minimal to not impede walking or distract attention;
- Safe environment – footpaths are wide, flat and non-slip, development is orientated to avoid creating dark shadows or bright glare.

Source: From RTPI 2017 p8.

Table 13.5 Forms of Provision Required per 1,000 of Relevant Populations 75+C

Form of Provision	Estimates Demand per 1,000 of Relevant Population
Conventional sheltered housing to rent	60
Leasehold sheltered housing	120
Enhanced sheltered housing (divided 50:50 between that for rent and that for sale)	20
Extra care housing for rent	15
Extra care housing for sale	30
Housing based provision for dementia	6

Source: ADASS 2011 p19.

An English local plan survey (Branson 2017) found that only 32 local authorities had identified a policy for older people and associated this with site allocations for housing. The survey found that 72 councils had a policy only and 22 had site allocations and no policy. They found that 203 local plans had neither a policy nor site allocations. When they examined this in more detail, reviewing the relationship between those councils with the highest number of older people that had policies or allocations in their local plans, they found that most of them had populations where the proportion of residents aged 65+ was well below the national average. Those councils with amongst the highest numbers of old people, including Christchurch, Wealden, King's Lynn and West

Norfolk, had no provision for older people in their local plans. The local plans that were in the highest category in the Branson survey of planning policies for older people included a range of issues, as illustrated in Box 13.1.

Box 13.1 Planning Policies for Older People: Some Examples from Adopted Local Plans in England

- Existing specialist accommodation should be protected unless it can be demonstrated that there is insufficient need/demand for that type of accommodation (Woking 2012)
- New specialist accommodation should be of high quality design, including generous space standards and generous amenity space. At least 50 per cent of schemes should have two bedrooms (unless the development is entirely for affordable units, when a smaller percentage may be more appropriate). Bed-sit development should be discouraged (Woking 2012)
- The council should allocate specific sites through the Site Allocations DPD to assist in bringing suitable sites forward to meet need (Woking 2012)
- New specialist accommodation should incorporate 'lifetime homes' standards and be readily capable of adaptation to meet the needs of those with disabilities and of the elderly. A percentage of new specialist accommodation should be required to be fully wheelchair accessible (Woking 2012)
- Provision should be made in new housing developments, sheltered housing and extra care housing to support older people living in their homes (East Hampshire and South Downs National Park 2014)
- Create public spaces and routes that are attractive, safe, uncluttered and that work effectively for all in society, including disabled and elderly people (Crawley 2015)
- Ensuring that new housing takes account of local need to create neighbourhoods where there is genuine choice of the right housing in terms of size, type and tenure, both at neighbourhood and borough-wide levels, is essential. The council should therefore encourage a mix of housing that will be appropriate to the needs of the community, taking account of the information within the SHMA and its updates, to provide a range of types, sizes and tenures, including housing for the elderly, lifetime homes and other specialist housing needs (Crawley 2015)
- Further education plays an important role in equipping young and older people with the skills and qualifications to find employment. The council should support proposals that seek to improve facilities and accommodate the increasing number of students wishing to enrol (East Staffordshire 2012)

- New housing will be needed for older people, including specialised accommodation and mainstream market housing. Over the plan period the following specialised accommodation is needed:

- 965 new extra care housing dwellings

- 558 new Retirement Housing dwellings
- 548 new places in Care and Nursing Homes
- In addition, 1,213 new units of housing for older people will be needed – mainstream properties designed to be especially suitable for older people, around 14 per cent of all housing approvals (East Staffordshire).

Some local authorities are preparing specific supplementary planning documents for accommodation of older people. One example is that adopted in Eastleigh (2011), which sets out principles for design and car parking and requires the location of sites for older people's housing to be near open space and within 400m of other facilities, including shops, post office, pharmacy, bank and general store. The SPD also requires that housing for older people be integrated into the community. Hambleton District Council (2015) points out in their Affordable Housing SPD, many older people are not eligible for smaller but more affordable homes and this is a specific issue in downsizing. Eastleigh also identified internal design standards for residential care homes and how these apply to existing, new and converted properties. Windsor and Maidenhead's SPD (2010) also considered a check-list of questions for any proposed development, including whether it meets the standards for lifetime homes as set out and whether the property will be within a lifetime neighbourhood, also defined in the SPD. The Mayor of London has produced supplementary planning guidance on housing, which includes issues related to older people; however, the Greater London Authority (GLA) (2016) research report showed that very few local plans in London had few or reference to older people. Asked why this was, there were a range of reasons, including seeing older people's issues as part of health and social care or that older people were too mixed as group to be able to plan for them appropriately.

Neighbourhood Planning for Older People

Older people spend more time in their own neighbourhoods than elsewhere (Phillipson 2012), so their design and legibility are important, particularly where the elderly population is a higher proportion of the residents. As neighbourhood and community plans become more widespread across the UK, it is useful to consider what types of neighbourhoods will be most appropriate for older people. Based on experience in the Netherlands, the ADASS (2011) have suggested a range of factors that can be considered in neighbourhood plans and these are shown in Table 13.6.

Table 13.6 Range of Factors that Can Be Considered in Neighbourhood Plans

- Are health and care services grouped in the areas of highest density?
- Are there nearby shops and banks and are shops and banks accessible to older people, particularly those with mobility scooters?
- Are neighbourhoods considered safe, e.g. what are the reaction times on street lighting failure; is access to property safe and secure?
- Are transport systems accessible?
- Is there a structured plan for the installation of drop curbs?
- Are there verified and police-checked local care and repair services?
- Is there easy access to a range of social activities and facilities? Development of neighbourhoods that 'work'

Source: ADASS 2011 p30.

References

ADASS (2011). *Strategic Housing for Older People: Planning, Designing and Delivering Housing That Older People Want*. London: ADASS and LIN. www.housinglin.org.uk/_a ssets/Resources/Housing/SHOP/SHOPResourcePack.pdf (accessed 19 August 2018).

Altman, I., Lawton, M. P., & Wohlwill, J. F. (Eds.). (2013). *Elderly People and the Environment* (Vol. 7). Springer Science & Business Media.

Alzheimer's Society (2017). Dementia friendly communities. www.alzheimers.org.uk/ get-involved/dementia-friendly-communities/making-your-community-more-dementia -friendly (accessed 9 July 2018).

Arno, P. S., Levine, C., & Memmott, M. M. (1999). The economic value of informal caregiving. *Health Affairs*, 18(2), 182–188.

Ball, M. (2016). Housing provision in 21st century Europe. *Habitat International*, 54, 182–188.

BBC (2014). Suffolk replica village boosts dementia patient memories. www.bbc.co.uk/ news/av/uk-england-suffolk-28061574/suffolk-replica-village-boosts-dementia-pa tient-memories (accessed 9 July 2018).

Blood, I., & Associates (2016). Housing & support partnership: Supported accommoda-tion. Review. https://assets.publishing.service.gov.uk/government/uploads/system/up loads/attachment_data/file/572026/rr927-supported-accommodation-review-summary. pdf (accessed 9 July 2018).

BPF (2015). *Investment in Care Homes*. London: BPF.

Branson, A. (2017). Planning authorities are failing to prioritise housing for older people in their local plans. *Property Week*, 20 July. www.propertyweek.com/professional/pla nning-authorities-are-failing-to-prioritise-housing-for-older-people-in-their-local-plans/ 5090453.article (accessed 4 January 2018).

BSI (2015). *British Standard Code of Practice*. https://shop.bsigroup.com/ProductDetail/? pid=000000000030300514 (accessed 10 July 2018).

Buffel, T., McGarry, P., Phillipson, C., De Donder, L., Dury, S., De Witte, N., ... & Verté, D. (2016). Developing age-friendly cities: Case studies from Brussels and Manchester and implications for policy and practice. In *Environmental Gerontology in Europe and Latin America* (pp. 277–296). Cham, Switzerland: Springer International Publishing.

Carter, M. (2017). This assisted living facility is designed to look like a small town from the 1940s, *Country Living*, July 21, www.countryliving.com/life/a39630/nursing-hom e-tiny-houses/ (accessed 10 July 2018).

DCLG (2017a). *National Planning Policy Framework: Draft Text for Consultation*. London: DCLG.

DCLG (2017b). *Draft Planning Practice Guidance*. London: DCLG.

DCLG/DWP (2017). *Funding Supported Housing: Policy Statement and Consultation*. London: DCLG and DWP.

DoH (2013). Statutory guidance on joint strategic needs assessments and joint health and wellbeing strategies. www.gov.uk/government/uploads/system/uploads/attachment_da ta/file/277012/Statutory-Guidance-on-Joint-Strategic-Needs-Assessments-and-Join t-Health-and-Wellbeing-Strategies-March-20131.pdf (accessed 4 January 2018).

Eastleigh Borough Council (2011). *Accommodation for Older People and Those in Need of Care Supplementary Planning Document*. Eastleigh: Eastleigh Borough Council.

Fernández, J. L., McGuire, A., & Raikou, M. (2018). Hospital coordination and integration with social care in England: The effect on post-operative length of stay. In press. www.sciencedirect.com.libproxy.ucl.ac.uk/science/article/pii/S0167629618301000?via% 3Dihub (accessed 10 July 2018).

Foster, S., Knuiman, M., Hooper, P., Christian, H., & Giles-Corti, B. (2014). Do changes in residents' fear of crime impact their walking? Longitudinal results from reside. *Preventive Medicine*, 62, 161–166.

Gale, C., Dennison, E. M., Cooper, C., & Sayer, A. A. (2011). Neighbourhood environment and positive mental health in older people: The Hertfordshire Cohort Study. *Health & Place*, 17(4), 867–887.

George, A., Metcalf, H., Tufekci, L., & Wilkinson, D. (2015). *Understanding Age and the Labour Market*. York: JRF.

GLA (2016). *Older Londoners and the London Plan: Looking to 2050*. London: GLA.

Graham, E., Fiori, F., & Feng, Z. (2015). To downsize or not? Household changes and housing consumption among older adults in Scotland. Centre for Population Change, University of Southampton. eprints.soton.ac.uk/383906/1/BP30_To_downsize_or_not_ household_changes_and_housing_consumption_among_older_adults_in-Scotland.pdf (accessed 2 November 2017).

Green, J., Jones, A., & Roberts, H. (2014). More than A to B: The role of free bus travel for the mobility and wellbeing of older citizens in London. *Ageing & Society*, 34(3), 472–494.

Hambleton District Council (2015). Affordable housing supplementary planning document. Adopted 7 April 2015. www.hambleton.gov.uk/info/20039/planning/288/supp lementary_planning_documents/2 (accessed 19 August 2015).

Hall, A. (2012). Welcome to Dementiaville: £17m village in Switzerland will keep sufferers in fake reality, *Daily Mail*, 31 January. www.dailymail.co.uk/news/a rticle-2094155/Dementiaville–17m-village-Switzerland-sufferers-fake-reality.html (accessed 10 July 2018).

Hill, A. (2017). Hidden carers: The sixty-somethings looking after parents and grandchildren. *The Guardian*, 13 February. www.theguardian.com/membership/2017/feb/13/ new-retirement-ageing-responsibility-carers-parents-children-care-crisis (accessed 1 November 2017).

Hosie, R. (2017). Australia's first dementia village planning in $25m project. *The Independent*, 23 July. www.independent.co.uk/life-style/health-and-families/australia-dem entia-village-korongee-project-complex-tasmania-glenview-elderly-a7855461.html (accessed 10 July 2018).

Hupert, W., & Galilee, J. (2015). The indirect health and mental wellbeing benefits of the Concessionary Travel Scheme in Scotland. *Journal of Transport and Health*, 2(2), 56.

IPSOS MORI (2015). *Later Life in 2015: An Analysis of the Views and Experiences of People Aged 50 and Over*. London: Centre for Better Ageing.

Kollewe, J. (2017). Number of women working past 70 in UK doubles in four years. *The Guardian*, 22 March. www.theguardian.com/money/2017/mar/22/number-of-women-working-past-70-in-uk-doubles-in-four-years-retirement (accessed 10 July 2018).

Lifetime Homes (2010). Design criteria. www.lifetimehomes.org.uk/index.php (accessed 1 November 2017).

Lorenc, T., Petticrew, M., Whitehead, M., Neary, D., Clayton, S., Wright, K., ... & Renton, A. (2013). Fear of crime and the environment: Systematic review of UK qualitative evidence. *BMC Public Health*, 13(1), 496–504.

Macguire, E. (2016). Young people given cheap rents in Finnish seniors home. CNN, January 21. http://edition.cnn.com/2016/01/21/europe/helsinki-seniors-home-oman-muotoinen-koti/index.html (accessed 10 July 2018).

Mackett, R. (2017). Older people's travel and its relationship to their health and well-being. In *Transport, Travel and Later Life* (pp. 15–36). Bingley: Emerald Publishing Limited.

McCarthy and Stone (2017). Our market. www.mccarthyandstonegroup.co.uk/investors/our-markets (accessed 10 July 2018).

McNair, S. (2006). How different is the older labour market? Attitudes to work and retirement among older people in Britain. *Social Policy and Society*, 5(4), 485–494.

Metz, D. (2003). Transport policy for an ageing population. *Transport Reviews*, 23(4), 375–386.

Morphet, J., & Clifford, B. (2017). Local authority direct provision of housing. RTPI & NPF. http://thinkhouse.org.uk/repository/natplanforum.pdf (accessed 20 July 2018).

Nathan, A., Pereira, G., Foster, S., Hooper, P., Saarloos, D. and Giles-Corti, B. (2012). Access to commercial destinations within the neighbourhood and walking among Australian older adults. *International Journal of Behavioral Nutrition and Physical Activity*, 9(1), 133.

NCVO (2016). Economic value of volunteering. https://data.ncvo.org.uk/a/almanac16/economic-value-2/ (accessed 1 November 2017).

OECD (2000). *Reforms for an Ageing Society*. Paris: OECD Publishing.

ONS (2017). Overview of the UK population: July 2017. www.ons.gov.uk/peoplepopulationandcommunity/populationandmigration/populationestimates/articles/overviewoftheukpopulation/july2017 (accessed 1 November 2017).

Pannell, J., Aldridge, H., & Kenway, P. (2012). *Market Assessment of Housing Options for Older People*. London: Shelter & Joseph Rowntree Foundation, New Policy Institute. www.npi.org.uk/publications/housing-and-homelessness/market-assessment-housing-options-older-people/ (accessed 10 July 2018).

Patterson, I. R. (2006). *Growing Older: Tourism and Leisure Behaviour of Older Adults*. Wallingford, Oxon: CABI.

Phillipson, C. (2012). Specs and the city: Planning for an ageing urban population. *The Guardian*, 25 July. www.theguardian.com/local-government-network/2012/jul/25/planning-ageing-urban-population-manchester (accessed 10 July 2018).

Robertson, G. (2016). Transitions in later life scoping research. Calouste Gulbenkian Foundation, UK Branch. https://gulbenkian.pt/uk-branch/publication/transitions-in-later-life-scoping-research/ (accessed 10 July 2018).

Royal Borough of Windsor and Maidenhead (2010). *Planning for an Ageing Population Supplementary Planning Document*. Maidenhead: RBMW.

RTPI (2017). *Dementia and Town Planning: Creating Better Environments for People Living with Dementia*. London: RTPI.

Rudgard, O., & Kirk, A. (2017). Silver splitters: What's fuelling the flurry of over 65s getting divorced and re-married? *Daily Telegraph*, 18 July. www.telegraph.co.uk/news/2017/07/18/silver-splitters-fuelling-flurry-65s-getting-divorced-re-married/ (accessed 2 November 2017).

Stula, S. (2012). Living in old age in Europe: Current developments and challenges. Working Paper No. 7. Berlin: Observatory for Sociopolitical Developments in Europe.

Toepoel, V. (2013). Ageing, leisure, and social connectedness: how could leisure help reduce social isolation of older people? *Social Indicators Research*, 113(1), 355–372.

UKMSA (2017). Men's Sheds. http://menssheds.org.uk/ (accessed 1 November 2017).

14 Planning and Smart Cities

Introduction

Smart cities are frequently considered as ends to be achieved by city governments working with suppliers of systems for IT or service delivery (Kitchin 2015). However, in this chapter, there will be a consideration of how the smart tools available can support planning policy and delivery rather than determining its agenda. Further, there will be some discussion of the ways that smart cities contribute to the achievement of the territorial and spatial planning objectives in the UN's New Urban Agenda (discussed in Chapter 2) and are being delivered through the EU and other countries.

The emerging literature on smart cities has yet to be fully considered within the context of planning policies and regulation (Batty 2013). Yet there are issues that are concerned with the decisions on what kinds of cities we want to achieve (Ballas 2013) and how these objectives can be delivered through all the tools that are available to local authorities and governments working together with communities. Smart cities have already shown that they are sites of the effective application of disruptive technologies (Cardone et al. 2013; Dixon et al. 2014), where using crowd sourcing and direct relationships with users can circumvent existing systems of institutional market regulation, which have been used to establish a fair platform of operation for all providers. Thus, for example, Airbnb manages to avoid existing regulations for planning, health and safety and taxation, using domestic properties as tourist and other accommodation (Zervas et al. 2017; McCarthy 2017; Gurran and Phibbs 2017).

There are other issues where autonomous vehicles have switched the discussion away from mass transit and sustainability into a different debate about increased usage of existing capacity (Firnkorn and Muller 2015). There are other issues to consider, such as the internet of things and smart energy grids (Lund et al. 2015) on the design and development of places. The chapter will also discuss the challenges of retrofitting existing buildings and environments to achieve resilience in the rise of climate change effects, including flooding, heating and cooling. It will also consider the provision of food and changing land management of rural areas.

Why Are Smart Cities Important in International Public Policy?

As growing numbers of people in the world live in cities (UN 2016) and the rate of urbanisation is continuing to increase, there are concerns about the scale of cities and how they can cope with their populations whilst maintaining their contribution to national GDP and growth in each country (Krugman 1991; 2011). There are also increasing concerns for urban resilience, particularly in terms of managing basic services such as water, food, flooding, energy and waste (Meerow et al. 2016; McPhearson et al. 2015). While this level of growth is being maintained, there is a concern to ensure that existing investment and sunk costs in infrastructure and services are optimised to make them efficient. Decisions to make new investment can be understood within the existing pattern of the city. There is also potential for economic and spatial growth that is optimal for the city and the country as a whole (Turok and Parnell 2009). Cities are also a key component in dealing with climate change (OECD 2010; Lee 2005; Bahadur and Tanner 2014).

What Is a Smart City?

Defining a smart city is difficult (Morphet and Morphet 2016). Batty et al. (2012) identify it as a city that has an information and communications technology (ICT) layer as part of its infrastructure and that this is used as a means of reporting on the city, its infrastructure and its citizens in ways that help to make the city more efficient and effective. However, this approach can be considered as narrow and does not take into account other issues about smart cities, including skill levels and the role of technology in supporting economic growth (Shapiro 2006; Kitchin 2015).

There are many definitions of a smart city, but it has increasingly become a generic or umbrella term that has more of an associational meaning than a precise definition. When reviewing the smart city literature, it is always useful to consider the provenance of the article and any associated research, as much of the literature in this field relies on specific technologies or approaches that are not necessarily universal in their application. In their review of smart city definitions, Albino et al. (2015) identify a variety of meanings that are associated with different genres of problem solving. Many of these are anchored on the contribution of ICT to city management (Nam and Pardo 2011). In some instances, there is an assumption that, to be smart, the city must fashion itself to optimise the system under consideration.

'Smart' is also an emotionally positive term (Harrison et al. 2010) and has been attractive to cities as part of their branding (Zygiaris 2013). Politicians want to promote their cities and countries as locations for future investment. In other cases, adopting a smart city objective has been a way of changing existing and possibly outdated practices (Söderström et al. 2014). There are also associations between the term 'smart cities' and the capacity, capability and intelligence of any city's population (Winters 2011). Glaeser and Berry (2006) have demonstrated the positive effect of the proportion of skilled workforce attracted to and available in cities and the role that this can play in enhancing the economy. They have also stated that, in cities that are not so attractive to skilled labour, there is what they describe as a 'brain gap'.

How Can Smart Cities Assist Planning?

What is the role of smart cities within the planning system? Batty (2013) argues that the provision of big data, collected through sectors in the city environment and through data collected through transactions, such as those for travel or via Twitter in real time. This data can provide an essential support and understanding of the ways cities work and this can assist in their near-term, if not necessarily their longer term, planning using data analytics. The RTPI views these approaches as particularly useful for strategic planning and transformational for the planning system, using constant monitoring of development and the use of models to predict change and to produce integrated infrastructure maps as part of a wider effective use of existing investment, as well as identifying locations for future growth (Harris 2017). This approach to smart cities can also consider the application of service supply standards as a key issue in their economies and while governments can establish public service criteria for the provision of broadband, for example (NIC 2017), local and combined authorities can identify where these are not being met or whether there are not spots, and request the regulator to act with service suppliers.

One of the bigger issues to consider is how different approaches to smart city thinking and initiatives can be useful in diverse types of cities. Where there are existing elevated levels of urban concentration, smart city analytics might assist in ways that improve the existing capacity of the city, whether this is through infrastructure or use of space (Kitchin 2014). It may also assist in developing models of locational redistribution and future areas of activity (Caragliu 2011). In cities that are less mature or still growing, the smart city approach might provide methodologies to prioritise investment and new growth areas through support to considerations of locations for development or growth or new investment in utilities and public transport. However, there are also issues about how this kind of modelling and investment in data is used in more market-driven, neo-liberal economies and planning systems. The market is expected to be the most efficient means of investment although this is not necessarily the case in practice, where the market follows other leaders rather than identifying new locations.

The ways in which smart city tools, including data analytics, can be used to support planning are considered in the following sections.

Sustainability

In considering the objectives of sustainability as set out in the Brundtland report (1987), Bătăgan (2011) discusses how smart city approaches can contribute to meeting the objectives of leaving the present so that it is at least as good as, if not better than, the past. The role of urban systems is seen to be important and data analytics can be used to further understand the internal city interactions and their possible vulnerabilities. This might be achieved using big data – that is, the data that is captured through everyday city movement on public transport, energy consumption or use of social media – to identity economic and growth clusters. At the same time, social media can be used to report on key issues of sustainability, including air quality (Stevens and D'Hondt 2010), or to use crowdsourcing methods that are the basis of citizen science (Wiggins and Crowston 2011; Haklay 2013).

In smart cities, the use of big data can assist in understanding when sustainable limits that have been set are close to being reached. This can then alert users to reduce consumption. In some systems, while it is usual to pay for energy consumption, at times of peak demand, users are paid to reduce consumption. The same can also occur when there are problems in the transport network due to weather or other disruptions. People can be advised to take different routes or use other modes of transport or be advised to work at home or, by providing information in advance, change their own plans for travel. These approaches can be personalised so that travel routes can be advised before leaving home or work each day. In some cities, drivers are requested to change routes to improve air quality. Using data analytics, individuals and companies can be advised about the point at which they are using more energy or consuming more resources than the limits they have set or whether they might need to do more (Lombardi et al. 2012; Gelazanskas and Gamage 2014).

In these approaches to sustainability, the smart city systems can only advise when critical points are reached if these limits have previously been set by politicians and policy makers. Smart city technology can advise when these limits are nearing their capacity or where there are specific incidents that might cause problems. However, the system must be managed and these interventions are critical to achieving sustainability through smart systems. The systems can also monitor use as well as consumption, monitor levels of waste and recycling and inform people of when they have improved their performance.

Efficiency

Efficiency is an important objective of smart city policy, not least as cities grow and populations may place increasing pressures on existing services. The provision of more efficient services may improve the capacity of existing resources (Angelidou 2015). As well as improving the efficiency of urban infrastructure systems, smart cities can improve service delivery to citizens, which can affect the number and range of facilities that are provided in fixed locations. For example, health services are located to provide ease of access to users but if more health care transfers to online delivery, then access to suitable levels of broadband, and the appropriate technology, plus training and confidence in using it, may be an alternative strategy to consider (DCMS 2017). The opportunity to provide services online and through social media also can be more effective in offering opportunities for people, communities and business to use services at various times that suit them.

The increases in efficiency that can be achieved through smart city approaches depend on improvements in the delivery of service methods at the consumer or user interface but will also need to be accompanied by improvements in the back office (Majchrzak et al. 2016). This might be evidenced through health record systems that might be available wherever any individual presents for treatment although these efficiencies can then be tempered by the needs for data protection and patient confidentiality (Silva et al. 2015).

Implementing efficiencies into smart city services can be achieved through transferring processes into more streamlined formats that are available through a variety of customer channels, including online, smart phones, phone, web and face-to-face (Piro et al. 2014; Pérez-Sanagustín et al. 2013). Those services that can be transferred online, such as finding information, booking appointments or buying tickets, can reduce costs in telephone answering or on front desks. However, some services may require telephone conversations with users and this might be achieved through a call centre or one-stop-shop or a ring back by a more experienced service provider (Batty et al. 2012). Some services will continue to be provided face-to-face.

Transferring any service into different channels will require piloting and an assessment of the business process. Also, transferring a failing service into a smart city method may only reinforce its weaknesses rather than address them. Each service needs to be tested by users and have the potential for customer feedback. This feedback needs to be addressed by staff delivering the service and there should also be reports on the service website on how this feedback has been considered. This will also ensure that others have confidence in making comments. Any sense that a customer feedback comment is a criticism of staff and is therefore ignored needs to be carefully monitored. Smart city services can be improved by many small comments and suggestions made by all who use and deliver them.

However, there are pitfalls in adopting an efficiency-focussed agenda. Firstly, services can be diminished or mis-transcribed into new systems that are offered online. Further, where services rely on responses to service requests, these must be dealt with swiftly and in ways that citizens can recognise. Where services are provided by third parties, through contractual or partnership arrangements, the smart city still retains the responsibility for their delivery and the costs of these services failing or insufficiently meeting the users' requirements.

Efficient services may be delivered within silos, with efficiency gains being generated by removing the complex components of service delivery, including interdependencies with other services that may or may not be available in smart city formats. The availability of efficient services may not be adequate for the users, who will also need to be aware of their availability, know how to use them and have trust in their operation. Some of these processes and data can be made available to others to generate new uses for them. Big data is an example of this, where information generated through the continual monitoring and storing of information about routine tasks or activities, such as transport journeys, can be used to support service improvements (Batty 2013).

The architecture of this data collection will be an important consideration in its subsequent use to consider the quality of the services and to make comparisons with other locations. The data may be collected in diverse ways, including through centralised information storage of all journey information, which will be used to monitor services, and, in the case of buses and trains, used as clearing house information for payment. Where older people receive free travel, the bus companies will be reimbursed for journeys taken. Data can also be collected from personal devices, including location via GPRS and personal activity levels for health and wellbeing. Big data may also be used to target individual purchasing profiles to improve the efficiency and effectiveness of infrastructure.

There are many ways that ICT can inform and improve the level of efficiency in the use of infrastructure (Kitchin 2014). This includes all kinds of smart phone locations for real time information on the availability of public transport systems, advising travellers in advance of potential disruption and acting as a means of finding alternative routes when this is the case. Travel data can also indicate the busiest times at any point in the transport system and can suggest alternative routes to overcome congestion. The system can also collect data on origins and destinations and, in the cases of some transport infrastructure, such as buses, it can respond to likely demands based on travel behaviour. Integrated ticketing can provide a means to assist people travelling around who do not know the city or who need to take short journeys (Lee et al. 2014).

All these approaches are important to planning, as they can inform the likely need for more investment in fixed transport systems. Buses, for example, can be used as an interim measure to help to demonstrate where there are new transport flows or patterns of movement. They can also demonstrate where there is surplus capacity, which might then be used as an alternative to new investment.

Optimisation

Smart cities are also about optimising space and existing investment (Letaifa 2015). Given the extent of existing development construction, methods may need to be tailored to specific sites and circumstances. This will include the role of intensification, which is a consistent process through urbanisation, as locations become absorbed into the city and then take on its characteristics (Williams 2004). This intensification may occur through the development of tall buildings or the more intense use of sites through redevelopment. While smaller sites cost more to develop or redevelop, as they may have difficult access or building costs, as property prices increase, the costs of building on smaller sites will be decided by local need or market price (Dovey et al. 2017). Existing buildings will also be used for other purposes, including change of use, where it is deregulated by the government, as in England, where office buildings may be used for residential purposes (Clifford et al. 2018) and where schools are no longer required to be housed in purpose-built accommodation with associated playing areas. However, urban densification also brings issues, such as pressures for loss of urban green space (Haaland and van den Bosch 2015) and for other resources, such as the supply of water (Gober et al. 2013).

Other responses have included modern methods of construction (MMC), which support speedier development at lower costs (Farmer 2016). In this approach, much of the development is constructed in a factory and can be prepared within greater accuracy standards than construction on site. This approach can also be helpful for smaller sites. Where there are many houses being provided, the first owners of these dwelling have a considerable choice about how they select the components for the disposition of the internal space and external appearance using technical specification methods. Further, the components for production using MMC can be ordered from the architects' drawings, while 3D models of the development can also be printed at the design stage.

Using these methods, interior units for apartments or student accommodation are constructed in factories away from the development site, in conditions that are weather-proof and where the requirements for finishing skills in building are fewer. From these factories, these units are transported to the development site and are then placed in situ within the frame that has already been built on site. This approach can be quicker and less expensive. However, there are also concerns about some forms of off-site construction. In the past, there have been building failures from modular contribution and UK Finance, formerly the Council of Mortgage Lenders in the UK, will not advance major loans to those wishing to purchase a house or apartment built using this method. Alternatively, the developer can use this kind of accommodation for rent if they are willing to bear any risk of construction failure. Others have been concerned about potential homogenised design although external walls can be clad in brick or another surface that make this modular development appear as if it has been constructed though more traditional means. In the UK, there is likely to be a dearth of building skills in the coming period driven by both the ageing of the existing buildings trades and the lack of certainty about free movement for citizens during and following Brexit. This will place a greater emphasis on off-site construction although many of those engaged in this type of building are also from Eastern Europe and may also be affected by changes in free movement of labour (Kollewe 2017).

Resilience

Smart cities have also been defined as being more resilient. This may be in terms of their ability to manage their physical environment, making them more sustainable and as a defence against natural disaster (Antrobus 2011). This might also lead to the use of selective smart city definitions or applications. Hence the US National Resources Defense Council identifies smart cities as those that safeguard natural resources and resilience of places against environmental threats. Planning can specifically support the development of resilient cities (Zygiaris 2013; Davoudi 2014).

A second use of the term 'smart city resilience' relates to its ability to cope with economic cycles (Batty 2012; Simmie and Martin 2010; Christopherson et al. 2010). This includes some consideration of the benefits of the circular economy. The

World Economic Forum (WEF) identified the circular economy as a mechanism for the intelligent use of assets (WEF 2016). Another view is to consider the approach of *Doughnut Economics* (Raworth 2017), which is concerned with a return to city management and its associated economy as a means of achieving political and societal ends rather than managing crises once they have occurred.

Another consideration of role of resilience in cities is through the role of on-street devices that may assist in 'designing out' crime and improving public safety, as well as more sustainable ends. This may be through cameras or other sensing devices located on street lights (Zanella et al. 2014), which may also be used to manage energy consumption and traffic flows. In Glasgow, as part of the Future Cities programme, street lighting columns are also being used to monitor air quality, provide street WiFi, detect noise disturbances and show footfall. These services are said to be of particular use to the city's planners in making policy for local areas (MacDonnell 2015).

Participative Governance

The capability and capacity of citizens and communities that are willing and able to engage with issues within an ICT-enabled environment can ensure that they are more involved in decision making. The ability to provide information and feedback systems on line for plans and planning decisions can enable citizens to engage in ways that suit them. These systems have also been used in conjunction with other smart applications, such as Facebook groups, for communities in favour of or against development or living in the same locality (Kleinhans et al. 2015; Afzalan and Evans-Cowley 2015). The Cityswipe application, which works on the same principles as Tinder, has been used to give users the opportunity to provide an immediate response to proposals and the use of Twitter can both inform a wider circle of influence and gather support for specific issues (Wainwright 2017). Crowdsourcing can enable groups to identify cultural heritage (Ridge 2013), raise funds to save an historic building (Oomen and Aroyo 2011) and use public petitions to raise matters in Parliament (Vicente and Novo 2014).

However, not all people will have the time or interest to engage online and many people prefer face-to-face encounters and deliverable discussions or charrettes (Condon 2012; Rogemma et al. 2017), so that they can hear what others have to say. There may also be expectations that everyone in an area will be able to contribute and engage in this way when that may not be the case. Online surveys may only attract a certain kind of respondent and that may not be typical of all the people who live within a specific area. It is also possible to have too much information to be able to engage with it in a meaningful way. The UK government has removed its own departmental websites and it is only possible to find information through press releases rather than any definitive explanation of the policy background. In this case, there is a secondary reliance on communications from other sources, such as the House of Commons Library, which provides regular and comprehensive briefings and debate packs for Members of Parliament (MPs), which are made available to all online, as being authoritative and definitive. There are other ways that the public can be swamped by information, such as through long environmental assessments that can extend over many volumes and be too technical for an eager member of the public to engage with. Systems of engagement may be supported by technology but some groups will need to have specialist assistance and funding to be able to engage in these ways.

Managing Change

Cities will change in their use, design and development. One of the most frequently discussed potential changes in city form is the potential use of electric and autonomous vehicles. The growth of electric vehicles has been slower than expected, not least because oil prices have been lower, but countries such as India are adopting stretch targets for the introduction of all electric vehicles by 2030 to deal with air quality and pollution challenges (Tomlinson 2018). One consideration is that the world has passed peak car levels (Metz 2013) and the many different initiatives that have been used worldwide to encourage transfer to public transport have begun to work. Although cars can be hybrid, these are more expensive and rely on charging points for cars in residential streets or homes as well as in city centres.

The introduction of testing for autonomous vehicles and the implications for the associated design of streets are major considerations. Autonomous vehicles are expected to be safer and more efficient. They provide the opportunity for personalised travel for those without driving licenses – young or old – and for the distribution of goods, including groceries, to specific locations. This type of delivery is also being supported by drone technology. In California, there is also innovative technology being explored that would allow vehicles to have vertical take-off and to fly between destinations. New city neighbourhoods, such as those in West London, are attempting to grapple with the design requirements of autonomous vehicles (OPDC 2017).

Monitoring and Evaluation

The provision of sensors and the collection of big data though transport and energy systems allow a considerable amount of monitoring on the effectiveness of city infrastructure and utility systems, what happens when the system breaks down temporarily and how to plan for additional capacity and maintenance. The data can also be used to demonstrate how land markets work in cities and where there are elevated levels of poverty or poor health and to model access to services for diverse groups of people. These are central to understanding how to plan growth and investments. However, this is tempered within a neo-liberal government ideology, where there is also a temptation to follow the market on the assumption that it is more efficient and effective in choosing where to invest than the public sector although this is not always necessarily the case. Where there are major transport or ICT investments, some locations will benefit businesses through connections that are nanoseconds quicker. Here, the market will follow investment. Elsewhere, other considerations, such as travel zones or market location incentives or clustering, can all overtake existing patterns of behaviour and recreate new markets and venues for property and movements.

The Future Role of Smart Cities

While most of the focus on smart cities is on their technological dimensions, there is already a shift in consideration of how technology can be harnessed to achieve wider city objectives. This is particularly important in consideration of the implementation of the principles and objectives of the New Urban Agenda (Taylor 2017) and the changing governance models that align functional economic area boundaries (Harkness 2017). These new areas, formed through combined authorities in England, are focussed on the efficient and effective use of existing infrastructure within the context of place making as cities drive national economies. The use of big data will be part of this management together with innovative approaches to using other smart approaches to support cities as they change and grow.

References

Afzalan, N., & Evans-Cowley, J. (2015). Planning and social media: Facebook for planning at the neighbourhood scale. *Planning Practice & Research*, 30(3), 270–285.

Albino, V., Berardi, U., & Dangelico, R. M. (2015). Smart cities: Definitions, dimensions, performance, and initiatives. *Journal of Urban Technology*, 22(1), 3–21.

Angelidou, M. (2015). Smart cities: A conjuncture of four forces. *Cities*, 47, 95–106.

Antrobus, D. (2011). Smart green cities: from modernization to resilience? *Urban Research & Practice*, 4(2), 207–214.

Bahadur, A. V., & Tanner, T. (2014). Policy climates and climate policies: Analysing the politics of building urban climate change resilience. *Urban Climate*, 7, 20–32.

Ballas, D. (2013). What makes a 'happy city'? *Cities*, 32(1), S39–S50. doi:10.1016/j.cities.2013.04.009.

Bătăgan, L. (2011). Smart cities and sustainability models. *Informatica Economică*, 15(3), 80–87.

Batty, M. (2013). Big data, smart cities and city planning. *Dialogues in Human Geography*, 3(3), 274–279.

Batty, M., Axhausen, K. W., Giannotti, F., Pozdnoukhov, A., Bazzani, A., Wachowicz, M., Ouzounis, G., & Portugali, Y. (2012). Smart cities of the future. *The European Physical Journal Special Topics*, 214(1), 481–518.

Brundtland, G. (1987). *Our Common Future*. UN Brundtland Commission Report. New York: United Nations.

Caragliu, A., Del Bo, C., & Nijkamp, P. (2011). Smart cities in Europe. *Journal of Urban Technology*, 18(2), 65–82.

Cardone, G., Foschini, L., Bellavista, P., Corradi, A., Borcea, C., Talasila, M., & Curtmola, R. (2013). Fostering participation in smart cities: A geo-social crowdsensing platform. *IEEE Communications Magazine*, 51(6), 112–119.

Christopherson, S., Michie, J., & Tyler, P. (2010). Regional resilience: Theoretical and empirical perspectives. *Cambridge Journal of Regions, Economy and Society*, 3(1), 3–10.

Clifford, B., Ferm, J., Livingstone, N., & Canelas, P. (2018). *Assessing the Impacts of Extending Permitted Development Rights to Office-to-Residential Change of Use in England*. London: RICS. www.rics.org/Global/PDR%20Research%20trust%20rep orts/22790%20RICS%20Assessing%20Impact%20of%20Office-to-Residential% 20REPORT-WEB%20(without%20notice).pdf (accessed 10 July 2018).

Condon, P. M. (2012). *Design Charrettes for Sustainable Communities*. London: Island Press.

Davoudi, S. (2014). Climate change, securitisation of nature, and resilient urbanism. *Environment and Planning C: Government and Policy*, 32(2), 360–375.

DCMS (2017). *UK Digital Strategy*. London: DCMS.

Dixon, T., Eames, M., Britnell, J., Watson, G. B., & Hunt, M. (2014). Urban retro-fitting: Identifying disruptive and sustaining technologies using performative and foresight techniques. *Technological Forecasting and Social Change*, 89, 131–144.

Dovey, K., Pike, L., & Woodcock, I. (2017). Incremental urban intensification: Transit-oriented re-development of small-lot corridors. *Urban Policy and Research*, 35(3), 261–274.

Farmer, M. (2016). *Modernise or Die: The Farmer Review of the UK Construction Labour Model*. London: Construction Leadership Council.

Firnkorn, J., & Müller, M. (2015). Free-floating electric carsharing-fleets in smart cities: The dawning of a post-private car era in urban environments? *Environmental Science & Policy*, 45, 30–40.

Gelazanskas, L., & Gamage, K. A. (2014). Demand side management in smart grid: A review and proposals for future direction. *Sustainable Cities and Society*, 11, 22–30.

Glaeser, E. L., & Berry, C. R. (2006). Why are smart places getting smarter?Rappaport Institute/Taubman Center Policy Brief, 2. Boston: Harvard University, Kennedy School of Government. www.hks.harvard.edu/sites/default/files/centers/taubman/files/brief_divergence.pdf (accessed 10 July 2018).

Gober, P., Larson, K. L., Quay, R., Polsky, C., Chang, H., & Shandas, V. (2013). Why land planners and water managers don't talk to one another and why they should! *Society & Natural Resources*, 26(3), 356–364.

Gurran, N., & Phibbs, P. (2017). When tourists move in: How should urban planners respond to Airbnb? *Journal of the American Planning Association*, 83(1), 80–92.

Haaland, C., & van den Bosch, C. K. (2015). Challenges and strategies for urban green-space planning in cities undergoing densification: A review. *Urban Forestry & Urban Greening*, 14(4), 760–771.

Haklay, M. (2013). Citizen science and volunteered geographic information: Overview and typology of participation. In *Crowdsourcing Geographic Knowledge* (pp. 105–122). London: Springer Netherlands.

Harkness, A. (2017). Stronger government for smarter cities. Keynote speech. New Urban Agenda New Urban Analytics Conference, UCL CASA Senate House, 29 November, London.

Harris, J. (2017). *Better Planning, Smart City Regions*. London: RTPI.

Harrison, C., Eckman, B.Hamilton, R., Hartswick, P., Kalagnanam, J., Paraszczak, J., & Williams, P. (2010). Foundations for smarter cities. *IBM Journal of Research and Development*, 54(4), 1–16.

Kitchin, R. (2014). The real-time city? Big data and smart urbanism. *GeoJournal*, 79(1), 1–14.

Kitchin, R. (2015). Making sense of smart cities: Addressing present shortcomings. *Cambridge Journal of Regions, Economy and Society*, 8(1), 131–136.

Kleinhans, R., Van Ham, M., & Evans-Cowley, J. (2015). Using social media and mobile technologies to foster engagement and self-organization in participatory urban planning and neighbourhood governance. research-repository.st-andrews.ac.uk/bitstream/handle/10023/10151/Kleinhans_2015_UsingSocialMediaMobileTech_AAM.pdf?sequence=1&isAllowed=y (accessed 7 January 2018).

Kollewe, J. (2017). Housebuilders issue Brexit plea as poll shows UK reliance on EU workers. *The Guardian*, December 5. www.theguardian.com/business/2017/dec/05/housebuilders-issue-brexit-plea-as-poll-reveals-uk-reliance-on-eu-workers (accessed 7 December 2017).

Krugman, P. (1991). Increasing returns and economic geography. *Journal of Political Economy*, 99(3), 483–499.

Krugman, P. (2011). The new economic geography, now middle-aged. *Regional Studies*, 45(1), 1–7.

Lee, K.N. (2005). Cities and climate change: Urban sustainability and global environmental governance. *Global Environmental Politics*, 5(4), 122–124.

Lee, J. H., Hancock, M. G., & Hu, M. C. (2014). Towards an effective framework for building smart cities: Lessons from Seoul and San Francisco. *Technological Forecasting and Social Change*, 89, 80–99.

Letaifa, S. B. (2015). How to strategize smart cities: Revealing the SMART model. *Journal of Business Research*, 68(7), 1414–1419.

Lombardi, P., Giordano, S., Farouh, H., & Yousef, W. (2012). Modelling the smart city performance. *Innovation: The European Journal of Social Science Research*, 25(2), 137–149.

Lund, P. D., Mikkola, J., & Ypyä, J. (2015). Smart energy system design for large clean power schemes in urban areas. *Journal of Cleaner Production*, 103, 437–445.

MacDonnell, H. (2015). Glasgow: The making of a smart city. *The Guardian*, 21 April. www.theguardian.com/public-leaders-network/2015/apr/21/glasgow-the-making-of-a-smart-city (accessed 17 December 2017).

Majchrzak, A., Markus, M. L., & Wareham, J. (2016). Designing for digital transformation: Lessons for information systems research from the study of ICT and societal challenges. *MIS Quarterly*, 40(2), 267–277.

McCarthy, J. (2017). Airbnb in Edinburgh. Conference panel paper presented at UK and Ireland Planning Research Conference, Belfast, 11–13 September.

McPhearson, T., Andersson, E., Elmqvist, T., & Frantzeskaki, N. (2015). Resilience of and through urban ecosystem services. *Ecosystem Services*, 12, 152–156.

Meerow, S., Newell, J. P., & Stults, M. (2016). Defining urban resilience: A review. *Landscape and Urban Planning*, 147, 38–49.

Metz, D. (2013). Peak car and beyond: The fourth era of travel. *Transport Reviews*, 33 (3), 255–270.

Morphet, J., & Morphet, R. (2016). New Urban Agenda, new urban analytics scoping paper. London: Centre for Advanced Spatial Analytics, University College London.

Nam, T., & Pardo, T. A. (2011). Conceptualizing smart city with dimensions of technology, people, and institutions. Proceedings of the 12th Conference on Digital Government Research, College Park, MD, June 12–15.

NIC (2017). *Data for the Public Good*. London: National Infrastructure Commission.

OECD (2010). *Cities and Climate Change*. Paris: OECD Publishing.

Oomen, J., & Aroyo, L. (2011). Crowdsourcing in the cultural heritage domain: Opportunities and challenges. In *Proceedings of the 5th International Conference on Communities and Technologies* (pp. 138–149). New York: ACM. https://dl.acm.org/citation.cfm?id=2103373 (accessed 10 July 2018).

OPDC (2017). Old Oak Common and Park Royal smart strategy report, April. www.london.gov.uk/sites/default/files/40._smart_strategy.pdf (accessed 9 January 2018).

Pérez-Sanagustín, M., Buchem, I., & Kloos, C. D. (2013). Multi-channel, multi-objective, multi-context services: The glue of the smart cities learning ecosystem. *Interaction Design and Architecture(s) Journal*, 17, 43–52.

Piro, G., Cianci, I., Grieco, L. A., Boggia, G., & Camarda, P. (2014). Information centric services in smart cities. *Journal of Systems and Software*, 88, 169–188.

Raworth, K. (2017). *Doughnut Economics: Seven Ways to Think Like a 21st-Century Economist*. London: Random House Business.

Ridge, M. (2013). From tagging to theorizing: deepening engagement with cultural heritage through crowdsourcing. *Curator: The Museum Journal*, 56(4), 435–450.

Shapiro, J. M., (2006). Smart cities: Quality of life, productivity, and the growth effects of human capital. *The Review of Economics and Statistics*, 88(2), 324–335.

Silva, B. M., Rodrigues, J. J., de la Torre Díez, I., López-Coronado, M., & Saleem, K. (2015). Mobile-health: A review of current state in 2015. *Journal of Biomedical Informatics*, 56, 265–272.

Simmie, J., & Martin, R. (2010). The economic resilience of regions: Towards an evolutionary approach. *Cambridge Journal of Regions, Economy and Society*, 3(1), 27–43.

Söderström, O., Paasche, T., & Klauser, F. (2014). Smart cities as corporate storytelling. *City*, 18(3), 307–320.

Stevens, M., & D'Hondt, E. (2010). Crowdsourcing of pollution data using smartphones. http://soft.vub.ac.be/Publications/2010/vub-tr-soft-10-15.pdf (accessed 10 July 2018).

Taylor, A. (2017). Address to the Implementing the New Urban Agenda Conference, 5 May. https://ministers.pmc.gov.au/taylor/2017/address-implementing-new-urban-agenda-conference (accessed 9 January 2018).

Tomlinson, H. (2018). Charge: India in ambitious drive for all cars to be electric by 2030. *The Times*. www.thetimes.co.uk/article/charge-india-in-ambitious-drive-for-all-cars-to-be-electric-by-2030-wrs8gr0nq (accessed 9 January 2018).

Turok, I., & Parnell, S. (2009). Reshaping cities, rebuilding nations: The role of national urban policies. *Urban Forum*, 20(2), 157–174.

UN (2016). *The World's Cities in 2016*. New York: UN.

Vicente, M. R., & Novo, A. (2014). An empirical analysis of e-participation: The role of social networks and e-government over citizens' online engagement. *Government Information Quarterly*, 31(3), 379–387.

Wainwright, O. (2017). Tinder for cities: how tech is making urban planning more inclusive. *The Guardian*, 24 January. www.theguardian.com/cities/2017/jan/24/tinder-cities-technology-making-urban-planning-interactive (accessed 7 January 2018).

WEF (2015). *Intelligent Assets Unlocking the Circular Economy Potential*. Geneva: WEF.

WEF (2016). Intelligent assets: Unlocking the circular economy potential. www3.weforum.org/docs/WEF_Intelligent_Assets_Unlocking_the_Cricular_Economy.pdf (accessed 10 July 2018).

Wiggins, A., & Crowston, K. (2011). From conservation to crowdsourcing: A typology of citizen science. In *44th Hawaii International Conference on System Sciences* (pp. 1–10). New York: IEEE. https://ieeexplore.ieee.org/abstract/document/5718708/ (accessed 10 July 2018).

Williams, K. (2004). Can urban intensification contribute to sustainable cities? An international perspective. *City Matters: Official Electronic Journal of Urbanicity*. http://eprints.uwe.ac.uk/9233 (accessed 10 July 2018).

Winters, J.V. (2011). Why are smart cities growing? Who moves and who stays. *Journal of Regional Science*, 51(2), 253–270. doi:10.1111/j.1467–9787.2010.00693.x.

Zanella, A., Bui, N., Castellani, A., Vangelista, L., & Zorzi, M. (2014). Internet of things for smart cities. *IEEE Internet of Things Journal*, 1(1), 22–32.

Zervas, G., Proserpio, D., & Byers, J. W. (2017). The rise of the sharing economy: Estimating the impact of Airbnb on the hotel industry. *Journal of Marketing Research*, 54(5), 687–705.

Zygiaris, S. (2013). Smart city reference model: Assisting planners to conceptualize the building of smart city innovation ecosystems. *Journal of the Knowledge Economy*, 4(2), 217–231.

Index